The Library of American Biography

EDITED BY OSCAR HANDLIN

Stephen A. Douglas

Defender of the Union

Gerald M. Capers

Stephen A. Douglas
Defender of the Union

Edited by Oscar Handlin

Little, Brown and Company · Boston · Toronto

LIBRARY OF CONGRESS CATALOG CARD NO. 59–5277

FIRST EDITION

Capers, Gerald Mortimer.
    Stephen A. Douglas, defender of the Union. Edited by
Oscar Handlin. ₁1st ed.₎ Boston, Little, Brown ₁1959₎
    239 p. 21 cm. (The Library of American biography)
    Includes bibliography.

    1. Douglas, Stephen Arnold, 1813–1861.

E415.9.D73C28   923.273   59–5277 ₎

Library of Congress

To my mother
Vivia Deane Capers

Editor's Preface

THE Civil War was the great failure in the history of the United States. At this point of crisis, American governmental forms proved inadequate to reconcile the contending forces which pulled the North and the South apart. A long tragic conflict, the consequences of which are still with us, was the result.

Since then, Americans have not ceased to wonder whether the failure was inevitable or not. Could more enlightened statesmanship have staved off the war or was the test of battle indeed the only form in which the clash of interests could have been resolved?

Stephen A. Douglas was among those convinced at the time that the divisions between the sections need not lead to war. For more than a decade he labored in Congress to find compromises acceptable to all in order to prevent a permanent rupture between the men of the North and those of the South. His whole active life in national politics was thus dedicated to the purpose of maintaining the Union.

His position was altogether understandable in terms of his background and experience. As a spokesman of the state of Illinois, he was aware of the connections of the area he represented with both the South and the Northeast. As a prominent member of the Democratic Party, he was anxious to preserve the national basis on which its strength rested. In both roles, he resisted the tendency toward sectional fragmentation.

Yet in the long run the compromises for which Douglas struggled were not effective. The successive settlements proved temporary; and after 1860 both the Democratic Party and the Union suffered the calamitous splits that led to war.

Perhaps the issues over which the divisions occurred were of such a nature that no compromise could have succeeded. By the middle of the nineteenth century slavery had become an anachronism in a free republic; and Douglas's opponents were beginning to question whether the nation could indeed remain half slave and half free.

But perhaps too mistakes of leadership contributed to the outcome. Sincere as he was in his devotion to peace and union, Douglas was also moved by ambition; and the American dream of a rise to power and wealth may subtly have influenced his decisions. In this regard, he was representative of the statesmen of his time, who were all inclined to interpret national interest in terms of their own human desires. Whether he and they failed as a result of forces beyond their control or through flaws in their own character remains a perplexing and intriguing question in the lively pages of Professor Capers's account.

OSCAR HANDLIN

Contents

Stephen A. Douglas
Defender of the Union

I

"Go West, Young Man"

FOR four centuries millions of Europeans took the long trek to the western hemisphere. From Hudson Bay to the Argentine pampas some of them found fame and fortune. This migration settled the two continents of the New World.

This success story is associated particularly with the United States, largest and richest in natural resources of the new nations which arose in the West. There the distribution of wealth, observed Benjamin Franklin in the eighteenth century and Alexis de Tocqueville in the early nineteenth, was more even than in Europe, and the standard of living higher. The most popular version of the success story, however, appeared later — after that nation's intensive industrialization began in mid-nineteenth century — in the novels of Horatio Alger. Their plot never changed: poor boy from the country starts as janitor in a bank, works hard, saves his money, eschews vice, and in time becomes the bank's president. Alger's legend, despite its exaggerations, had some relationship to hard fact; this was the story of native-born John D. Rockefeller and Scotch immigrant Andrew Carnegie. The legend remained in the folklore of the country long after it ceased to be as true to life, once the captains of industry consolidated the American economy.

There were also earlier American success stories, the circumstances of which differed considerably from those of the Alger tales. Down to the Revolutionary War a steady migration from Europe produced the populous English colonies along the Atlantic seaboard with their affluent minority of planters and merchants. From Independence until the Civil War, European migration continued and the soil remained the chief source of wealth, but the central movement of people was over the Appalachians into the Mississippi Basin and across the Rockies to the Pacific. Less than fifty years separated the purchase of Louisiana and the acquisition of California. Since the Civil War Americans have completed the process of settling this vast area, have moved from the country to the city, and have turned more and more from farming to manufacturing and financial investment.

The middle period supplied a setting for the life of Stephen A. Douglas. In this period the great interior valley of the American West was the land of opportunity. It grew more rapidly in economic and political importance than any other section; and from it came the national heroes Henry Clay, Andrew Jackson, and Stephen Douglas. Like these three men, the typical westerner was born on the seaboard but migrated early in life into the interior, with which he almost completely identified himself.

The magnet which drew men westward was largely economic opportunity. Jackson from South Carolina, Clay from Virginia, and Douglas from Vermont, all practiced a little law upon their arrival from the East and all soon realized considerable wealth from speculation in land. They were as typical for their day as Rockefeller and Carnegie later. Unlike their successors, however, these early heroes spent more of their energy in politics and less in the accumulation of wealth. Some Americans who chose to remain along the seaboard also acquired either wealth or political position. Daniel Webster remained in New England and John Calhoun in South Carolina, but amassed no fortunes of their own. John Jacob Astor and John McDonough grew rich in the West but never entered politics. But the national heroes associated by later generations with this era had two common experiences: they were migrants to the West, where they prospered,

and they became political leaders of national prominence.
Stephen Douglas is usually remembered as the statesman who,
taking the middle ground on the eve of our civil conflict between
his fellow westerners Abraham Lincoln and Jefferson Davis, failed
in his effort to prevent a needless war. In a real sense his career
typifies the American success story when the West was young.

Stephen Douglass (he dropped the final "s" after moving to
Illinois) was born in a plain one-and-a-half story house in Brandon, Vermont, in 1813. A few weeks later his father, a doctor and
a college graduate, died from a stroke, and his mother moved the
family to a nearby farm which she and her bachelor brother had
inherited from their father. Thus the future Senator from Illinois,
like most of his contemporaries, was reared on a farm. But when
he wrote a brief autobiography in his twenties he barely mentioned his forebears, although he came from an old New England family; and in later years he rarely alluded to his eastern
nativity and residence, although he did not migrate until he was
twenty. Adaptability was ever one of his most conspicuous and
advantageous traits. Indeed, as he himself later remarked, he became to a degree unequaled among public men "a Western man,
with Western feelings, principles and interests."

The farm lad attended the local district school three months a
year and intended at the proper time to enter Brandon Academy.
When that time arrived his uncle, having acquired a wife and
heir, was unable to afford the expense. Instead he urged his
nephew to continue as a farm hand, arguing that the farm hand's
income was more secure than that of a professional man. But the
fifteen-year-old Stephen chose rather to walk fourteen miles to
Middlebury and apprentice himself to a cabinetmaker, Nahum
Parker. At the end of a year, piqued at his employer's insistence
that he perform menial household duties, he returned to Brandon
and labored as a journeyman workman in a similar shop for another year. Allegedly he abandoned cabinetmaking because of a
physical breakdown.

Later he called these two years the happiest of his life. But before they were over he had probably rejected both farming and a trade for politics and law. In addition he had formed an attachment to Andrew Jackson and the Democratic Party, and heated arguments with his employer, a stanch Whig, contributed to the break between them. The whole nation had resounded in 1828 with the charges of "Bargain and Corruption" which ousted President Adams and put Jackson in the White House. Like his hero the young Vermonter early took the side of the people, and to prepare himself for the law entered the local academy, using funds he had saved.

In 1830 his mother married Gehazi Granger, a well-to-do farmer of Clifton Springs, New York, and Stephen moved with them to a new home across the Hudson. There his stepfather entered him in Canandaigua Academy, where he began his study of the classical languages. Never a profound student, he had a quick and retentive mind that enabled him to acquire the type of information that he wished. His formal education, in fact, was superior to that of most Americans of his day. His fondness for and excellence in political debate increased, and his fellows remembered him chiefly for a speech before the debating society for Jackson in 1832, the year of the general's re-election. That same speech he would repeat as his initial effort in Congress a decade later. In January, 1833, he left the academy and began his law studies in a local office; the following June he departed for the West. In reply to his mother's query as to when they would see him again, according to tradition he replied, "On my way to Congress." Ten years later he made his promise good.

By his own account, Douglas made the decision to move west because New York required seven years of legal and classical study for a law license, and his family was unable to meet the expense of the additional four years of school. In Cleveland, where he first stopped on his journey, only a year of study in a law office was required for a license; in Illinois, where he finally settled, the license could be had for the asking. Although it revealed his pride, independence, and impatience, his action was neither unusual nor particularly risky; in the boom era of the

1830's young easterners by the thousands were leaving their homes all along the Atlantic seaboard. By contemporary standards a man of twenty was fully mature, and Stephen had by no means led a sheltered life. Five feet tall and a hundred pounds in weight, with a massive head on a frail body, he appeared much younger than he actually was. This boyish appearance, no less than his winning personality, elicited the sympathy and help he was so often to receive from strangers on his wanderings.

At his departure from Clifton Springs he had in mind no particular destination, but he did carry with him letters of introduction to certain residents of Cleveland, and there a leading local attorney offered him the use of an office and library for the necessary year of study. Fate determined otherwise, however, for in a few days Douglas contracted malaria and for four months his recovery was highly uncertain. Advised by physicians to find another climate, still weak from the fever, and with only forty dollars in his pocket, in October he moved on by canal and river boats to Cincinnati — then to Louisville and St. Louis, unsuccessfully seeking employment as a clerk in a law office where he might continue his studies. Too proud to return home or appeal for funds and too weak for manual labor, he took a stagecoach for Jacksonville in central Illinois, hoping for more luck in a small town. But the legal business of its one thousand inhabitants was already divided among a dozen lawyers, one of whom advised him to go on to Pekin, farther up the Illinois River, and offered to furnish him sufficient law books on credit.

After selling a few books of his own to pay for his lodging, Douglas proceeded to the nearest landing on the river, only to learn that the single steamboat had recently exploded. With but a few cents left, he decided in desperation to teach school. A friendly farmer put him up for the night and next morning drove him to a neighboring village, but he could find no pupils. Hearing that Winchester ten miles away sought a teacher, he walked the remaining distance, and there at long last his luck turned. The local tavernkeeper introduced him to residents and shortly he obtained forty students for a three-months session.

Meanwhile he replenished his finances by serving as clerk at an auction sale. The village storekeeper, a fellow Vermonter, invited him to share his quarters.

Winchester's new schoolmaster began at once to make friends and to learn the customs of his adopted state. Since Illinois law permitted anyone to practice in justice of peace courts without a license, he handled a few cases. Regularly he attended the weekly meetings of the Lyceum, at one of which he defended Jackson's attack on the Bank against his future rival Josiah Lamborn, Whig lawyer from Jacksonville. To Jacksonville he returned himself in March, a hundred dollars richer and his health restored. A justice of the State Supreme Court granted him a license, but warned him that "he must apply himself closer to the study of the law." Thereupon he rented an office in the Morgan County Courthouse and announced himself by an ad in the local press.

In 1833 Illinois had been in the Union but fifteen years. Only the southern half of the state could be called settled and the vast majority of its inhabitants had come from south of the Ohio. Chicago was a village three years old and Morgan County, in the center of the state where Douglas landed quite by accident, was on the northern fringe of the settled area. Since it was one of the two wealthiest and most populous counties, however, it had a relatively high proportion of Whigs in a state that usually had been and would continue to be Democratic. In view of the number of veteran lawyers in Jacksonville, the fact that the young attorney selected it as his residence indicated that he had a political rather than a legal career in mind, although the two were supplementary. That was true also of Abe Lincoln in adjacent Sangamon County, who entered politics about the same time and in the same manner.

Central Illinois was just passing from the frontier stage of hunting and trapping into that of settled community life. Hunting shirts and moccasins were beginning to go out of style. The future was full of opportunity for the energetic, the astute, or the lucky, but the roughness and friendliness of frontier society long survived. Such an environment was ideal for a youngster of Douglas's temperament and purpose; from the beginning he loved it. He urged his family to join him, pointing out the sure return on almost any type of investment; "Equality and equal rights prevail and no man acknowledges another his superior." It required no effort on his part to doff his eastern dress and speech — he did so spontaneously. Ambition, intelligence, and skill in debate were all factors in the rapidity of his rise to political leadership in state and nation; but it is unlikely that his personal conduct and the manner of his association with people would have been at all different had he instead become a merchant or a farmer.

Within a decade Douglas held a number of elective and appointive offices in the state. At the same time, with the assistance of colleagues over whom he soon came to exercise an undisputed leadership, he organized the Democratic Party in Illinois into an effective machine. In the process he developed a set of techniques and attitudes — a political personality — which were to influence his later actions on the national stage. His Illinois career, exciting and colorful as it was, merits attention as much for its immediate as for its ultimate consequences.

In Jacksonville the young lawyer struck up a warm friendship with S. S. Brooks, editor of the *News*, and by one means or another became known to other party leaders in Morgan County. But the morale of the Democrats was low because of the local unpopularity of their President's vetoes of the Bank recharter and the Maysville Road bills. Douglas induced his friends to hold a mass meeting on a Saturday afternoon, when most farmers from the county came to town, at which resolutions were introduced boldly defending all of Jackson's actions. He presented the resolutions himself when at the last minute the prominent Democrat selected for the task refused. In an hour's speech he defended the party record with such vigor that he routed his opponent Lamborn, who attempted to reply. The electrified crowd carried Douglas triumphantly around the square on its shoulders; and he now acquired the sobriquet "Little Giant." The sarcastic attacks of the local Whig press upon the young upstart brought him more legal business than he could handle, and made his name famous throughout the county and in much of the state.

This prominence, for which he and his Whig critics were equally responsible, led indirectly to his first political office. A feud developed between his friend Captain John Wyatt, member of the legislature, on one hand and Democratic Governor Joseph Duncan and State's Attorney John Hardin of the local district on the other. Wyatt sought to remove Hardin from office by transferring the appointing power from the governor to the legislature. "If I can only beat him with little Douglas," said Wyatt, "it will be too good." The Little Giant drew up the bill, became Wyatt's candidate against Hardin, and was elected to the office by the legislature by the close vote of thirty-eight to thirty-four.

Enchanced in prestige and undismayed by the technicalities of the law — with which he was only slightly acquainted — the new district attorney more than made up for his limited knowledge by his energy and his persuasiveness. He soon began to develop a facility for influencing juries and even judges that was later to make him known as the best lawyer for a bad case in the state. The size of his district enabled him to increase the number of his friends of both parties and of all degrees, as well as to preach the convention system of party nominations to a larger audience. Whatever office Douglas held in these early years, he spent fully half his time, both openly and behind the scenes, in party organization.

When the parties squared off for the state election of 1836, the Democrats of Morgan County found they had no one else who could match Hardin of the Whigs on the stump. A place on the ticket for the legislature was made for the Little Giant, who toured the county debating Hardin. When the returns were in, five of the six new Morgan representatives to the lower house were Democrats, Douglas among them.

The ex-state's Attorney transferred the scene of his activity to the legislature in Vandalia in one of its more memorable sessions. The delegation from neighboring Sangamon County, led by

Lincoln, pushed through a bill to move the capital to Springfield, their county seat. On this matter Douglas was apparently neutral, but on other issues he continued his warfare with the Whigs. In the campaign both parties had wildly pledged themselves to internal improvements; this was the height of the Jackson boom. Consequently a bill was passed appropriating ten million dollars for railroads and canals, largely as a result of log-rolling by the different counties. The young representative from Morgan preferred a smaller expenditure and a more moderate plan of public works, but he dared not offend his constituents by voting against so popular a measure. When the depression of 1837 broke shortly, the state became bankrupt, but he spoke out strongly against repudiation.

In reward for his service to the party, at the end of the session President Van Buren appointed him Register of the Land Office at Springfield. "We are told the little man from Morgan," noted the Sangamon Whig *Journal,* "was perfectly astonished at finding himself making money at the rate of from one to two hundred dollars a day." The job acquainted him at firsthand with the intricacies of public land policy, a subject to which he later devoted much attention in his long career in the Senate. Residence in the state capital enabled him to keep in touch with legislators and to direct various maneuvers which he thought would strengthen his party. This was the chief reason, no doubt, for his intimacy with the editors of the Springfield *Republican,* the leading Democratic paper. He did his work well, for when the district convention met in 1838 to nominate a candidate for Congress, it passed over the incumbent William L. Mays and chose Douglas, who would barely have attained the required age when the House met. The substitution was clearly the work of the machine, and the statement of the Little Giant's friends that he accepted without hope of success merely to "consolidate the party" is hardly credible. But not even the lucrative income from the land office could turn him aside from his goal.

The Whigs had chosen as their candidate an "Old Resident," Major John T. Stuart, Lincoln's six-foot law partner. For months the two opponents traveled together over the thirty-four counties in the district, debating wherever they found an audience, in a campaign that became legendary in Illinois history. When the votes were counted Douglas lost by the narrow margin of thirty-five votes in a total of more than 36,000. At first inclined to challenge the election on grounds of fraud, he decided otherwise when he discovered the cost of such a contest. For a while he returned to the practice of law in Springfield, but the approach of the presidential election a year later found him as active in politics as ever. Chairman of the State Central Committee, he directed the campaign and joined in hectic debate over the state with Lincoln and numerous other Whigs. Illinois was one of the few northern states which went for Van Buren; the Little Giant received his well-deserved reward when the governor appointed him Secretary of State of Illinois. Several months later he was elevated to the newly constituted State Supreme Court.

The act of 1840 reorganizing the court, in control of the Whigs at the time, and Douglas's appointment to it were both a matter of partisan politics. In 1838 the Court had denied the right of a Democratic governor to remove the secretary of state, a Whig. Subsequently a move was initiated to vacate the office by legislative enactment; the incumbent thereupon resigned and Douglas received the appointment. Meanwhile a decision of the Circuit Court denying aliens the franchise, which would have cost the Democrats thousands of votes in the 1840 election, had been appealed to the Supreme Court. Anticipating an adverse decision, under the leadership of the Little Giant as counsel for the appellants the Democrats drove through a bill abolishing the Circuit Courts and adding five new judges to the Supreme Court. Each of its justices would preside over a separate circuit.

Douglas was appointed to the Quincy circuit, where the Mormons held the balance of power, probably with the objective of winning their votes for the party. At any rate, although his judicial record was quite creditable, he granted the Saints virtual autonomy and won the confidence of Joseph Smith. As a judge he was still a potential candidate for any office, and in 1842 he

actively sought election to the United States Senate but lost in
the legislature by five votes. The next year, when one of the three
new congressional districts acquired by the state was set up in his
circuit, he permitted himself to be drafted by the party. He resigned his office, and after forty successive days of campaigning
he defeated his Whig opponent by more than four hundred votes.
Thus upon his third attempt, at the end of ten years of strenuous
politics, the Little Giant at last realized his ambition and rose to
national office.

That young Douglas at the end of the next ten years was a
leading contender for the presidential nomination of his party was
evidence of his unusual political talents. In 1856, when he almost
won the nomination over Buchanan, Abraham Lincoln testified:
"Twenty-two years ago, Judge Douglas and I became acquainted.
We were both young then. . . . Even then we were both ambitious, — I perhaps, quite as much as he. With me the race of
ambition has been . . . a flat failure; with him it has been one of
splendid success. His name fills the nation. . . . I would rather
stand on that eminence than wear the richest crown that ever
pressed a monarch's brow."

Making friends and influencing people came as naturally to
Douglas as breathing. It was a necessary expression of his personality which required no motivation of ambition or self-interest; but
a man of his sophistication and intelligence recognized its value
in the quest for public office. "I live with my constituents," he
confessed, "eat with my constituents, drink with them, lodge
with them, pray with them, laugh, hunt, dance and work with
them; I eat their corn dodgers and fried bacon and sleep two in
bed with them." A Massachusetts editor on the same train with
him during one of his campaigns gave a detailed description of
his technique, observing that he spoke to every man, woman, and
child in a disarming and personal manner: "He can talk religion
with the priests as well as politics with the statesman. . . . At
every station, more regularly than the conductor, Mr. Douglas is
on the platform with a good-bye to the leaving, and a welcome to

the departing traveler — a shake of the hand with one man that stands at the depot and the touch of the hat to another. He knows everybody; can tell the question that affects each locality; calls the name of every farm-owner on the way. . . . Now such a man as that, in contact with everybody, knowing everybody, and at the bottom wrapped up with the one idea of preferment, power and dominion over men, is not easily to be put down. . . . He would be popular in Boston or anywhere else."

But the Little Giant was no mere baby-kisser or professional glad-hander; his personal magnetism was felt by his political opponents as well as by his intimates. Undoubtedly his youth and his diminutive stature won him sympathy, and his courage, his general good nature, and his friendliness drew men closer to him as they knew him longer. Douglas was a man's man. Except for some slight participation in the polite society of Springfield, he lived a bachelor life in the company of men. He was more often to be found with the boys in the bar, the newspaper office, or the lobby of the capitol than at his own desk. In a day of hard drinking, when candidates were expected both to provide and consume more whisky than their opponents, he rarely came off second best. In one famous exploit, at a banquet celebrating a friend's election to the Senate, he and General James Shields danced the whole length of the table singing and kicking off dishes. Moreover, he was willing when the occasion required to fight physically as well as verbally. He and Major Stuart began their canvass in 1838 in friendly fashion, but towards its close in a debate in Springfield, Stuart seized his little opponent by the neck and carried him around the square. The Little Giant retaliated by biting his assailant's thumb until it was half-severed.

Douglas's increasing number of close friends contributed to his personal success and that of his party. They saw to it that he was nominated to office and some of them stepped down in his favor. Personal loyalty to him became loyalty to the party; it permitted him to build an organization and a regularity that otherwise would have been impossible in such an individualistic society. He was one of the early leaders in the successful movement to induce the party to adopt the practice of choosing only one candidate for each office instead of several, and of selecting the nominee by a convention at the county, district, or state level. Usually these conventions were rump affairs, controlled by Douglas and his cohorts.

But the efficiency of the Illinois Democratic machine could not have been achieved merely by the popularity of its leader; rather it was his adroitness in the undercover maneuvers of politics, the strategy and tactics of campaigns, the division of the spoils of office, the various ruses to embarrass or divide the opposition, the log-rolling essential to the passing of desired bills, and the selection of issues which would win votes. Douglas's personal honesty was never questioned; he paid his own campaign expenses or lived off the land as he could; his sole reward was the attainment of office. But in the more practical arts of politics he became as adept as a Boss Platt or a Boss Quay of a later day. He beat his opponents at their own game, and his methods were not generally considered unethical by his western contemporaries.

Certainly his outstanding attribute — the one which contributed most to his own success and that of the party — was the oratorical power and skill in debate which brought him his initial fame. From his schooldays until the presidential campaign of 1860, a year before his death, the Little Giant influenced his fellow men chiefly through the spoken word. Few national political figures were so effective on the stump; in the Senate he was more than a match for Seward or Benton. In his day Americans took their politics seriously, both local and national. Listening to long political speeches between rival candidates was their chief form of amusement. In the boisterous West such contests were more gladiatorial combats than rational debates, and the premium was upon showmanship, not logic.

On the whole Douglas's methods on the stump were typical rather than original. He gesticulated so wildly that his clothes became disheveled; he wore himself into a frenzy. He used invective and sarcasm upon his opponents, but unlike Lincoln apparently he never told jokes. His ear for issues popular in the local community was acute. In his debates with Stuart, for example, he told the Irish canal-workers that he was a descendant of the "Mc-Douglases." But the device at which he excelled was that of misrepresenting the opposition and of twisting logic which, however obvious to the present-day reader of his speeches, seems usually to have convinced his audiences. As in physical contests in frontier areas there were simply no rules of fair play; one caught one's opponent as one could and took all the advantages offered, though when the bout was over the loser was expected to accept the outcome with good grace. Rival politicos were putting on a show for the public, and the Little Giant became a master showman.

Douglas's versatility and ability assured him a successful career, but it was characteristic of the man that he used his talents with a rare singleness of purpose and energy. Politics was both his vocation and his avocation. Not until he was past thirty did he marry; he neglected and then abandoned what surely would have been a lucrative and distinguished law practice. He did not turn, as he well might have, to the acquisition of easy wealth from commercial enterprise, although in the fifties his land holdings in Chicago were estimated to be worth almost a million dollars.

The Little Giant was not a simple man, although he could make people so regard him, and he was much more than a politician. His motives were mixed, like those of most human beings. He was not mentally or physically lazy. Few men, and no lazy ones, could have survived the incessant traveling and grueling campaigning of the Illinois years. Nor was his success due simply to his luck in associating himself with the Democratic Party, which in that era was more popular in Illinois than the Whig; rather the Democrats were usually successful because they had Douglas in their ranks. Undoubtedly he chose politics largely because he enjoyed it, but he was also motivated by his desire to serve his state, his section, and his nation, to all three of which he felt an intense loyalty.

His personality definitely changed as he grew older and after he went to Congress, but his methods and attitudes were permanently influenced by the circumstances of his decade of apprenticeship in Illinois. To mention only one instance, as a young state's attorney he misspelled the name of McLean County in an indictment (McClean) and a lawyer for the defense moved that the indictment be quashed. Nettled by his opponent's manner and his colleague's amusement, for revenge Douglas asked the court to withhold its decision until an official copy of the statute in question could be procured. Two days later when the copy arrived from an adjacent county, to his and everyone else's surprise it appeared that he had spelled the name of the county correctly, and he won his point. Eventually he learned that this was the result of a printer's error, but the incident led him, so he said in his autobiography, to resolve that in the future he would admit nothing and always force the opposition to prove its point.

His early career revealed that he possessed considerable common sense as well as intelligence. To the surprise even of his friends his record as State Supreme Court Judge — the only one of his numerous offices which he held long enough for a valid evaluation — was good. Of the cases appealed from his circuit, fifteen of his decisions were affirmed and fourteen were reversed, but reversals were frequent in Illinois in that period. As Supreme Court Judge himself he rendered opinions in sixteen cases, in seven of which he dissented from the majority. True, his conduct was informal: it was alleged that he had been known to leave the bench to sit on the knee of a friend and chat. "The judge of our circuit," observed a somewhat dismayed newcomer from the East, "is S. A. Douglas, a youth of 28. . . . He is . . . a man of considerable talent, and, in a way of dispatching business, is a perfect 'steam engine in breeches,' . . . the most democratic judge I ever knew." But more pertinent was the testimony of the cynical Whig, Justin Butterfield, prominent member of the Chicago bar. "I thought I could handle him," Butterfield admitted, "but damn that little squatty Democrat — he is the very best and most acute judge in all this Democratic State. He listens patiently, comprehends the law and grasps the facts by intuition; then decides calmly, clearly and quietly and then makes the lawyers sit down. Douglas is the ablest man on the bench today in Illinois." When it was called for, the Little Giant was a man of dignity.

"Judge" Douglas constantly followed congressional debates and contemporary newspapers. He had read generally in American political history; for example, the *Federalist Papers* and John Adams's *Defense of the Constitutions*. But during his apprenticeship he was not a careful student of the facts nor a seeker of abstract knowledge to be gleaned from books and the written word. Realist that he was, he learned rather from people. Having decided upon a certain policy — for whatever reasons, personal, party, or national — he sought to win support for it by appealing to emotions or by rationalization, because his experience had taught him that such methods were more effective than cold logic. Usually in his early career he looked not at all the facts, but took the first ones he found which supported his particular point. Upon occasion he was guilty of error and often of distortion. Lincoln completely demolished a speech of his in 1840 defending the Van Buren administration, in which the Little Giant's statements about national appropriations were utterly fallacious. This was intellectual sloppiness but hardly deliberate dishonesty, the product of a pragmatic habit of mind. Yet in a national statesman it could prove a dangerous vulnerability, and the older Douglas was more careful with his facts.

A vitriolic account of one of Douglas's first speeches in Congress, not entirely without justification, was recorded by ex-President John Quincy Adams in his famous diary. "He now raved out his hour," observed the old man, "in abusive invective upon the members who had pointed out its [a report that Douglas had drawn up for a committee of which he was a member] slanders and upon the Whig Party. His face was convulsed, his gesticulation frantic, and he lashed himself into such a heat that if his body had been made out of combustible matter, it would have burnt out. In the midst of his roaring, to save himself from choking, he stripped off and cast away his cravat, and unbuttoned his waistcoat, and had the air and aspect of a half-naked pugilist. And this man comes from a judicial bench, and passes for an eloquent orator."

Intellectual consistency, or abstract principles like state rights and strict construction to which he and his party might be committed, never bothered the young Douglas if they stood in the way of a measure he supported. He simply got around them by ignoring them or by some specious argument designed to convince his audience. Here again he was on safe grounds, for most people were willing to forget consistency when it conflicted with ends they desired. At this stage in his career he was ever an advocate, an amazingly effective one. Primarily he was a politician. He spent most of his time working for the party.

These traits were in large part due to youthful impetuosity and the influence of a frontier environment which placed major emphasis upon success. The mature Senator of the fifties, although still a pragmatist, had acquired caution, consistency, self-control, and considerable objectivity. His later speeches were generally logical and heavily buttressed with facts, but to carry a point upon occasion he resorted to the debater's trick of shifting the argument and twisting his opponent's contentions.

I I
Neophyte Congressman

As AN energetic and ambitious new congressman, Douglas pursued two main lines of action. He had to express the views of his constituents on national issues and obtain the passage of some legislation they desired. At the same time he had to impress his colleagues with his ability and gain the confidence of the party leaders.

He accomplished both objectives in his four years in the House of Representatives. Twice re-elected from his district in Illinois by large majorities, he was elevated to the Senate by the state legislature at the end of 1846, without opposition from his own party. In his second session in Congress he had become chairman of the Committee on Territories and one of Presidents Polk's confidential advisors. In general the young congressman was an ardent and effective supporter of the administration's program, and the President offered him the leadership of the Democratic Party in the House. Such success resulted more from political acumen than from luck. Although the Little Giant matured somewhat during his apprenticeship in the lower house and his manners became less brazen, he remained a stanch party man and followed the party line.

Douglas first drew attention and attained a reputation as a debater by a speech on a bill to remit the fine imposed on General

Jackson for contempt of court in declaring martial law in New Orleans years before. The theme was hackneyed, but the Whigs were in office, a presidential election was approaching, and Old Hickory's name still commanded respect. Unware that Douglas had made the same speech many times before, congressmen were impressed by his rhetoric and his sophistry. He disposed of all technicalities by stating, amid fulsome praise of Jackson and appeals to patriotism, that even if the General had violated the Constitution by declaring martial law, he had not committed contempt of court. When he met the General in Nashville the next year, Jackson told Douglas that he had always felt that he was right but that he could never make out a legal justification for his action. The Little Giant having done this for him, he could "now go down to the grave in peace."

The Illinoisan's next oratorical effort was on a more practical matter. In violation of a recent act requiring representatives to be elected by districts, four states had chosen them on a general ticket. All but two of the twenty-one new members were Democrats. Douglas drew up the majority report of the committee to which the matter was referred. The states had clearly violated the law, yet the report recommended the seating of the new members. An ingenious argument took the high ground (popular with the southern wing of the party) that Congress had no power to district the states, since that power was among the rights reserved to them.

His next venture was not so successful. Appropriations for improvement of the Illinois River, a project vital to his constituents, were included in a western harbors bill. Although the Democrats were strict constructionists and Jackson in his Maysville veto had killed a similar bill, the Little Giant nevertheless argued that the current measure was constitutional. During his unavoidable absence, however, his western colleagues removed the appropriation for the Illinois River in order to increase that for the Ohio. He had forgotten that building one's fences behind the scenes was as essential to parliamentary action as speeches.

When the Democrats nominated James K. Polk of Tennessee in

1844, Douglas found an opportunity for a campaign speech in Congress. The nominee was "emphatically a Young Hickory — the unwavering friend of Old Hickory in all his trials — his bosom companion — his supporter and defender on all occasions, in public and private. No man living possessed General Jackson's confidence in a greater degree. . . . He is the very man for the times — a 'chip of the old block' — of the true hickory stump." During the campaign the Illinois congressman toured Tennessee and Missouri making similar speeches, and as a Nashville newspaper commented, "he was equaled by few men" as a popular debater.

Political maneuvering of this sort required no great surrender of principle, for Douglas was in complete agreement with the candidate, the party, and his own state on the central issue of expansion. On this matter the South and West had united in the recent convention; by it the Democrats would shortly return to power. More Americans than ever before talked about and advocated a "Manifest Destiny," a folk belief that God had ordained the United States because of its superiority to take over the entire continent, proving in the process the virtue of democracy. This destiny was soon fulfilled by the acquisition of Texas, Oregon, California, and New Mexico — all within half a decade.

From the outset of his national career Douglas made it plain that an American Empire was his major objective. He would not violate treaties or international law. But to those who would proceed cautiously for fear of war with England he replied, "Assert our right to the last inch, and then, if war comes, let it come. . . . I would blot out the lines of the map which mark our national boundaries on this continent, and make the area of liberty as broad as the continent itself. I would not suffer petty rival republics to grow up here, engendering jealousy of each other, and interfering with each other's domestic affairs, and continually endangering their peace. . . . I will never be satisfied . . . while Great Britain shall hold possession of one acre on the northwest coast of America." Ascendancy on the Pacific Ocean and Oriental markets were his ultimate goal.

Throughout most of his life, expansion remained Douglas's primary interest, and for a long time he viewed all other questions in relation to it. In the House he introduced bills for the annexation of Texas, the organization of the territory of Nebraska, and the establishment of military posts in Oregon. He voted for the admission of Florida and Iowa as states. Because of his zeal and experience in the matter, when he rose to the Senate that body made him chairman of its newly created Committee on Territories. Since western empire was his dream, he backed all types of measures to encourage more rapid settlement of the new areas: liberal immigration laws, easy terms for the purchase of land, protection from Indians, and government assistance to transcontinental railroads. In 1844 the Little Giant was as eager as Polk for the reannexation of Texas and the reoccupation of Oregon.

His original approach to the slavery question was determined, therefore, largely by the fact that it proved the chief impediment to expansion. In view of the strength of the southern wing of the Democratic Party and of southerners of both parties in Congress, an ambitious northern politician must seek their support by compromise — particularly if he was an expansionist.

When Douglas entered Congress the Whigs were in power, having won the election of 1840. The Democrats regained the ascendancy in 1844, only to lose it again four years later. Already both parties were subject to the strain of sectional differences over slavery, which in the next decade would cause their disintegration.

The Republican Party of Thomas Jefferson had split in the 1820's into two wings. One under Adams and Clay became the National Republicans (later the Whigs) and won the presidency in 1824; the other under Jackson and Calhoun became the Democratic Republicans (later the Democrats) and came to power in 1828. The Jackson Party, a coalition of groups opposed for various reasons to the Adams-Clay policies, were internally divided on major issues. Cleavages developed when it won office but did not prevent the election of Van Buren in 1836, though they became more serious when depression hit the country the next year. Meanwhile the coalition of out-groups became the Whigs, opposed to Jackson and the Democrats but even more internally divided.

During his two terms Jackson took positive action on the major questions over which classes and sections divided. He vetoed the recharter of the Second Bank of the United States and then broke it by removing Federal deposits to state banks. (The establishment of an independent treasury under Van Buren severed the connection between the Government and all banks.) The General also vetoed the Maysville Bill, committing the party to opposition to Federal subsidy of internal improvements. In 1833 the tariff was lowered. Thus the Democrats definitely took a strict constructionist, state rights position on the Constitution. They pronounced slavery a domestic matter under the exclusive control of the states. Yet the party was unionist: in the nullification crisis over the tariff it denied the right of a state to interfere with a constitutional action of the national government, and it denied the right of a state to secede. The party was avidly expansionist: it recognized the independence of Texas immediately and urged its annexation; it moved the Indians out to the Great American Desert; it defied John Bull at every opportunity. In subsequent platforms the Democrats reiterated their stand on these issues. But the Whigs, a majority of whom were in opposition on most of them, never dared commit themselves formally in a platform.

The National Republicans had taken the name Whig for propaganda purposes, claiming they sought to preserve liberty from the executive tyranny of King Andrew I. Still disunited in 1836, they supported three candidates — each in different sections — but four years later they united on General William Henry Harrison from the Northwest. In view of the depression they probably would have won in 1840 regardless of their nominee, but they clearly copied earlier Democratic strategy by nominating a western general who had won fame by fighting Indians and who allegedly had been born in a log cabin. To win the southern votes they selected Virginian John Tyler as the vice-presidential candidate. In their inner circles it was well understood that Henry Clay would lead the party and direct its program in Congress.

The plan miscarried when Tyler became Chief Executive upon Harrison's sudden death. A state righter who joined the Whigs because of Jackson's effort to coerce South Carolina in the nullification crisis, the Virginian vetoed much of the legislation which Clay got through Congress, especially the bills rechartering the bank. The net result of the Whigs' efforts was a repeal of the independent treasury and an increase in the tariff, but both actions were shortly reversed under Polk. The single Whig measure which survived was the Preemption Act of 1841, which they had passed only to retain western votes. But by advocating the acquisition of both Texas and Oregon in 1844 the Democrats won the West back.

Both parties were national, not sectional; since they were strong in all sections, contests between them were usually close. From 1840 to 1856 neither held the presidency longer than one term. On the whole the Whigs were the party of the classes, though with manhood suffrage they did their best to conceal it, and the Democrats the party of the masses. The Whigs tended to be stronger in the East and the Democrats in the West. Both sought to avoid the slavery issue. Then as always, men's motives for party affiliation were complex, and emotional rather than rational. They varied from person to person, state to state, and section to section. Lincoln could easily have been a Democrat and Douglas a Whig; their initial choice may have been due simply to the admiration of the one for Clay and of the other for Jackson. Once established, party loyalties often became intense, and the minority which shifted its affiliation determined the change in party fortunes.

In the 1840's the older issues were still very much alive. They were both involved in and transcended by the newer issues of expansion and slavery which arose over Texas, Oregon, and the Mexican Cession — questions to which Douglas directed most of his attention. Purely aside from its moral aspects, sections and interests engaged in power politics approached the question of slavery with a view to getting votes for or against the tariff, the bank, subsidies for railroads and canals, or cheap land. On most issues slave states tended to take a position opposite to that of free states. New western states would thus swing the balance, and whether they entered the Union slave or free determined the disposition of these other vital matters.

But the situation was not simply one of slave and free states. If anything, sectional conflict was as complicated as that between parties, and the two were closely related. At least five distinct sections existed: the three older ones along the Atlantic seaboard — New England, the Middle Atlantic, and the South Atlantic states — and the newer but rapidly growing Northwest and Southwest in the interior. No two sections saw eye to eye on all issues, and on each issue the sectional pattern differed. In each section a minority dissented from the stand of the majority, and all were in the throes of rapid social and economic changes. Bargaining between them to enact or to block legislation was constant, but alignments were not permanent. Congressmen often voted with their section and against their party on crucial issues.

The earlier sectional alignment had been one of East against West, since all of the older sections were injured to some degree by western migration. Yet the older sections were forced to bid for the votes of the West. The War of 1812 and the election of Jackson reflected the growing political influence of the newer region. Later the two sections in the Northeast came to hold similar views on most issues: the Southwest, which had previously agreed with the Northwest, moved closer towards the position of the Southeast (Old South) as slavery was put more and more on the defensive. The stand of the Northwest — the fastest growing section at midcentury — would determine the outcome of the struggle between the older sections. Keenly aware of this development, as a rising leader of his section Douglas worked for compromise between northern and southern interests.

The Democratic Party had its own internal scissions, chief of which was the rivalry between Calhoun and Van Buren. The

New Yorker had replaced the Carolinian as heir-apparent during Jackson's first administration and had succeeded the General for one term. When Calhoun broke with the party over nullification in 1833, he took with him a number of southern Democrats into an irregular association with the Whigs. Later he brought them back when Van Buren came out for the independent treasury and indicated his concurrence with their views on slavery and the tariff. In 1843 Calhoun actively sought the Democratic nomination against Van Buren, but seeing that he would be defeated in the convention dropped his informal efforts rather than injure his chances for 1848. But the party convention the next year rejected Van Buren because of his opposition to the annexation of Texas and nominated Polk, a southern moderate and expansionist.

Calhoun's complicated strategy profoundly affected the Democratic Party. Driven by an unadmitted ambition for the presidency and a sincere desire to preserve the Union by giving the South full security for slavery, he followed two main lines of action. Since parity between free and slave states in the Senate was maintained down to 1850, the South possessed in effect a veto, but the lower house could be controlled at any time by the more populous free states if they united on an issue. In nullification — rejected by all southern states except South Carolina — he sought the acceptance of an interpretation of the Constitution that would make it almost impossible for a northern majority, even if it should capture all branches of the national government, to interfere with the peculiar institution of the South. Failing to get nullification accepted, he strove thereafter on all matters for the maintenance of a state rights, strict construction precedent; if the Federal Government could not build roads or charter a bank, then it could not emancipate slaves. In a Senate speech in 1838 he declared slavery a "positive good" and introduced resolutions stating that neither the national government nor the free states could interfere with it, nor could they discriminate against southern states because of its existence.

As a second line of action, in practical politics the Senator from

South Carolina adopted balance of power tactics. He urged southerners to unite behind a set of minimum demands and support the
party which would accept them. Enough did so to enable him to
exert strong pressure on the Democrats when he returned to them
after his Whig flirtation in the 1830's. By alliances with other sections or groups in other sections, he forced the Democratic Party
to accede to much of the southern program; for example, on Texas.
But as antislavery and antisouthern sentiment increased in the
faster growing free states, the party found itself subjected to a
strong counterpressure. Like Polk, Douglas tried constantly to reduce these pressures in order to preserve the unity and the
strength of the party. The main political developments of the
1840's, therefore, were produced by the interaction of the forces
of party development and expansion.

The Texas question was the first big issue on which Douglas
took a leading part in Congress. Whatever title the United States
had to Texas by the purchase of Louisiana was surrendered by
the Florida Treaty of 1819, which recognized the Sabine River as
our western boundary. President Adams made futile efforts to buy
it. When Texas successfully rebelled against Mexico in 1836 Jackson at once recognized its independence. Two years later Congress
rejected its request for admission to the Union. In 1844 a treaty
of annexation drawn up by Tyler's secretaries of state, Upshur
and Calhoun, was defeated in the Senate after both the prospective presidential candidates Clay and Van Buren had come out
publicly against it. The next fall the Democrats won the election
on a platform advocating acquisition of both Texas and Oregon.

Opposition to slavery kept Texas out of the Union for nine
years, but many sincerely objected to its admission on the grounds
that it would involve us in war with Mexico, which refused to
accept the independence of its former province. Its admission was
defeated in 1838 in the House by a three-weeks' filibuster by John
Quincy Adams, a fellow traveler of the abolitionists. The heart
of the matter was the fact that Texas might be divided into several slave states, thus increasing the number of senators to vote

against the Whig program. On the other hand, southerners realized that these slave states would offset the free states which in the course of time would enter from the large area in the Louisiana Territory north of 36° 30′, in which the Missouri Compromise had prohibited slavery. Politicians who feared that any stand on slavery itself would lose them votes in either North or South could oppose annexation on the grounds of the danger of war. This, in fact, was what Clay and Van Buren both did.

In pressing the issue Tyler and Calhoun sought to win a political following in the South. But by that time the matter had acquired international ramifications. Pursuing her old policy of blocking the expansion of the United States, England took diplomatic steps to guarantee the independence of Texas from both neighboring republics and encouraged her to emancipate her slaves. Calhoun's emphasis on the necessity of protecting southern interests may have alienated some northern support, but at the same time he sought to acquire Oregon by negotiation. Many Americans had their eyes on Oregon, California, and Texas; in each region England was our real antagonist. Thus the Democratic platform of 1844 was more than a clever ruse to get both southern and western votes by coupling Texas and Oregon. It took a strong national position in keeping with the expansionist tradition of the party.

This coincided exactly with the views of Congressman Douglas, as he cogently explained in the House. Shortly after the election of 1844 he introduced on his own a series of eight resolutions for the annexation of Texas. They were passed over in favor of the joint resolution from the Committee on Foreign Affairs, for which he made one of the leading speeches. In addition to the general arguments for expansion quoted above, he spoke to the specific question. Faith had been broken with the residents of the Louisiana Territory when Texas had been surrendered by the Treaty of 1819. In answer to the Whigs' charge that the measure was devised by the Democrats "for sinister purposes," he retorted that John Quincy Adams — one of their current leaders — had himself as Secretary of State claimed title to the whole area north of the

Rio Grande under the Treaty of 1803. The same Adams as President had sought to purchase it. To those who argued that a treaty, not a joint resolution, was the proper procedure, he replied by a broad construction of the Constitution. *Congress* may admit new states — not the Senate or the President. States cannot be admitted unless territory is acquired; consequently Congress (the House) may annex territory under the power to pass acts necessary and proper to carry out its specific powers.

In view of later events, however, the Little Giant's most significant proposals were those dealing with the question of slavery. In his original resolutions he suggested an extension of the Missouri Compromise line through Texas, since the area according to his view was included in the Louisiana Territory. Opposition to the joint resolution arose from a group of southerners led by the Whig Alexander Stephens of Georgia, who would assent only if the rights of the slave states were fully protected. Douglas then suggested that not more than three states besides Texas should be admitted from the area, the people of each to decide the status of slavery upon their admission. This was clearly a step in the direction of popular sovereignty, which became his ultimate position. His suggestion induced the southerners to introduce a substitute stating that five states might be formed from the area; those south of the Missouri Compromise line might be admitted with or without slavery as their citizens should decide. To remove northern opposition, Douglas offered an amendment prohibiting slavery in states formed from the area north of 36° 30′. The bill thus amended passed the House.

The Senate changed it by giving the President discretion to decide whether to proceed by treaty, which would require the two-thirds vote of that house alone, or to act under the terms of the House bill, which required only a majority vote in each house. It was assumed that the decision would be left to Polk, but Tyler hastened to accept the second alternative before he went out of office. Negotiations were quickly concluded with the Republic and Polk accepted its annexation. Within a year Texas was admitted as a slave state.

In this matter, and later on Oregon and other territorial questions, Douglas's course was consistent. In each case his end was expansion, his means the removal of opposition to it. In general there were three types of opposition: eastern opposition to any western expansion, northern opposition to the acquisition of regions where slavery was probable, and southern opposition to those where it was not. Once an area was acquired, those who wished to discourage settlement for the same reasons would block the formal establishment of territorial government. All obstruction, from whatever source, the Little Giant attempted to overcome by argument and by compromise.

But he could hardly have failed to see how the seemingly safe efforts of Clay and Van Buren to dodge the slavery issue backfired. When the New Yorker came out against Texas, without committing himself on slavery but undoubtedly to please his northern following, the southerners in his party blocked his nomination. After his initial statement opposing annexation, Clay hedged in a letter accepting it conditionally, and thereby lost enough votes in New York to the small Liberty Party to throw the state to Polk.

In the Oregon matter, to which Douglas moved with customary vigor once the Texas business was settled, he was not as successful. Accepting at face value the insistence in the Democratic platform upon 54° 50′, in January, 1846, he made one of his most vehement anti-British speeches as the new chairman of the Committee on Territories. He would have the whole of Oregon, even at the risk of war with England. In the place of the joint resolution terminating joint occupation of the region, he was one of a small group who would substitute a stronger declaration that Oregon was no longer a subject for either negotiation or compromise. When the substitute motion was defeated, he was among the few who passed between the tellers crying "54° 40′ forever." He further stated that if negotiations were reopened "sooner let his tongue cleave to the roof of his mouth than he would defend that party which should yield one inch of Oregon."

On this, as on other matters, the House and Senate did not agree. The original division found the expansionists and Polk — who seemingly at this time would have the whole area even at the risk of war — opposed by the conservatives of both parties who felt that it was not worth such a risk, particularly since a strong probability of war with Mexico existed. Actually Polk consciously took no such chance, but diplomatic and political considerations prevented him from revealing his course frankly to congressional leaders.

It must be remembered that the President was dealing simultaneously with England and Mexico, and that he had his eye on California, which he regarded as more valuable than that portion of Oregon north of the forty-ninth parallel. He was not so foolhardy as to chance a war with two powers. He knew that to compromise on Oregon would cause repercussions in the West, but he was willing to do so to avoid hostilities with Britain. (He vetoed the Rivers-and-Harbors Bill of 1846, knowing that it would subject him to recrimination from that section.)

Despite the formal Democratic commitment to the *whole of Oregon* (jointly occupied with England since 1818), in his inaugural address the new President simply stated that "our title to the *country of Oregon* is clear and unquestionable." The omission went unnoticed at the time. Polk proceeded secretly to offer British minister Pakenham a compromise on the forty-ninth parallel, out of deference he said later to his predecessors in the White House who had several times unsuccessfully made such a proposal. Pakenham rejected the offer without referring the matter to Foreign Secretary Aberdeen, who now had decided upon compromise and who expressed the fear that the Americans would not repeat the offer. Learning of this, Polk decided that by applying pressure he could force England to take the initiative, thus hoping to absolve himself of the charge of betraying the West. He was certain that the conservatives in the Senate would compel compromise.

Knowing that England would probably yield, in his message of December, 1845, he asked for an act giving England the required twelve-month notice of the termination of joint occupation, and extending the laws of the United States to our settlers in the area. This set off a four-month debate in which the westerners charged the southerners, who had gotten all of Texas, with "Punic faith." In April the Senate amended the House bill terminating joint occupation by giving the President power to give notice "at his discretion." Shortly Polk sent notice and the British proposed compromise. A treaty dividing the region at the forty-ninth parallel was quickly drawn up, which in June the President submitted to the Senate for advice. By that time the war with Mexico was on; the Senate advised acceptance and Polk "yielded" to its wishes. But the treaty intensified sectional bitterness and led directly to the introduction of the Wilmot Proviso forbidding slavery in any territory acquired from Mexico.

Douglas failed in his effort to prevent the division of Oregon, and his temporary coolness towards Polk was genuine — aggravated no doubt by the President's refusal to accept certain of his recommendations for Federal offices in Illinois. But upon reflection he decided not to let personal pique affect his loyalty to the party and the administration. Shortly after the Oregon Treaty he had a long conversation with the President, assuring him of his full support. Polk then told him he could lead the party in the House. In the next two years, both in the House and in the Senate, the neophyte from Illinois was a leading defender of his chief's course in the war, which gave promise of even larger territorial spoils.

During the debate over Oregon the Little Giant joined in the heated charges against his Democratic colleagues from the South. The issue was simple: the South got all of Texas and its admission as a slave state (shortly even a war to insure the Rio Grande as its boundary), but failed to fulfill its bargain when the Oregon question arose. "The Oregon and Texas annexation projects," he stated, "had their birth in the Baltimore convention. . . . They were 'cradled together' with a distinct understanding that if the West sustained the South in securing Texas, the South would sustain the West in her claims to Oregon." He for one openly accused the southerners of an attempt "to play a game treacherous to the West." But here again he refused upon reflection to let his passions cloud his judgment. The southern alliance was essential to the success of the party; disputes over slavery were a divisive force. Therefore he repeatedly voted against the Wilmot Proviso, supported for revenge by disgruntled westerners.

Like the War of 1812, the war with Mexico was unpopular with a large minority of Americans (mostly on the Atlantic seaboard) and the administration was constantly under attack. Unlike the previous war, it was quite successful. Naturally many Whigs, even some western ones like Lincoln who was then spending his single term in Congress, opposed it as a Democratic venture. Antislavery groups, particularly in the East, denounced it as a plot to enlarge the area open to slavery. This was true only to the extent that it was fought to gain more territory for the state of Texas. In the rest of the southwestern region acquired by the war Mexican law forbade slavery, and the area seemed unsuited to the growing of cotton. Partly for this reason Calhoun and others in the South Atlantic region opposed the war; it would not enlarge the slave area and actually states from the new region might enter free. In their view it was better to maintain the *status quo,* since Texas might be divided to offset free states coming in from the region north of 36° 30'.

This opposition was enhanced by the fact that Polk's actions before the outbreak of hostilities definitely exposed him to the charge of aggression. At worst, it can be argued that when Mexico refused to sell California and New Mexico he incited her into war in order to take that region by force. At best, it can be said that he permitted a situation, which with more forbearance might have been compromised, to result in hostilities because he foresaw that victory would insure acquisition of the desired territory. True, Mexicans appeared more eager to fight than he. They warned the United States that annexation would mean war and had broken off diplomatic relations when it occurred. Yet they did not attack for more than a year, and then only after Taylor moved his troops into the disputed region between the Rio Grande and the

Nueces. Mexico's claim to this region was superior; the Republic of Texas had never extended its authority over it.

Polk formally agreed to protect Texas's claim to this area. He first thought to acquire it in return for assumption of unsettled claims of American citizens against the Mexican government. Yet he was clearly playing for higher stakes and time was of the essence. Mexican authority in California was so weak that it might at any time be taken by a European power. He ordered Taylor to advance into the disputed area, and by appointing John Slidell as *minister* to Mexico instead of *commissioner* he made it impossible for the current Mexican administration to receive an envoy. So strong was anti-American feeling there at the time that any resumption of diplomatic relations — which reception of a *minister* meant — would have overthrown the government responsible. Upon the rejection of Slidell — who was sent to buy California and New Mexico as well as to settle the boundary dispute — Polk and his cabinet decided to ask Congress for a declaration of war on the morning before news was received of the attack on Taylor. It is highly doubtful whether Congress would have voted for a declaration. With news of the attack, which came over the week end, Polk simply stated that Mexico had shed "American blood on American soil," and asked for recognition of the existence of war by the act of Mexico. Congress did so.

Political expediency alone would have induced Douglas, party man that he was, to aid and to justify the Democrats' war. The fact that its object was his own cherished dream of a continental empire surely whetted his enthusiasm. Already a valued confidential adviser of the executive, he became prominent in the Democratic high command which planned the strategy for promoting the war and for overcoming obstruction. For some time he considered asking for a military commission. His most important service was the defense of the war against its enemies in Congress, where Polk was under attack from the Whigs and from two elder statesmen of his own party, Senators Calhoun and Thomas Hart Benton of Missouri.

The Little Giant made two main speeches: one more or less impromptu in the House at the outbreak of the war and a second, carefully prepared, in the Senate on the Ten Regiment Bill. First he appealed to the sentiment of patriotism: "All who, after war is declared, condemn the justice of our cause, are traitors in their hearts." American blood had been shed on American soil. To prove this Douglas used all his skill as an advocate, citing sometimes spurious evidence to support his case and ignoring facts which refuted it. The region between the Rio Grande and the Nueces belonged to the United States, he argued, because it belonged to Texas. (The Nueces had been the boundary of the state of Texas in the Mexican Republic.) The Texas Republic had extended authority over it after the war of independence. (It had not.) After the battle of San Jacinto, he said, Santa Anna by treaty had accepted the Rio Grande as the boundary. (Mexico had never ratified the treaty nor recognized the new republic.)

His cleverest stroke was in rebuttal against John Quincy Adams, his constant heckler and bitterest of the Whig critics. He quoted Adams verbatim as secretary of state in 1819 as stating that our title to the Rio Grande was "as clear as to the island of New Orleans." The old man replied with a lame quibble, but his young opponent convinced the House. Nothing could have so increased the prestige of the apprentice congressman as this victory over an elder statesman, particularly one so formidable and eloquent as Adams. In the carefully prepared Senate speech two years later he went over the same grounds, producing a copy of the Santa Anna Treaty which agreed neither with the published version — already printed in Niles' Register — nor the secret treaty itself. Certainly he was careless in his zeal to justify his party's action.

His reason, and that of Polk, for opposing the Wilmot Proviso was in part that it was attached to an appropriation bill for funds to buy territory and hasten victory. Polk had other troubles: his two victorious generals, Taylor and Scott, were supposedly Whigs who might be chosen by that party as candidates for the presidency in 1848. To offset this danger he yielded to Benton's insistence that he recommend the creation of the rank of lieutenant general and appoint the Missourian to it. Douglas and the congressional advisers could not dissuade the President, and when the Senate rejected the recommendation, Benton blamed Polk.

Polk decided upon an offensive, not a defensive war. Shortly after Scott captured Mexico City in the fall of 1847, Commissioner Nicholas P. Trist drew up and sent to the President a treaty ceding New Mexico and California for fifteen million dollars and the Rio Grande boundary in return for our assumption of the claims of American citizens. By this time sentiment was growing for the acquisition of all of Mexico; needless to say, Douglas shared it. But Polk hastily presented the treaty to the Senate, which ratified it.

The new senator from Illinois objected strenuously to the fifth article, stating in regard to the new boundary line that "no change shall ever be made therein except by the express and free consent of both nations." He alleged this implied some guilt on the part of the United States in the recent conflict, but later he revealed his true reason: "It pledges the faith of the Republic that our successors shall not do that which duty to the interests, and honor of the country, in the progress of events, may compel them to do." In other words, at some later date Manifest Destiny might dictate another bite on our southern neighbor!

In the midst of preoccupation with these high matters of state the Senator, at the age of thirty-four, took for himself a southern belle as wife. This marriage involved him even more with the problem of slavery, which would become increasingly significant in the future. When he first came to Washington he formed a close friendship with his seat-mate, David S. Reid of North Carolina. Shortly Reid's planter uncle, Colonel Robert Martin, visited Washington with his two daughters. At once a mutual attraction developed between the Little Giant and Martha Reid. Soon he visited the Martins at their plantation on the upper Dan, and three years later he married Martha. During the courtship he dropped many of his rough western ways; he gave up liquor and his cigar and became careful of his dress. Immediately after the wedding he took his bride to Chicago, where he now moved his residence.

Mrs. Douglas returned to the capital with him when Congress reopened. Before she died in childbirth six years later, she bore him two sons. In the interval her husband, for the first time in his hectic career, enjoyed the full pleasures of a settled domestic life. This experience, and her early death which probably shook him emotionally more than any event in his life, inevitably changed his personality. Already wise in the ways of politics and in the ways of the male world of the barroom and the capitol lobby, now that he had his own hostages to fortune he was forced into a human insight and understanding previously absent from his make-up.

The effect of a southern marriage upon Douglas the politician and the emerging statesman was equally great. Before entering Congress he had never been south of Louisville. He did make speaking tours there in the campaigns of 1844 and 1848, but by intimate association with his wife's family and their friends he was exposed to an aristocratic culture and to the southern point of view. At least he saw southern life as it was lived firsthand, not through the eyes of William Lloyd Garrison or Harriet Beecher Stowe.

But his new relationship submitted him to serious criticism from his northern enemies. As a wedding gift Colonel Martin gave him the deed to a plantation on the Pearl River in Mississippi worth one hundred thousand dollars. The son-in-law courteously refused. He explained that he was no Abolitionist, but as a prod· uct of a northern environment he was incapable of handling property in slaves. A lesser man would have accepted the gift and sold it. Colonel Martin respected his wishes. Upon the Colonel's death a year later it was discovered that he had named the Little Giant manager of the property, left by will to Martha Douglas, and directed that his son-in-law be paid one-fifth of the income as a fee. For years the Senator was charged in the North with the ownership of slaves.

His attitude in the matter was well-expressed in a letter he wrote to his friend Charles Lanphier, editor of the *Illinois State Register:* "It is true that my wife does own about 150 Negroes in Mississippi. My father-in-law in his lifetime offered them to me and I refused to accept them. *This fact is stated in his will,* but I do not want it brought before the public, as the public have no business with my private affairs, and besides anybody would see that the information must have come from me. My wife has no Negroes except those in Mississippi. We have other property in North Carolina, but no Negroes. It is our intention, however, to remove all our property to Illinois as soon as possible."

The lad who arrived almost penniless in Illinois fifteen years before was well along the road to success. He had become a member of the United States Senate and he had acquired a wife. Already the most prominent citizen of his state, a resident of the city destined to become the hub of the Mississippi Valley, and still in his middle thirties, he had good reason to view the future with confidence and with optimism.

I I I
Compromise of 1850:
The Statesman Emerges

POLK was not a tool of the "Slave Power." To a greater degree than Jackson he spoke for the expansionist democracy of the Mississippi Valley, both south and north of the Ohio. To the ultras of each section he said "a plague on both your houses." Like Jackson he vetoed internal improvements and he succeeded in getting Congress to lower the tariff. By luck, nerve, and persistence he accomplished most of the objectives with which he entered the White House, and he stuck by his announced resolve not to seek a second term. But he alienated prominent elder statesmen in his party; in his administration the split between South and West, which produced the Republican Party, began. Despite the heat of the debates over the Wilmot Proviso, however, it did not seem at the time that this split was more than the normal trouble of the party returning to power.

Behind the scene in the Democratic Party an old feud between Calhoun on one hand and Van Buren and Benton on the other dated from the Jacksonian era. Now it became even more bitter. Polk, a trusted Jackson lieutenant himself, attempted to remain neutral among the three and ended by alienating them all. Van Buren was unhappy when Polk was selected over him in 1844. Further disgruntled by cabinet appointments, he gave the administration little support and in 1848 helped defeat the Democrats by accepting the Free-Soil nomination. The President refused to retain Calhoun as secretary of state; and the Carolinian fought back on Oregon and Mexico. Benton went into opposition when Congress refused Polk's request for a lieutenant generalship for him and the administration decided upon court-martial of his son-in-law, John Frémont. Benton was largely responsible for the canard that such actions were evidence of Calhoun's influence over the President. Becoming bitterly antislavery, the Missourian in a few years was retired from the Senate by his own state.

Anxious to restore party harmony, Polk was dismayed at the furor set off by the Wilmot Proviso. His own solution was the extension of the Missouri Compromise line through the new territory. He at once pronounced the Proviso vicious: "a mischievous and foolish amendment. . . . If persisted in it will be attended with terrible consequences to the country, and cannot fail to destroy the Democratic Party, if it does not ultimately threaten the Union itself. Slavery was one of the questions adjusted in the compromises of the Constitution. It has, and can have, no legitimate connection with the war with Mexico."

Wilmot was a Pennsylvania Democrat who had western support; the Proviso had been introduced by northern ultras for political purposes and would be used by southern ultras as a further excuse for a southern party. "There is no patriotism on either side," Polk concluded. "It is a most wicked agitation that can end in no good." At the same time he called Calhoun "the most mischievous man in the Senate . . . governed more by his personal and political interests than by the public good." He pointed out that slavery was impossible in the territory acquired from Mexico for geographical reasons, so the Proviso was unnecessary; he urged immediate organization of government in the new area. For Douglas and the President extension of the Missouri Compromise line to the Pacific would eliminate from Congress debates over slavery, which blocked other legislation and aroused passions.

As a result of Calhoun's strategy, southern obstruction became serious in the 1840's. As early as 1838 he had insisted upon meeting the abolitionist attack head-on. He proposed, not a southern party, but a southern bloc in the Democratic Party which would force concessions to slavery by obstructionist tactics. Earlier abolitionists had attempted the same method of sabotaging legislation, but since they controlled practically no votes Congress had been able to dispose of their obstruction by such devices as the Gag Rule, which excluded debate on their petitions. The Calhoun group did control votes and could force compromise. Many southerners suspected both Calhoun's motives and his method, preferring to wait for a frontal attack on slavery before unified action, and southern Whigs blocked the full application of his strategy until after 1850. But the tactics of his group were increasingly irritating. Douglas, like many northerners who had no use for abolitionists, undoubtedly agreed with one congressman, who blurted out the truth: "From morning to night, day after day and week after week, nothing can get a hearing that will not afford an opportunity to lug in something about Negro slavery. . . . Sir, I am heartily tired of this nigger business. I want a change. I beg gentlemen to remember there are some white people in this country, and that these white people are entitled to some consideration."

These words were spoken in 1848, when the southern obstruction policy had been answered in kind by the northern obstruction of the Proviso. The southern chickens had come home to roost. Now a vehement northern opposition, supported by many in Douglas's own Northwest, prevented the extension of the Missouri Compromise and the establishment of territorial government. The chairman of the Senate Committee on Territories had to deal with two, instead of one, obstructionist groups.

For some time the Little Giant sought simply to ignore or play down the slavery question. But as a new senator brashly inclined to put the venerable Calhoun and Webster in their places, he expressed his sentiments candidly in one dramatic instance. Abolitionist Senator John Hale of New Hampshire in 1848 aroused the ire of Mississippi Senator Henry Foote and of Calhoun. Foote invited Hale to come to Mississippi to "grace one of the tallest trees of the forest, with a rope around his neck." The Carolinian said he would as soon argue with a maniac from Bedlam as with the Senator from New Hampshire.

Here Douglas entered the debate. He had already condemned remarks like those of Hale as a form of northern fanaticism responsible for the increasing sectional rancor; now he said the same to his southern colleagues. Foote, he charged, had given the abolitionists ten thousand votes: "It is the speeches of Southern men, representing Slave States, going to an extreme, breathing a fanaticism as wild and as reckless as that of the Senator from New Hampshire, which creates Abolitionism in the North." Since Foote and Calhoun now turned their attack on Douglas, he developed his position fully for the first time.

He had no sympathy, he said, either for the Abolitionists or the southern ultras. Northern Democrats would not permit themselves to be destroyed by the violence of the latter. Hale "is upheld at the North because he is a champion of Abolition; and you are upheld at the South, because you are the champion who meets him; so it comes to this, that between those two Ultra parties, we of the North who belong to neither are thrust aside." He knew southern life from personal observation and understood their resentment: "We stand up for all your Constitutional rights, in which we will protect you to the last . . . but we protest against being instruments . . . puppets . . . in this slavery excitement, which can operate only to your interests and the building up of those who wish to put you down."

Foote had warned the Senator from Illinois that he was only deluding himself if he thought he could remain neutral in the dispute over slavery. He was not, Douglas replied, speaking either for or against the institution, the existence or the absence of which depended upon local opinion. "In the North it is not expected that we should take the position that slavery is a positive good — a positive blessing. If we did assume such a position, it would be a very pertinent inquiry, why do you not adopt this institution? We have moulded our institutions at the North as we have thought proper; and now we say to you of the South, if slavery be a blessing, it is your blessing; if it be a curse, it is your curse; enjoy it — on you rests all the responsibility! We are prepared to aid you in the maintenance of all your Constitutional rights, and I apprehend that no man, South or North, has shown more consistently a disposition to do so than myself. . . . But I claim the privilege of pointing out to you how you give strength and encouragement to the Abolitionists."

In these remarks Douglas was already moving to popular sovereignty, or nonintervention as he was to call it, as a method of removing from congressional debate the question of slavery in the territories. Later in the second session of the same Congress he left no doubts about his conversion to the new doctrine. To settle the question, he said, "Let us banish the agitation from these halls. Let us remove the causes which produced it; let us settle the territories we have acquired, in a manner to satisfy the honor and respect the feelings of every portion of the Union. . . . Bring those territories into this Union as States upon an equal footing with the original States. Let the people of such States settle the question of slavery within their limits, as they would settle the question of banking, or any other domestic institution, according to their own will."

There was little new in this; few denied the right of a *state* to act on the matter for itself. Then he advanced to the newer proposal: "No man advocates the extension of slavery over a territory now free. On the other hand, they deny the propriety of Congress interfering to restrain, upon the great fundamental principle that the people are the source of all power; that from the people must emanate all government; that the people have the same right in these territories to establish a government for themselves that we have to overthrow our present government and establish another, if we please, or that any other government has to establish one for itself." In short, the people of the territories, not Congress, should have the exclusive right to determine the status of slavery within their own boundaries *prior to their admission as states.*

This proposal, already suggested by Democratic candidate Lewis Cass in 1848, came at a critical point in the history of the territories and of slavery. Seven of the original thirteen states — from Pennsylvania northward — abolished slavery within a generation after the Revolution; the six southern states retained it. By the Northwest Ordinance of 1787 the Confederation Congress prohibited slavery in the Northwest Territory (the area west of the Alleghenies and north of the Ohio surrendered by the states to the national government in 1781), thus applying to it the approximate geographic line already dividing free and slave states. The ordinance also provided for admission of territories, after a period of limited self-government and upon sufficient growth in population, into the Union as states equal to the original thirteen "in all respects." By 1819 Congress had admitted seven new states, accepting without alteration the constitutions drawn up by their residents prior to statehood. All those in the region from which the Ordinance of 1787 excluded slavery became free states. But Kentucky and Tennessee, the western parts of Virginia and North Carolina respectively, entered the Union with the consent of the parent states and like them gave legal sanction to slavery. Southwestern territories, formed in the area later surrendered to the national government by Georgia and from which slavery was *not* excluded, were likewise admitted with constitutions which legalized slavery.

At this point free and slave states were equal in number and thus shared control of the Senate, though the more populous free states had a sizable majority in the lower house. When Missouri, the second territory organized in the Louisiana Purchase, applied for admission in 1819 with slavery, Congressman James Tallmadge of New York introduced an amendment requiring gradual emancipation. Passed by the House, this amendment was rejected by the Senate. Like the Wilmot Proviso later, it set off a bitter sectional debate. But in spite of strenuous northern opposition Congress finally adopted a compromise which permitted Missouri to enter without restriction on slavery as she desired. To preserve the existing parity in the Senate Maine was admitted as a free state, and slavery was prohibited in the remaining Louisiana Territory north of latitude 36° 30' (the new state's southern boundary). Congress thereby prohibited slavery in the territories a second time through the extension of the older geographic line.

By tacit agreement the precedent of offsetting each new slave state with a free one was followed thereafter, maintaining a potential southern veto in the upper house. Obviously the balance of power in the Senate between the sections depended directly upon the disposition of slavery in the territories, for those in which the institution did not exist were unlikely to incorporate it in their constitutions when applying for admission as states. The annexation of Texas gave the South a means of matching the greater number of free states which could be brought in from the Louisiana Territory, since the compromise line of 1820 had designated a much larger area for free soil than for slavery. Northern insistence upon the Wilmot Proviso in the Mexican Cession of 1848 and northern refusal to extend the 36° 30' line put the South — already a "conscious minority" because of its increasing loss of representation in the House — again on the defensive. Popular sovereignty, on the surface at least, would give southern states an even break in the new region.

Several simultaneous developments — in the South and the West, in Congress, and in his own state of Illinois — caused Douglas to shift his position. It was a shrewd parliamentary maneuver and ultimately a successful one. By it he sought to counteract the growing antisouthern feeling in his own section and to develop a western feeling that would rise above sectionalism. Growing antislavery sentiment in the West and the Northeast undoubtedly led to the introduction of the Wilmot Proviso. Western desire for revenge for the Oregon compromise was also a cogent factor. But the Southwest had kept its bargain with the Northwest in this matter, for seven of its nine Democratic Senators voted against the forty-ninth parallel compromise. Groups in the Southeast and Northeast, as well as the Whigs generally, had put through the Oregon treaty.

Still a third important cause for western pique against the

South, for which it again was unjust to blame the Southwest, was the fact that the Polk administration lowered the tariff and then vetoed the Rivers and Harbors Bill, an internal improvement measure dear to the West. In 1845 Calhoun, serving as president of a Memphis railroad convention where delegates from the entire Mississippi Valley united in demanding internal improvements by the Federal Government, departed from his strict construction by finding constitutional warrant for them in the commerce clause, and he later spoke for such a bill in Congress. This was a typical bit of Calhoun maneuvering: he sought support from the West for a lower tariff by a bargain on internal improvements, he was seeking votes for his anticipated candidacy in 1848, and he was trying to substitute the western farmer for the northern working man (then becoming more antislavery in his views) as southern allies. Yet the upshot of the matter was that the South got all of Texas, its admission as a slave state, and a lower tariff; but the West got no internal improvements, only part of Oregon, and the establishment of territorial government there was held up by southern votes. Votes of slave states were blocking legislation desired by other sections. Protectionist areas noted that the lower tariff of 1846, which passed in the Senate by one vote, received the support of both Texas Senators. Why not reduce southern power in the future by prohibiting slavery in new territories?

The most direct influence upon Douglas in his shift of position, however, was his failure as chairman of the Senate Committee on Territories to induce Congress to adopt his specific recommendations. He had introduced bills for territorial governments in Minnesota and Nebraska in the older area, and for Oregon, California, Utah, and New Mexico in the newer. Southerners opposed the organization of territories in the older area made free by the Missouri Compromise, and in Oregon, unless they received concessions in the new region recently acquired from Mexico; Proviso men from the North would make no concessions. In short, the House, where the North held control, rejected any Senate bill which did not prohibit slavery; the Senate, where the South had parity, insisted upon an extension of the Missouri Compromise line or some similar compromise and refused to act upon the House bills. For several years the two houses were deadlocked, but action was essential after the Gold Rush of 1849. Otherwise it was possible that California might decide to remain an independent republic.

Northern sentiment in the House blocked the extension of the 36° 30' line through the new region, which even Calhoun would have accepted. In response to the Proviso, southern ultras moved to make slavery legal in all territories. The Carolinian looked again at the Constitution and came out with the necessary logic — logic which the Supreme Court accepted ten years later in the Dred Scott Decision. The territories were held in trust for the states by the national government. The Constitution recognized slaves as property; the fifth amendment prevented the national government from depriving a person of property without due process of law. Slaves like mules could therefore be taken into all territories; Congress could not prohibit slavery in them as it had done in the Missouri Compromise.

In this impasse Cass and Douglas advanced their new proposal: Let the people of the territories decide about slavery for themselves. This solution had the virtue of conforming with the American tradition of self-government and democracy; its more practical consequence would be the removal of debates over slavery from the halls of Congress. Its disadvantage, as some southerners ultimately realized, lay in the fact that where soil and climate in the new region made it unsuited for cotton, its residents would probably outlaw slavery. Parity in the Senate, the South's last defense against the northern majority, might then be lost. Yet popular sovereignty was preferable to the Proviso, and at first acceptable to many southerners.

Douglas's parliamentary maneuvers to overcome the opposition of ultras in both sections to the organization of territorial or state governments, or both, during the several years before 1850 were unsuccessful. Their failure was highly important in conditioning his mind to an acceptance of popular sovereignty as the only means of preventing the debate over slavery from disrupting the parties. No existing law on slavery applied to Oregon and the Mexican Cession, unless the courts should retain the Mexican law prohibiting slavery in the latter. Congress, of course, could settle the matter by statute, as it had in similar situations in 1787 and in 1820. Each of the ultra groups was suspicious of the other and both were afraid of committing themselves to a precedent. Both were also very much aware that the ultimate consideration was balance of power in Congress.

In January, 1848, the chairman of the Committee on Territories introduced in the Senate his fourth Oregon Bill, but before he could defend it he was called to the deathbed of his father-in-law. His committee was deadlocked. The southerners conceded that the people of that territory did not want slavery, yet if Congress exercised the power to exclude slavery from Oregon it could use that power to keep slavery from other areas also. A special committee, with Senator Clayton of Delaware as chairman, reported a compromise. The territorial legislature of Oregon could act on slavery as it desired, but the prospective legislatures of territories of California and New Mexico were forbidden to pass laws on the subject. The issue there would be settled by the courts, with the right of appeal to the Supreme Court. Upon his return Douglas supported this bill, which the Senate passed and the House rejected.

He next pressed his original bill, with an amendment prohibiting slavery because the "said territory is north of the parallel of 36° 30'." He told the senators that their vote would not commit them to a precedent, but they would have none of it. Then he proposed extension of the line through all of the new territories to the Pacific. The Senate passed the measure but the House remained adamant. At the end of the long session the upper house finally gave way and accepted the bill of the lower, organizing the territory of Oregon and prohibiting slavery therein. It was identical with the original bill which the Senator from Illinois had introduced in the House several years before.

Persistence at length won out on Oregon, but not on the more critical matter of California and the rest of the Mexican Cession, to which Douglas next turned his attention. He had recently patched up a quarrel with Polk and had consulted with the President about his final message. (By this time the Democrats had suffered defeat in the presidential election of 1848.) Having agreed, however, with Polk's recommendation that either the Missouri Compromise line be extended or that the question of slavery in the new territories be left to the judiciary for settlement, the Senator made a radical and ingenious proposal of his own when Congress met: admit all the new territory at once as a state, skipping the territorial stage. He confessed that he did so because he had no hope for the passage of a territorial bill in that session. The measure was referred, not to his own committee, but to the Judiciary Committee on which southerners were in a majority. There it died, after Douglas got into arguments over the nature of sovereignty. Without success he then proposed the admission of the western part of California as a state, or the admission of California and New Mexico as two states.

At the end of the session Senator Walker of Wisconsin added a rider to the appropriations bill authorizing the President to set up a quasi-territorial government in the whole new area. With Douglas voting in the affirmative this measure passed the Senate, but the House still insisted upon its territorial bill for California excluding slavery. When conference produced no agreement Douglas urged acceptance of the House bill by the Senate, the same ruse that had finally worked on Oregon. "I have tried to get up State bills," he said in answer to the charge of inconsistency, "territorial bills, and all kinds of bills in all shapes, in the hope that some bill, in some shape, would satisfy the Senate. . . . Now I wish to make another and final effort . . . towards giving a government to the people of California." But at the last minute Congress passed the appropriations bill without the rider. The net accomplishment of the chairman of the Committee on Territories, after several years of effort, was only bills organizing the territories of Oregon and Minnesota. At this point the Whig administration of Zachary Taylor took over.

The defeat of Douglas's immediate objective in Congress in 1848 — the organization of formal government in California — was the consequence of a crisis in the nation and in Illinois state over slavery. In that year, in fact, the Illinois legislature instructed its representatives in Congress to vote for the Wilmot Proviso; the Senator had consistently voted against it. Both parties were split internally over slavery, but to the Democratic Party the division brought defeat in the presidential election. The bitter recriminations which followed threatened to produce the passage of the Proviso, supported by northern Democrats in revenge for alleged southern desertion; its adoption might well have induced embittered southerners to attempt secession. The career of the Senator from Illinois, as well as the fate of California and possibly the Union, was at stake. To save all three he must find some means of restoring harmony in his state, his party, and the nation.

Both national parties in 1848 sought to offset the divisive force of the dispute over slavery. The Democrats, on the record more pro-southern, nominated the northerner Cass of Michigan, who offered the South the concession of popular sovereignty. The Whigs chose the slaveholding southerner, General Zachary Taylor. Proviso men and Free-Soilers formed a third party, nominated ex-President Van Buren who received almost 300,000 votes, and took enough Democrat votes in New York from Cass to give that state and the election to Taylor. Both the popular appeal of the hero of the recent war and the inroads of the Free-Soil Party influenced the outcome. Northern and southern Democrats each blamed the defeat upon the other. Undoubtedly some southern Democrats voted for Taylor because he was a southerner and some northern Whigs voted against him because he held slaves. Northern Democrats also voted against Cass because he rejected the Proviso, or because his party had failed to acquire all of Oregon.

Soon after the election a bill to abolish the slave trade in the District of Columbia passed the House. Southerners under Calhoun's leadership called a caucus to present a united front on the various controversial issues before the nation. Regarding this move as a ruse to rob them of the fruits of their recent victory, southern Whigs opposed the Calhoun tactics and only two of them signed the address finally drawn up by the caucus. Undaunted, the Carolinian continued to urge a convention of the southern states; in the fall of 1849 the state of Mississippi issued such a call for a meeting at Nashville in June, 1850. Failure of the northern states to return fugitive slaves as required by the Constitution, proposals for interference with the slave trade, the imminence of the passage of the Proviso and of California's admission as a free state — all disturbed southern Whigs and Democrats alike. They differed chiefly as to the proper methods of resisting current evils. Calhoun was probably feinting secession to wrest greater concessions from the North when Congress got around to the business of compromise. But to produce the necessary effect the South had to appear to mean business.

As in 1841 the Whigs were soon split, and Henry Clay found himself again fighting a President from his own party. But southern Whigs were disillusioned first. They discovered that the President had fallen under the influence of William Seward, the radical Senator from New York; that he had secretly sent an emissary to urge California to draft a constitution and planned to ask Congress for its admission as a state. Soon after Taylor's messenger arrived the Californians elected delegates to a convention, which later drew up a constitution excluding slavery. Southern Whigs were prepared to accept the admission of California but only in return for concessions on other matters. The President would make none and in a private meeting he told them in no uncertain terms that he would answer a move towards secession by force, as Jackson had formerly met South Carolina's threatened nullification. Douglas knew of these developments, and when he drew up his plan for averting the crisis he was in close contact with these same southern Whigs.

For various reasons the Wilmot Proviso had a strong appeal in the North — not just to its small minority of abolitionists. Led now by fiery agitators like Garrison instead of mild Quakers, this group exercised an influence out of proportion to its size. Abolitionists proposed immediate emancipation, either with compensation to slaveowners or without. As a third party they never won more than 67,000 votes, though there were fellow travelers in both major parties. In general they were unpopular, particularly since their radical wing urged secession from an "unholy" Union, and their leaders were frequently handled roughly. The majority of the northern public admitted the constitutional obligation which protected slaves as southern property, though personal liberty laws passed by northern states impeded the return of fugitive slaves. Yet even this majority regarded the institution of slavery as immoral, un-Christian, and inhuman — a national disgrace — and favored its exclusion from territories as a step towards its ultimate decline in the South itself.

A third attitude, equally significant, was simply an anti-Negro one. Strong in the Northwest and among northern laborers, it had no concern for morality or humanity. Farmers and laborers who wished to attain greater economic opportunity and affluence by migrating to the new territories of the West wished to exclude the black race as well as slave labor and aristocrats. (The Illinois Constitution of 1848 prohibited the immigration of free Negroes.) In addition many northerners, in response to the utterances of southern hotheads, became antisouthern, and therefore in effect antislavery. Changes in the attitude of the Northwest were largely the result of economic developments of the 1840's.

The Ohio Valley had been settled first. Its commercial ties, by the edict of geography, were at first exclusively with the lower Mississippi Valley. Its early residents, in Illinois in particular, were largely southern in origin. Some migrants crossed the Ohio because they disliked Negroes, some actually took their slaves along — seven hundred Negroes were held in indenture in Illinois when it entered the Union. Many of them were small farmers who had been forced out when planters moved into the southern interior. But when the states built canals in the 1830's connecting the Ohio with the Great Lakes, the region developed economic connection with the Northeast by the Erie Canal; thereafter the upper part of the Northwest was settled and grew more rapidly than the lower. These new settlers came mostly from the Northeast, and many after 1848 were foreign immigrants, whose views on government and slavery differed from those of earlier residents. A conflict ensued in each of the northwestern states, accentuated by a lively commercial rivalry. State leaders like Douglas, who moved to Chicago in 1847 for economic reasons, were caught in the middle of this conflict. Naturally they sought to reduce it by compromise.

Southern Illinois has been mistakenly regarded as prosouthern. Like most areas it followed the dictates of self-interest and rationalized its legislative program in terms of the national interest. But its residents were better conditioned to understand the point of view of southerners and to compromise with them, as the Memphis Railroad Convention in 1845 revealed. Not so in the northern part of the state, where moral antipathy to slavery was growing. Douglas realized, however, that Illinois was a microcosm of the nation, that the ties which bound its sections together were stronger than those which divided them. He proposed, therefore, Federal subsidy of an Illinois Central Railroad to run from Chicago to Cairo, and an extension of it to the Gulf of Mexico, to reduce the friction between southern and northern Illinois, between the Northwest and the Southwest. This project, indeed, he considered as important and as mandatory as the admission of California, and it too was initially blocked by the slavery controversy. That controversy must somehow be settled to clear the way for both these pet measures.

In 1848 Illinois went Democratic by a small margin: 56,300 to 53,047 for the Whigs and 15,774 for the Free-Soilers. Compared with the election of 1844, this represented a tremendous gain for the third party, an increase of 7519 for the Whigs and a decline of 1620 for the Democrats. The strength of antislavery men among the Democrats was soon reflected in the instructions of the Democratic legislature that state representatives vote for the Proviso in Congress. Up to this point Douglas had voted against the Proviso and for the extension of the Missouri line or some other compromise. He thereafter made some pretense of following the instructions in his votes, but spoke against them in speeches and fought for their repeal in his home state.

Since public opinion in the state would no longer support an extension of the compromise line, at this point he shifted to popular sovereignty. The new plan would accomplish the identical purpose of the Proviso, he argued, for the territories in question were by nature unsuited to slavery. Within a year he had the satisfaction of seeing the decline of the Free-Soil Party in Illinois and the repeal of the instructions. Popular sovereignty proved effective also in the South, since it implied home rule — that is, state control — over slavery. Most important of all, it got rid of the Proviso which was inciting so much furor south of the Ohio.

When Congress met late in 1849, the nation was facing an ugly crisis. Northern legislatures with few exceptions had passed resolutions urging the Proviso and the immediate admission of California as a free state; most southern legislatures had responded with resolutions to the contrary. Mississippi had called for a southern convention which, by all indications, would decide upon secession of the South should the northern majority succeed in pushing its program through Congress. For once it seemed that the public was as aroused as the politicians. Weeks were required for the House to elect a speaker, largely because of the tactics of the Free-Soil minority, which held the balance of power. Passions reached a new heat as threats of violence became frequent and open. A climax came when the politically moderate Robert Toombs of Georgia succumbed to the intense feelings of the moment. "I have as much attachment to the Union of these States," he told his colleagues, "under the Constitution of our fathers, as any freeman ought to have. I am ready to concede and sacrifice for it whatever a just and honorable man ought to sacrifice. [But] I do not . . . hesitate to avow before this House and the Country, and in the presence of the living God, that if by your legislation you seek to drive us from the territories of California and New Mexico . . . I am for disunion."

That the crisis was resolved, that counsels of appeasement at last prevailed in the North and attachment to the Union at last prevailed in the South, there can be no doubt. Yet the triumvirate of the statesmen of America's Silver Age — Clay, Webster, and Calhoun — were correct, so events proved, in believing that the sectional conflict over slavery would disrupt the Union. The younger generation then coming into power were generally not as disturbed; Seward even poured fuel on the flames in power-politics fashion, and Douglas from the first predicted that compromise would be the outcome. Despite the long deadlock between the two houses, the failure of his efforts for California in the last session, and the obvious increase in the intensity of sectional bitterness, the Senator from Illinois was confident that the conflict would be peacefully resolved. "The Union will not be put in peril," he assured the Senate. "California will be admitted; governments for the territories must be established; and thus the controversy will end, and, I trust, forever." All along he voiced similar sentiments in private conversations with his lieutenants.

Why this optimism? The Little Giant realized that events had taken a turn for the worse when Congress assembled in 1849: "He must be blind who does not see that there is really danger in it." Yet already he was in the process of forming a coalition which he believed would arrive at a satisfactory settlement. Undoubtedly he thought that the politicians had gotten ahead of the people, that in the end the sentiment of nationalism would prove stronger than that of sectional particularism. He was aware that in a parliamentary struggle extreme positions taken for effect could be abandoned overnight. He discounted heavily the vituperative and passionate language of congressmen and editors because he himself used such language in debate when he did not at all mean it. Finally, as a successful man, Douglas believed in his own ability to win others to his proposals.

His plan was to have all measures pertaining to territories referred to his committee, and having worked out in advance terms of settlement acceptable to a majority in the lower house, to present bills to the Senate. Since the southern wing of his own party under Calhoun and Davis was recalcitrant, he approached the moderate southern Whig group under Toombs which had recently broken with the President. Southern Whigs would concede California in return for certain concessions on slavery. Not all southern Democrats followed the Calhoun-Davis leadership; the hothead Foote now urged compromise, broke openly with Calhoun in the Senate, and fully supported the effort of Douglas. Accordingly, at a meeting between the Little Giant's lieutenants and the southern Whig leaders in the House, terms were agreed upon and put in writing. California was to be admitted under its free constitution; territorial governments were to be organized in the rest of the area and the residents allowed to legislate as they pleased on slavery; Congress was to admit these territories without restrictions on slavery; and attempts to abolish slavery in the District of Columbia would be opposed. (A more stringent fugitive slave bill had already been introduced.)

Before Douglas could proceed with his plan, Clay, after obtaining Webster's concurrence, introduced his own resolutions in the Senate. These were referred — not to the Committee on Territories — but to a select committee of thirteen which presented all the territorial provisions in one bill: an Omnibus. The Little Giant objected to this procedure but acquiesced when he was outvoted. He correctly predicted that such a bill would be defeated because it would unify the opposition; he refused to become a member of the committee in order that he might be free to proceed with his own method when the other was defeated. He did magnanimously allow Clay to use two of his own bills. Allegedly this led the Kentuckian to assert, "You are the most generous man living. I will unite the bills and report them; but justice shall nevertheless be done you as the real author of the measures." At the moment the Senator from Illinois was more interested in action than in credit.

Many senators spoke during the hectic months of debate, but the arguments of five illustrate the main positions: those of Clay, Webster and Douglas for the compromise, and those of Calhoun and Seward against it. In his January resolutions the Kentuckian proposed the following measures: California should be admitted as a state and New Mexico organized as a territory without congressional restrictions on slavery (this meant California would come in as a free state as provided in the constitution already drawn up by its residents); Texas should surrender some disputed territory to New Mexico in return for Federal assumption of its pre-annexation debt; slavery should not be abolished in the District of Columbia without the consent of its residents and of the state of Maryland, but the slave trade should be forbidden in the area; a Federal statute should be passed for the recovery of fugitive slaves, and the absence of any congressional power to interfere with the interstate slave trade should be confirmed. The territorial provisions, it should be noted, were identical with those already arranged by Douglas.

Webster and Clay pleaded eloquently for Union, but their arguments differed little. They asked the North to surrender the Proviso, since the new territory would in any event become free soil. "What more do you want?" asked Clay. "You have got what is worth a thousand Wilmot Provisos. You have got nature itself on your side." They warned the South that secession would result in war, and they appealed to moderates in both sections to support reciprocal concessions as essential to peace and to Union. In return for acceptance of a free California, the South would get a Federal guarantee that the Constitutional recognition of slave property would be honored.

Calhoun spoke for the southern extremists. The rights of his section in the territories must be conceded, the North must return fugitive slaves and cease all agitation about slavery. An amendment to the Constitution must be passed to restore the equilibrium of power between the two sections, which would be broken by the admission of California as a free state.

Seward spoke for the extremists of his section: he called for an end of the appeasement of the "slavocracy." California must be admitted as a free state and the northern majority should use its power to abolish slavery both in the territories and in the nation. The struggle was between "right and wrong"; slavery, if not contrary to the Constitution, violated an even higher law. No concessions should be made to the South.

Douglas gave the Omnibus his full support and argued for it with his customary exuberance. Perhaps his chief contribution was the clarity with which he developed the doctrine of nonintervention, aware as he was that by it he stood the best chance of winning the necessary votes of western Democrats and southerners of both parties. In his first major speech he defended the consistency of the northern Democrats and chided Webster for his tardiness in recognizing that, as Cass had argued in 1848, a law of nature made the territories free. But his most effective efforts were his answers to Calhoun and Davis.

"What share has the South of the Territories?" he asked Calhoun, "or the North? or any other geographical division unknown to the Constitution? I answer, none — none at all. The Territories belong to the United States as one people, one nation, and are to be disposed of, according to the principles of the Constitution. . . . It is no violation of the Southern rights to prohibit slavery, nor of Northern rights to leave the people to decide the question for themselves." He went on to argue that no congressional legislation on slavery had ever been effective, neither the Northwest Ordinance of 1787 nor the Missouri Compromise. Despite the Ordinance, slaves had been held in Illinois and the institution had later disappeared in that state only because natural laws so ordained it. Congress, in effect, could not legislate against climate.

For this reason the Carolinian's proposed equilibrium between the sections was "a moral and physical impossibility." In time all the border states would adopt a gradual system of emancipation; from the vast trans-Mississippi West at least seventeen states would enter the Union. "I think I am safe in assuming that each of these will be free Territories and free States, whether Congress shall prohibit slavery or not." But this inevitable minority status for the South in no wise endangered her peculiar institution; the Constitution protected it in states where it existed. The democratic and the wisest procedure was to allow residents of territories to settle the question in their own area for themselves.

His most powerful defense of popular sovereignty, however, was presented in debate with Jefferson Davis, who proposed an amendment prohibiting territorial legislatures from passing any laws in regard to slavery and who accused his Illinois colleague of refusing to protect legal property. "I wish to allow these people to pass such laws as they deem proper respecting their rights in property without any exception," replied the Little Giant. "He might just as well say that I am opposed to protecting property in merchandize, steamboats, in cattle, in property of any other description; for I desire to put them all on an equality. . . . I do not hold to the doctrine that to exclude any species of property by law from any territory is a violation of any right to property. Do you not exclude banks from most of the territories? Do you not exclude whiskey . . . gambling tables, which are properly recognized as such in the states where they are tolerated? I am opposed to any provision in this bill prohibiting the people of the territory from legislating in respect to African slavery."

By the end of July the Omnibus was stripped down to a mere measure organizing the territory of Utah. The defeat, which Douglas had earlier predicted, was the result of the "union between the Free Soils and Disunionists and the Administration of Gen'l Taylor which had brought all the power and patronage of the Gov't . . . to bear against us." Even the leadership of Clay had hurt the measure. "If Mr. Clay's name had not been associated with the bills," observed his younger colleague, "they would have passed long ago. The Administration was jealous of him and hated him and some Democrats were weak enough to fear that the success of his bill would make him President. But let it always be said of Old Hal that he fought a glorious and patriotic battle. No man was ever governed by higher and purer motives."

With Taylor and Calhoun dead, Webster elevated to the cabinet, and Clay absent because of poor health, Douglas took command. He called up, in order, his California bill, the Texas boundary measure, the New Mexico bill, all of which passed the Senate within two weeks. Amendments which restricted the territories' action on slavery, or their entrance later as states, were rejected. Soon the Fugitive Slave Act and the bill abolishing the slave trade in the District were similarly passed, though not under his direct leadership, as these were not territorial matters. All along his lieutenants were pushing the same measures in the lower House, where there was greater opposition. But early in September it too adopted the several measures and the Compromise became law.

After nine months of wrangling Congress thus effected a compromise acceptable to a majority in both sections. The Proviso was rejected, the Nashville Convention fizzled out, and calm was generally restored. But the traditional explanation of the outcome is inadequate: that the aging Whigs Clay and Webster, by their eloquence, won the North to forbearance and the South to acceptance over the pleas of extremists like Seward and Calhoun.

Actually Cass of Michigan, Foote of Mississippi, and Douglas — to mention only three of the Democratic leaders in the Senate — all proposed and were working for compromise before Clay introduced his resolutions in January. His terms were constantly opposed by a majority of the northern Whigs and by President Taylor, despite Webster's Seventh of March speech. By midsummer the Omnibus had been rejected in the Senate except for a minor item. Then the Little Giant, with the support of other Democratic leaders, the rank and file of his party, and the southern Whigs, reintroduced the rejected measures one by one. A minority of the northern Whigs shifted their votes, since President Fillmore gave the effort his unreserved support, and the separate measures passed both houses by small but sufficient margins.

Many men of good will had worked for compromise. But Jefferson Davis, its opponent, asserted in the final debate that "if any man has a right to be proud of the success of these measures, it is the Senator from Illinois." Credit for the victory, added Clay, was due "to Douglas more than to any other individual." But the Little Giant told the Senate that "no man and no party has acquired a triumph, except the party friendly to the Union triumphing over abolition and disunion."

The fact that public opinion, North and South, had become more moderate, and that the death of President Taylor reduced the Whig opposition which had defeated the Omnibus, cannot detract from the brilliance of Douglas's parliamentary achievement. Once he took over he made but a single speech. Behind the scenes, however, he was constantly at work whipping congressmen of both houses in line for each bill as it came up. Wisely he let his lieutenants do much of the actual bargaining, but it is probable that his influence in the lower house was as great as in the upper. Obviously concessions were made. A majority of Democrats had voted for the Compromise from the beginning; in the final month many Whigs, who had previously voted in the negative, simply absented themselves to save face. From the outset the Little Giant knew, recalling the deadlock which had blocked action in 1849, that pressure upon the House was as essential to success as upon the Senate. Had his objective been partisan his tactics could accurately be described as log-rolling, but since the Union and peace hung in the balance they can objectively be pronounced statesmanship of the highest order. Surely he was justified in expecting as a reward the recognition of his leadership by his party.

One final incident caused him no little embarrassment. Being assured that the debates on the Fugitive Slave bill would last a week, he went to New York to attend to a personal note which had become due. When the Senate voted in his absence his opponents said that he had absented himself to avoid disfavor with his constituents by an affirmative vote. His friends prevented him from answering the charges, but he soon made his good faith clear in a spectacular manner. On his return to Chicago in October he found that the City Council had adopted resolutions denouncing the law and northern congressmen who voted for it as "fit only to be ranked with the traitors, Benedict Arnold and Judas Iscariot." City police were forbidden to assist in the arrest of fugitive slaves, and a huge mass meeting was called to ratify the resolutions. Douglas boldly attended the meeting, read to it the section of the Constitution on fugitive slaves, explained again his doctrine of popular sovereignty, and insisted that the Union depended upon justice being done the South. The meeting then unanimously adopted his counterresolutions that every provision of the Constitution and the laws on fugitive slaves be obeyed. Soon he expressed the same sentiments over the state in the current congressional campaign, with such success that the legislature repealed its earlier Proviso instructions and formally commended the Senator's compromise stand. Rarely had his power to change the convictions of men by the magic of his words and personality been so dramatically exhibited.

Using the same strategy and tactics, the Little Giant in this congressional session secured the passage of another measure of national significance, one to which he was equally attached: the subsidy of a north-south railroad from Chicago to the Gulf of Mexico by the transfer of Federal land to the states through which the road would run. The project illustrated his enlightened self-interest, the breadth of his objectives, and the skill with which he overcame almost insuperable opposition. Such a road increased greatly the value of the real estate he had been buying so intensively in Chicago, but it also reduced the friction between the northern and southern sections of his own state — and no less between the upper and lower Mississippi Valley — which was embarrassing him politically and dissipating the power of his party. By the railroad no less than by the compromise he consciously sought to check the rising sectional intensity which threatened the Union.

His first fight was within the state of Illinois itself. Speculators, including his former colleague in the Senate, Sidney Breese, had invested heavily in the Holbrook Company, which was petitioning for direct grants for a road from Cairo to Galena. The company had even bribed a clerk to smuggle into the acts of the state legislature a transfer to it of any lands ceded to the state by the Federal Government. Douglas objected to the project for two reasons: it would not serve Chicago or a large portion of northeastern Illinois, and the speculators would be enriched at the expense of the people. Finally his alternative was adopted; the land would be transferred directly to the state, which in turn would arrange with a private company for the road's construction, and a branch of the Cairo-Galena route would be extended to Chicago.

To get around the precedent of presidential vetoes of internal improvements, the positive stand of his party in the matter, and the constitutional scruples of southerners, the Senator introduced a bill in Congress ceding to Illinois the public domain within its boundaries. On his second try he put the bill through the Senate, but it was blocked in the lower house by a combination of opponents from the East, from the landless states, and from the South. Thereupon, on a trip to Mobile, he met with southern railroad men from Mississippi and Alabama who were having trouble financing their road to Cairo, and proposed that their states, as well as Illinois, be included in a Federal land grant bill. Congressmen from these states, previously opposed to the Illinois Central Bill on strict constructionist grounds, were now instructed by their respective legislatures to reverse their position. With additional votes from Kentucky and Tennessee, which would benefit from the road but where there was no Federal land left to cede, the enlarged measure passed, though only by the barest majority in the House. Rejection was prevented there, in fact, only by a clever parliamentary maneuver. But the work was his and he took the credit. "If ever a man passed a bill," he later boasted, "I did that one."

As soon as the bill passed the Senator was bedridden by an operation for an abscess in his thigh. The promoter Holbrook called on him with an offer to deed him half the land granted, over two million acres, if he would surrender the release. Incensed, the Little Giant rose from his bed, grabbed his crutches, and drove Holbrook from the room. At his suggestion the Illinois legislature required the eastern capitalists with whom it contracted to build the road to pay the state 7 per cent of their gross earnings.

Thus Douglas overcame the congressional deadlock which had blocked his program for several years. In the process he emerged as a leading national statesman and the parliamentary chief of his party. By the great Compromise and by his railroad bill he hoped that he had checked the debate over slavery and that he had reunited the South and the West.

I V

Calm before the Storm

THE Compromise of 1850 saved the Union. The alliance between the West and the Northwest, represented later by the Republican Party, was years in the future. Had the South attempted secession then, as the minority who called the Nashville Convention wished, it is doubtful if the rest of the nation would have responded by coercion. Since the railroads from the Atlantic to the Mississippi so essential to troop movements and to a more productive economy had not been built, in all probability the North would have failed to prevent southern independence.

A majority in both sections accepted the Compromise in good faith. A rump session of the Nashville Convention reassembled in the fall after Congress acted, but its call for another southern convention was ignored. On the contrary, in state elections throughout the South Whigs joined compromise Democrats in defeating ultra candidates who had prominently opposed the Compromise; in Mississippi (the state which had called the convention) the moderate Foote defeated the ultra Davis. South Carolina secessionists, who had started the movement, admitted that "to secede now would be to secede from the South." The platform of the Georgia Convention best expressed the southern attitude for the moment. It admitted the many advantages the state derived from the Union. Therefore it accepted the Compromise "as a permanent adjustment of the sectional controversy"; yet it warned that the preservation of the Union depended upon "the faithful execution of the Fugitive Slave Bill."

Opposition in the North generally, and certainly among northern Whigs, had been stronger, but there too a majority declared vehemently for the Compromise. Business interests in the East and farming interests in the West, aware of the value of the southern market and of the relation of peace to prosperity, were immensely relieved by the passing of the crisis. Mass meetings in large cities gave the measures their enthusiastic approval. A vocal minority, it is true, announced from the outset its opposition to the Fugitive Slave Act. Conspicuous instances, chiefly in New England, in which the public forcibly prevented the execution of the act, suggested that trouble lay ahead. Webster was excoriated for his support of the bill and probably as a result was passed over for the Whig nomination in 1852. Yet able northern lawyers defended the constitutionality of the law and in the vast majority of instances it was obeyed for several years.

Since the South was definitely the loser under the terms of the Compromise, southern acceptance was more surprising than northern. What did the South get? A bill for the return of fugitive slaves, but the obligation was already expressly enjoined by the Federal Constitution. Her other alleged "gains" were actually concealed losses. The slave trade, but not slavery, was abolished in the District of Columbia. Slavery was not forbidden in Utah and New Mexico, but, as time would prove, its protection there was by no means insured. Texas surrendered territory where slavery was lawful to New Mexico, where its status was uncertain. To offset these "concessions" California entered as a free state, thus ending parity in the Senate between slave and free states. The last sure check upon legislation favored by a growing northern majority was gone. At best it can be said that in losing the South was spared the indignity of the Wilmot Proviso, but the Missouri Compromise principle was abandoned in the new territory. Whether the North, in view of the southern strength in the Senate, could have obtained more is doubtful.

The South accepted the Compromise because nationalism was still stronger there than particularism; many southerners were as yet unwilling to face the conflict between their loyalty to their nation and to their section. Furthermore, the fact that southerners controlled the next two administrations, and indeed reached the height of their political power in this decade, kept many of them from realizing the extent of their loss by the Compromise. Prosperity was an equal if not a more potent reason. With the gold discoveries, the construction of railroads, and the expansion of foreign and domestic markets, the nation enjoyed a period of real economic progress in which the South participated. The price of cotton rose considerably in the 1850's, and the brief depression later in the decade was scarcely felt in that section. The boom, however, was ultimately the undoing of the South and the Democratic Party, for the business interests of the North, fearful of the threat of secession, long permtited southern domination of the party as the price of peace. The rival national party became hopelessly divided between "cotton" and "conscience" Whigs.

Nevertheless, after four years of calm, the slavery dispute was resumed even more vigorously upon the passage of Douglas's Kansas-Nebraska Bill in 1854. This dispute continued unabated until a new northern party opposed to the extension of slavery, the Republican, captured the presidency in 1860 and half of the southern states seceded. After several years of harmony, the bitter debates over slavery broke out anew.

Many Americans in 1850 actually believed that the Compromise had solved the sectional issues and had removed the slavery debate from the halls of Congress. Probably a larger group fervently hoped that it had done so and thought that by reiterating the finality of the Compromise they could achieve finality. In 1852 the Democratic Party and candidate Franklin Pierce gave the Compromise their unqualified endorsement; but the Whigs only "acquiesced" in its terms and promised to "maintain" them until experience revealed the necessity of change. In that year the Free-Soil Party received only half as many votes as in 1848. Douglas certainly expressed the sentiment of most westerners when he told a party gathering "the North and South may quarrel and wrangle about a question which should never enter the Halls of Congress. But the great West will say to the South: 'You must not leave us,' and to the North, 'You must faithfully observe the Constitution with all its Compromise.' "

Foremost among the reasons why the Compromise failed was the fact that a minority group in both North and South, temporarily rejected by their respective sections, worked for its undoing. Later events played into their hands. Seward and new antislavery senators like Charles Sumner of Massachusetts and Salmon P. Chase of Ohio had determined to abolish slavery. On the other hand southerners like Robert Barnwell Rhett of South Carolina and William L. Yancey were convinced that the only salvation for their section lay in secession. Both groups bided their time but each worked single-mindedly towards its objective.

Perhaps the chief reason for the failure of the Compromise was its own ambiguity. Its proponents claimed that the principle adopted was that of nonintervention. To Douglas and the West this meant popular sovereignty: that the people of a territory alone could settle the status of slavery in a territory, and that Congress could place no restrictions upon their entrance as a state because of their action on slavery. But to most southerners nonintervention meant the older Calhoun doctrine (for which the Supreme Court decided seven years later) that Congress could not, as Toombs said immediately after the adoption of the Compromise, interfere with "the right of the people to hold slaves in a common Territory." If Congress could not interfere, could a territorial legislature do so? Some of the compromise leaders had been aware of this acute discrepancy, but simply had not pressed the matter to a decision for fear of defeat. The Democratic Party for the same reason remained deliberately ambiguous on the matter in its later platforms.

The usual statement that the territories of Utah and New Mexico were organized by the Compromise without mention of slavery ignores certain sections of the territorial bills which did implicitly and explicitly refer to that subject. One section extended the Constitution and laws of the United States to the territories. It would have protected slavery there should the Calhoun nonintervention doctrine be accepted and it compelled the return of fugitives. A second provided that "cases involving title to slaves" in the territory should be determined by the local courts, subject to appeal to the national Supreme Court. (Both of these amendments were taken from the earlier unsuccessful Clayton Compromise that the Senate had passed.) A third stated that "said territory, when admitted as a state, shall be received with or without slavery as its constitution shall prescribe." Most important of all, a fourth section specified that "the legislative power of the Territory shall extend to all rightful subjects of legislation," but subjected the exercise of this power to the governor's veto or disallowance by Congress. Since the prohibition in the original bill upon territorial action on slavery was later removed by amendment, the legislatures were granted definite though limited power to act on slavery. Certainly these four sections confused the issue and allowed different interpretations.

Later the larger question was raised whether these laws were retroactive; that is, did they apply just to New Mexico, or to all the new territories, or to all territories? Did this compromise, whatever its meaning, supersede the Missouri Compromise? * Both compromises were laws passed by Congress. That body, obviously, could repeal or clarify them by later statutes, but until such action was taken the Supreme Court could, if a case arose, decide the meaning of the law. With such confusion in the Federal statutes the conflict over slavery was almost certain to be resumed whenever new territories should be organized.

The Fugitive Slave Act, because of its unpopularity in the North, eventually proved the undoing of the Compromise. It did not provide a jury trial for fugitives, who could simply be taken for trial before a Federal Commissioner. The Commissioner could issue a certificate returning the Negro to bondage without appeal; if he did so his fee was ten dollars, if he failed to do so it was only

* See Chapter V, pp. 99-108.

five. Marshals were subject to heavy fine if they failed to execute the law, and persons who interfered with enforcement were subjected to heavier penalties. When Harriet Stowe's novel, *Uncle Tom's Cabin,* in 1852 dramatized the worst feature of slavery — the slave trade — enforcement became increasingly difficult, and later Wisconsin formally nullified the act. Since this law was the only major concession to the South, and since it was the price of southern acceptance of the Compromise, naturally there were southern repercussions. Some southern ultras had voted for so stringent a measure hoping for just such an outcome.

The South had accepted the Compromise partly because the Unionists in both parties favored it, but also because a large group, called "Cooperationists," felt that the terms of compromise did not warrant secession at that time. They did not reject secession as an ultimate resort; their acceptance of the Compromise, as the Georgia platform indicated, was conditional. In the course of the subsequent decade most of this group shifted their position when they found themselves in the position predicted to one of them, Speaker Howell Cobb, by his fellow Georgian Henry Benning:

"You know well," wrote Benning during the calm of 1852, "that it has been my conviction for the last two years that nothing we could do, short of general emancipation, would satisfy the North. Your idea was that the measures of the Compromise would substantially effect that object, and you went for them for that reason chiefly, I think. Should it turn out that I am right and you are wrong it will not be long before it must be known. And it is, therefore, now time for you to be making up your mind for the new 'crisis.' Suppose the Whig Party shall be beaten [in the presidential election of 1852], and especially at the North, will not that disband it and send the elements of which it has been composed into union with the late Pittsburg free-soil anti-slavery concern? Manifestly. What then? That concern takes the North. The Democratic Party there, in conjunction with pretty much the whole South, may be able to make one fight, say in 1856 — a grand Union rally — but then the thing will be out. Is it not so?

You must have thought of all this. Have you made up your mind as to what is to be done?"

The dispute over slavery grew in intensity and led at last to secession and war. Different views about slavery openly split the Protestant Churches in the 1840's; the persistence of these views led directly in the next decade to the split in the political parties. The wisest of American statesmen recognized the probability of this outcome. Jefferson in his old age, observing the heated debates set off by the effort in 1820 to prohibit slavery in the Louisiana Territory, declared that "this momentous question, like a fire bell in the night, awakened and filled me with terror." A generation later Webster and Clay made the same diagnosis and sought with all their powers to avert the impending tragedy. But their old opponent Calhoun, who in his own way was as eager as they to save the Union, prophesied most exactly the subsequent course of events.

"The Union is doomed to dissolution," he told his friend, Senator James Mason of Virginia, a few weeks before he died in the spring of 1850, "there is no mistaking the signs. I am satisfied in my judgment even were the questions which now agitate Congress settled to the satisfaction and concurrence of the Southern States, it would not avert, or materially delay, the catastrophe. I fix its probable occurrence within twelve years or three Presidential terms. You and others of your age will probably live to see it; I shall not. The mode by which it will be is not so clear; it may be brought about in a manner that none now foresee. But the probability is it will explode in a Presidential election."

No two American figures are so similar in their public and private personalities as Stephen Douglas and Henry Clay. Both were contenders and unsuccessful candidates for the presidency, but by comparative standards moderate rather than extreme in their ambition. Both had long, distinguished congressional careers, both were leaders who dared fight a President of their own party. Yet despite sufficient provocation, neither broke with his party when lesser men had been chosen over him. Both were orators of great force, who moved their fellows deeply. They stood unswervingly for compromise and for Union; to combat the centrifugal pull of geography they advocated national economic planning. Men's men, they drank and gambled, speculated in land, and won to themselves a large and devoted following, though inevitably in the course of their hectic careers they made bitter enemies. Their virtues were big, their vices small. Most of all, in times of crisis they throve on punishment and rose above the considerations of party and of section.

The Senator from Illinois had more detractors in his own day, though Alexander Stephens called him the "foremost patriot and statesman of his time." The Little Giant carried on the identical Clay position and arguments after the Kentuckian's death in a bitterer decade, when public opinion North and South became extreme rather than moderate. Inevitably the compromiser, the stanch supporter of the middle of the road, made enemies where Clay had made friends; the outcries of his opponents in both sections were louder. Douglas was the proponent of appeasement who fought for the losing cause when the North in 1860 — by a narrow margin — rejected his position. Enemies in his own party, in his three contests for the presidential nomination, placed the worst interpretation upon his motives. At the end he was overshadowed by Lincoln.

Chiefly because the Little Giant took an official position of unconcern over the morality of slavery, though privately he condemned the institution,* his opponents in the 1850's repeatedly directed at him a barrage of accusations consisting of outright untruths and some irrelevant half-truths. He owned slaves, it was charged, and conspired to force slavery upon the entire nation. He was a dishonest schemer who would sacrifice anything for the presidency. He was a drunkard who would turn the wealth of the nation over to speculators. He was uncouth, unfair in debate, inconsistent, and he associated with unsavory characters. He sent his sons to a Catholic school. The pattern of this defamation is not unusual in American politics, but it was completely ground-

* See Chapter V, pp. 98-99.

less. Not a shred of evidence exists to convict Douglas in any way of moral turpitude. Circumstances made the Senator vulnerable, however, and he became a whipping-boy for the Republicans.

Like Seward, Toombs, and many respectable public servants of his day, he drank freely and at times to excess, but never to the detriment of his public duty. He was tricky and shifty in debate, but Lincoln was equally so. He indulged in personalities in his speeches, as did most westerners, but he never matched the studied vituperation of Charles Sumner of Massachusetts; yet Sumner posed as an idealist because he wished to abolish slavery. He accepted the political support of the unsavory George Sanders in 1852 (Sanders later deserted him for Buchanan), but he was also the social political intimate of a large number of southern and eastern gentlemen.

The Little Giant was a man of integrity, charm, and intelligence, and he continued to grow in stature. Contemporaries of both parties held him in high esteem — men as different as Robert Toombs of Georgia, Pierre Soulé of Louisiana, August Belmont of New York, and Buchanan's confidante, John Forney. Calling him the "acknowledged leader of the Democratic Party in the Senate," Whig Senator Archibald Dixon of Kentucky observed that he bore "the honors which encircled him with sufficient meekness."

As a party leader he used the patronage, both in his own state and in others, for the interests of his party and his own advancement. Such procedure is normal, ethical, and inevitable under the American governmental system. By and large he kept his host of friends happy; and he followed strictly the rule of never appointing relatives to office. A land speculator on a large scale, because of his long tenure as Chairman of the Committee on Territories he refused to buy land in those areas. A realist in politics, he took every advantage of his opponents and accepted support from whatever quarter it was offered. His exuberance, his craft, and his use of invective in debate were regarded as quite proper and not at all in bad taste by most citizens of his day. He conformed to the western code of sportsmanship which held any method fair in a fight, but which required that contestants shake hands when the encounter was over. Magnanimous to an extreme, he rarely harbored grudges and rarely complained when he was the victim of similar tactics. After Horace Greeley excoriated him in the *Tribune,* a mutual acquaintance asked the Senator if he objected to meeting that temperamental editor. "Not at all," was the reply. "I always pay that class of political debts as I go along, so as to have no trouble with them in social intercourse and to leave none for my executors to settle."

A lesser man, rejected twice by his party in favor of mediocrities before it finally nominated him for the presidency, might have bolted or at least given only halfhearted support. Not so Douglas. He campaigned for Pierce and Buchanan with his usual ardor; once in office they ignored him. When he later fought Buchanan on a matter of principle, he was cold to the overtures from the new Republican Party. Yet in crisis he cooperated fully with the Whigs in 1850 and with Lincoln once secession occurred.

One of the reasons why Douglas's leadership was widely accepted was the recognition of his objectivity and insight in matters political. Senator R. M. T. Hunter of Virginia, proposed as his running mate early in the preliminaries of the 1852 convention, called him "one of the coolest observers, even when he himself is concerned, that I ever saw." But what impressed his fellows in Congress equally was his prodigious memory of facts. "He had at his fingers' ends," wrote a biographer of Jefferson Davis, "all the *Congressional Annals* and *Globes, National Registers,* and political encyclopedias of every sort from Clusky's Text Book to the briefest *vade mecum*. In this intricate field of knowledge he had no rival; his illustrations gathered there were weapons, and they sometimes bore down the most formidable arrays of the intellect, and scattered the literary ornaments and flowery language of his cultivated competitors." Some of his most effective speeches were impromptu.

As a showman Douglas cultivated a public personality that would win votes. Yet, despite the demands of his active political and business life, he retained to a surprising degree an independent private life. Somehow he found a little time to indulge his appreciation of the arts and sciences. Having written poetry as a precocious lad, he even composed several poems in middle life. More attracted by art, he became the patron of several young sculptors and painters. He frequently discharged books from the Library of Congress (he had twenty out at the time of death), and apparently found time to read them. Science appealed most to him, particularly electricity, the telegraph, and the railroad, but he also read the classics, contemporary novels, history, politics, economics, and even Calhoun's speeches. A regent of the new Smithsonian Institution, he became a close friend of its scientist head, Professor Joseph Henry. Hardly an avid student, he had an open and inquiring mind. Once he chided the Senate for its mirth at a petition he presented from an inventor asking government aid for experiments with dirigibles. Always interested in education at higher and lower levels, he donated the land for the site of the proposed University of Chicago, and he received honorary degrees from two small colleges in his native state. All these activities were undertaken quietly, without consideration of their effect upon his career.

More to the point, when he lost his young wife early in 1853, he sought solace, not just in drink, but in a long trip to the continent of Europe. Publicly a vehement jingoist and Anglophobe, he had recently proclaimed Europe "antiquated, decrepit, tottering on the verge of dissolution. When you visit her, the objects which enlist your highest admiration are the relics of past greatness." The action suggests that he partly had tongue in cheek when he made such utterances. True, he was not presented to Queen Victoria, because he refused to don court dress or even wear a short sword, but John Bright called him an "intelligent looking person . . . evidently a man of superior mental power." He traveled through France, Italy, Greece, and ended his journey in Russia, where the Czar invited him to a grand military review. This country, so physically similar to his own America, interested the Senator most and he went by carriage from St. Petersburg down into Asia Minor. No intelligent man could fail to be impressed and stimulated by such an extensive tour of the Old World. "I know not what our destiny may be," he wrote, "but I try to keep up with the spirit of the age, to keep in view the history of the country, to see what we have done, whither we are going, and with what velocity we are moving, in order to be prepared for those events which it is not in the power of man to thwart."

He attended church and Cartwright's revivals as a youth, but as an adult Douglas was a deist unaffiliated with any denomination, and made caustic remarks about preachers when they entered the slavery debate and whetted the nativism of the middle fifties. Despite his eloquent profanity and his appreciation of the bottle, many ministers were his friends. In the midst of the bigotry of the Know-Nothing movement he spoke boldly for tolerance. His second wife was Catholic and he permitted her to raise her stepsons in that church; but he gave land to a Baptist college. In the presidential campaign of 1860 he scorned advice that he remove his sons from a Jesuit school.

The Little Giant began to speculate in land almost upon his arrival in the West. He would make his initial purchase with borrowed money, then sell part of his holdings to meet payments. Consequently, though he was financially comfortable most of his life and finally made a large fortune, upon occasion he was hard pressed. The depression of 1837 left him in debt for several years. Most of his profit came from Chicago real estate; his sales in the year 1856 alone brought him one hundred thousand dollars. His most lucrative outside venture was Superior City on Lake Superior, which he expected to be the eastern terminal of the northern transcontinental railroad. Other congressmen joined in the project and he included some of his friends; it proved so successful that in 1854 he was asking ten thousand dollars cash for half a share. Since he long favored a central route, not a northern, this speculation did not unduly influence his political position. As senator from Illinois he had to press the advantage of Chicago, an action which indirectly increased the value of his property there. His judgment in business matters was equal to that in politics.

Douglas's first wife was too busy with infants during their brief marriage for much social life, but he maintained extensive domiciles both in Chicago and in Washington. When he left his home in the capital in charge of his sister, Sarah Granger, upon his departure for Europe, she found there eleven servants. Grief over the loss of Martha made him for a time careless in his personal habits and curt even with his friends; it undoubtedly contributed to the bitterness of his speeches in the controversy with the Whigs over the Clayton-Bulwer Treaty. Four years later he married Adele Cutts, Washington beauty and a grandniece of Dolly Madison. With her as a hostess the Douglas home became a leading salon of the capital. She traveled with him on his campaigns, supported his every endeavor, and was largely responsible for his personal mellowness in his last years. That two women of such charm and breeding became his happy wives argues for the breadth of his personality.

For all his conviviality, the Little Giant was punctual in his congressional duties. His vigor and energy was all the more surprising in view of the persistence of physical malady. For ten years after his severe attack of fever on his trip west as a young man, his health remained so poor that he thought of retiring from the Illinois Supreme Court. The strain of speaking, once he began his arduous congressional life, produced a chronic throat irritation which required an operation in 1855 when he was fighting enemies on all sides. It was in the character of the man to ignore all such infirmities, but had he been able to move at a slower pace he might not have died at the early age of forty-eight.

In the session of Congress which met in the winter after the Compromise had passed, Foote introduced in the Senate a discussion of the finality of the measure which could have proved dangerous. Soon Douglas made a speech insisting upon finality and defending his own consistency. "The Democratic party," he affirmed, "is as good a Union party as I want, and I wish to preserve its principles and its organization, and to triumph upon its old issues. I desire no new tests — no interpolations into the old creed." He had resolved, he said, never again to speak on the slavery question; his protests suggested that he was one of those who realized the ambiguity of the Compromise and who sought to preserve harmony by reiterating its finality.

The Democrats at once began to set the stage for their return to power in 1852, which appeared a certainty in view of the Whig cleavage. But they must also choose their candidate from many hopefuls. Cass had the inside track, but Douglas, then only thirty-seven, as the leader of a new group calling itself "Young America," had definite ambitions. Like the belligerent wing of the isolationists of the next century, the Young Americans advocated a vigorous, unilateral foreign policy by the United States. Extreme exponents of Manifest Destiny, they would make their country, as Douglas said years before, "an ocean-bound republic, and have no more disputes about boundaries, or 'red lines' upon the maps."

Both Douglas and Cass appealed to the current sentiment of Manifest Destiny to oust the Whigs from office. The emphasis upon the slavery dispute has obscured the fact that the expansionist spirit of the Roaring Forties carried over undiminished into the next decade. Such a development was natural in view of the recent war and the acquisition of territory that resulted. Formal diplomatic efforts (after the Democrats came back in office under Pierce) and private filibustering forays sought Cuba from Spain, more land from Mexico, and footholds in Central America. Greeley's *Tribune* urged the annexation of Canada, though many in the North were not eager for Cuba or other Caribbean annexations which might make slave states. Politicos vied with each other in twisting the Lion's tail. All of this hurt the Whigs, as it was intended to, since they were reluctant expansionists and firm proponents of compromise with England. But it was down the Little Giant's alley, for who had been a more consistent and vociferous expansionist than he?

Much American sympathy existed for the short-lived European

republics which sprang from the Revolutions of 1848, and the visit of the Hungarian exile Louis Kossuth brought the sentiment to its peak. Leaders of both parties rode with the tide, but after much talk no action was taken; the Hapsburgs suppressed the Hungarian rebellion with the help of Czar Nicholas. Seward and Cass proposed resolutions which hinted at joint intervention with England, but Douglas, though sympathetic with Hungary, objected to that method until England recognized the rights of Ireland. He would defy all of Europe. "I think it is time America had a foreign policy" — he thundered at the Jackson Day dinner in 1852 — "a foreign policy predicated upon a true interpretation of the laws of nations — a foreign policy in accordance with the spirit of the age — but not such a foreign policy as we have seen attempted to be enforced in this country in the last three years. We have been told, and you are told every day, that neutrality is the true American policy; and that plea has been the excuse for the acts which have been performed by the existing Administration in connection with the Cuban question."

This broadside was an attack upon the Whig's efforts to check the Lopez filibustering forays in Cuba, and upon the Clayton-Bulwer Treaty in regard to the Isthmus of Panama, which the Democrats charged was a surrender of national rights and honor to John Bull. The Little Giant's Young American friends followed up with articles in the *Democratic Review,* notably one entitled "Eighteen-fifty-two and the Presidency," which called for a man not "trammeled with ideas belonging to an anterior era, or a man of merely local fame and local affections, but a statesman who can bring young blood, young ideas, and young hearts to the councils of the Republic. He must not be a mere general, a mere lawyer, a mere wire-puller." Clearly these articles were an attack upon Cass and other Democratic candidates, most of whom were many years older than the Little Giant. But Cass yielded nothing to Douglas in the aggressiveness of his speeches in Congress.

Since the days of President Monroe, the United States had refused to tie its hands in regard to Cuba but had accepted Spanish ownership for the time being. Polk's efforts to buy the island met an emphatic refusal from Madrid. The Whig administrations of Taylor and Fillmore, taking the earlier attitude, sought to check filibustering (Lopez's second invasion in 1851 ended in his own death and that of scores of the young Americans under him) and to soothe Spanish pride by apology and indemnity. But they rejected a proposal by England and France late in 1852 of a tripartite treaty guaranteeing Spanish possession. All along the Democrats had favored annexation, seeing in the Lopez raids the same tactics which had earlier induced Spain to sell Florida. Two years later the prosouthern Pierce administration, by the Ostend Manifesto, overtly threatened the use of force as a last resort. In 1853, by the Gadsden Purchase, it had obtained from Mexico the Gila Valley for ten million dollars, thus giving a great advantage to the proposed southern route.

The diplomatic issue which most aroused Democratic ire was the Clayton-Bulwer Treaty of 1850. The Gold Rush of '49 produced heavy traffic across Panama and Nicaragua, an area in which both Great Britain and the United States had vital interests. In each area treaties had been signed during the Polk administration (but not ratified) giving the United States exclusive rights had she chosen to use them, but the Whigs, as in Oregon, preferred compromise to the risk of a collision with the world's leading sea power. Occupying Belize in Honduras and the port of Greytown in Nicaragua, England had assumed a protectorate over the Mosquito Indians on the coast. Clayton and Bulwer agreed to the joint construction and control over any isthmian canal which might be built, pledging their nations to insure the neutrality of the area. The American diplomat also agreed specifically to the exclusion from this agreement of Honduras and small islands nearby.

The erection of some islands in the Bay of Honduras into a crown colony by England, soon after the election of 1852, set off a heated congressional debate. Cass made public the exclusion agreement, to which he objected, and introduced a resolution reaffirming the no-further-colonization statement of the Monroe

Doctrine. But his colleague from Illinois, who had refused to serve on the Foreign Relations Committee because he opposed the treaty, reached new heights of Anglophobia in an attack on this resolution as well as on the perfidy of the Whigs. Why repeat such talk about a policy which we had so recently repudiated in Oregon, he sneered. He for one would stop all truckling to any European power and go it alone. Polk's treaty that the Whigs had ignored, he pointed out, had met the requirements of international law for such a course in Central America. He would have no entangling alliances, least of all with our "unnatural mother" whose subjects continued to libel us in every way. As in the Mexican treaty he refused to bind the hands of the next generation of Americans: "You may make as many treaties as you please to fetter the limits of this giant Republic, and she will burst them all from her, and her course will be onward to a limit which I will not venture to prescribe."

All of this the Little Giant had said as eloquently before, if not so bitterly. He must have been aware of the popularity of his position in the South and in much of the West, and of its relation to a future nomination by his party and his re-election in his own state. He was for taking Cuba as he had been for taking Texas; with new free states coming in from the West, sectional balance in favor of the North was not endangered. But probably he was seeking most of all, by emotionalizing the issue, to divert the feelings of his fellow citizens from the dangerous slavery debate into safer channels, to enhance patriotism as a unifying force. Even Seward, when the South called his bluff by seceding, would propose to Lincoln in 1861 that he get the nation quickly into a foreign war.

After some hesitation the Little Giant decided to enter the race for the Democratic nomination in 1852. The contest was wide open. With more than half a dozen candidates, it soon appeared that the leading contenders would be Cass, Douglas, and James Buchanan of Pennsylvania. Certain astute politicians judged correctly that these three would block each other, and accordingly began grooming Franklin Pierce of New Hampshire, not even mentioned as a possibility at the outset, as the dark horse whom they would bring forward when the convention tired of deadlock. Other candidates receiving support in the preliminaries were Judge Levi Woodbury, William L. Marcy of New York, and General William O. Butler of Kentucky.

As it turned out Douglas's youth hurt him, chiefly because of the errors of his friends. He had started young, had moved up fast; his experience was as broad as that of his rivals. (The Washington editor Andrew Donelson thought he had the inside track.) It was in keeping with his drive and impetuosity to make the attempt in 1852, even if he did not expect to win the nomination until four years later; he had tried once for the Senate and the House before he succeeded. A real difficulty lay in the fact that Cass was certain to divide the Northwest with him — this and the opposition of Senator Jesse D. Bright of Indiana contributed much to his defeat — but Douglas had a wider national following, particularly in the South, and a more brilliant congressional record. Anything could happen in such a many-sided race. Once he made his decision, he exerted himself with usual vigor and persisted until the end.

The Little Giant's original strategy was an alliance with Senator R. M. T. Hunter of Virginia, who had opposed the Compromise, as a running mate. He urged his friends not to attack any of the other candidates; he himself cultivated leaders in all states and sections, hoping to become their choice in the later balloting of the convention. Even when Hunter backed down, his prospects remained strong. Then came the fatal blow, just as the Young American propaganda seemed likely to move him ahead of the field. George N. Sanders, whom he had helped to buy the *United States Democratic Review,* savagely attacked all the other candidates as "Old Fogies" in the most insulting language. Here was the kiss of death; Douglas's rivals held him personally responsible and they united in a tacit resolve to defeat him at all costs. Meanwhile the Senator pleaded with the editor to no avail: "If you cease now and make no more attacks upon anybody, and especially none on General Cass, possibly I may yet regain my lost position. If these attacks are repeated, my chances are utterly hopeless, and I may be compelled to retire from the field and throw my influence in favor of one of these whom the *Review* strives to crush." Sanders refused, and the effort of one of the Little Giant's friends in Congress to exonerate him for the attacks proved completely unconvincing. Yet at this point, when the Buchananites offered him second place on their ticket with the promise that he would be scrupulously rewarded four years later, he refused to yield.

This contest, and this particular incident, made for Douglas many permanent enemies in his own party who continued to believe the worst of him. John Slidell of Louisiana, who managed the Buchanan campaign, became his implacable foe. Like his rivals, the Senator must have indulged through his friends in the bargaining and infighting that occurs during the prelude to a party convention. Officially he denied that he had promised anyone an office. Lobbyists and others on the make, who according to his opponents would "disembowel the treasury, disgrace the country," had flocked to him because he appeared for a while the likely victor; he was too realistic to refuse their support. His methods were direct and his friends were uninhibited; he let his headquarters, famous for its whiskey and cigars, coin epigrams like "Cass whose reputation was beyond the C."

The Democratic convention began balloting in Baltimore on July 3. Within two days thirty-three ballots were taken. The first showed Cass in the lead with 116, Buchanan next with 93, Douglas third with 20, and 31 for the rest of the candidates. Buchanan's vote reached 104 on the twenty-second ballot, but Marcy of New York refused to throw him his support. Douglas's vote reached 93 at one point and on the thirty-first ballot he received a plurality; Cass soared to 133 on the thirty-third. The Buchananites had been playing Cass and Douglas off against one another. Under the two-thirds rule they could block any nomination, and now they attempted a clever ruse. Pennsylvania and five southern states agreed to give the minor candidates a play, to convince

their followers that none of them could be elected, hoping there-
after to rally them behind Buchanan. But the move backfired;
Pierce (who at the right moment had come out by letter for the
Compromise and the strict enforcement of the Fugitive Slave
Act) showed so much strength that he was nominated on the
forty-ninth with 282 votes to 2 each for Cass and Douglas.

The Old Fogies had stopped the Little Giant, even if they
failed to win for Buchanan. Henry A. Wise of Virginia exulted
that "the brandy bottle is smashed, the Champagne bazaars are
closed, and Douglas has crept out of town like a whipped dog
with his tail between his legs." But William H. Bissell of Illinois
thought differently about the Senator's failure. "With one-fourth
the effort on the part of his friends, and no more," he wrote Sidney Breese, "he would have been the nominee. Henceforth he will
have to *struggle,* like other aspirants to the Presidency, and like
them take his *chance.* The prestige of *universal good feeling* has
gone from him, and forever. But he will come up again."

Feuds were forgotten as the party joined in the fight against
General Winfield Scott, whom the Whigs chose over Webster and
Fillmore. As usual the Little Giant took the stump, sure of his
own and his party's success in Illinois, and he spoke in a majority
of the states. In his opening speech at Richmond he referred to
"Politician" Scott under the command of "General" Seward; if
Taylor "had lived one more year than he did," he asked, "would
this Union be extant at the present time?" Scott and Seward
favored measures which could lead only to civil war; how could
a nation recently rescued by Providence "from our first and only
military Administration" turn to another general? It did not;
though the Democrats won a popular majority of less than
300,000 they carried every state but four.

With his re-election to the Senate by a vote of 75 to 20 in the
Illinois legislature, Douglas became the complete master of the
Democratic Party in that state. Thereafter he gave insurgents no
quarter and exercised his local power in dictatorial fashion. In
the national party he was more and more inclined to the same
method, with the result that he added some enemies to those he

had previously made. Such a trait was natural in a vigorous man, sure of himself; as in war, insistence upon discipline wins more victories for a political leader, whatever else it does to his reputation.

Pierce ignored Cass and Douglas in his cabinet appointments and the distribution of patronage. He offended the two New York factions by trying to satisfy both, but he did somewhat placate Buchanan by the ministership to England. Moderates were dismayed by his appointment of Jefferson Davis, outspoken opponent of the Compromise, as secretary of war, and of Caleb Cushing, ardent prosoutherner from Massachusetts, as attorney general. The southern bias of the President's program, which became increasingly apparent, was due to his almost complete reliance upon these two cabinet members for advice. Soon after the inauguration his weakness became evident and his appointments opened the old wounds of his party. Could it avoid the disaster which had overtaken the Whigs because of their North-South cleavage? Inevitably Douglas's friends surveyed the situation and began to make plans for 1856. Post-mortem on the recent convention pointed up his failure to carry the Northwest. Senator David L. Yulee of Florida warned him against Bright of Indiana, who was seeking a reconciliation, as a rival sure to "defeat this desirable 'solidarity' of the N.W. if he can; . . . He does not mean that you shall rise if he can prevent it." Yulee went on to add that the Little Giant stood "well with the State's Rights men — with New England — with the South — and with the party at large." The Northwest had never had a President. Were it united its claim would be "yielded to at once, and your nomination effected without contest."

But the chastened Douglas was not ready to move so early, nor did he wish to add to party troubles. "The party is in a distracted condition," he cautioned his editor-friend Charles Lanphier, "and it requires all our wisdom, patience, and energy to consolidate its power and perpetuate its principles. Let us leave the Presidency out of view for at least two years to come." As for the talk in the press about his candidacy, "I do not wish to occupy that position.

I do not think I will be willing to have my name used. I think such a state of things will exist that I shall not desire the nomination. Yet I do not intend to do any act which will deprive me of the control of my own actions. I shall remain entirely non-committal, and hold myself at liberty to do whatever my duty to my principles and my friends may require when the time for action arrives. Our first duty is to the Cause — the fate of individual politicians is of minor consequence."

Despite Pierce's ingratitude he was ready to work with the administration: "If it stands firmly by the faith, if it is sound and faithful in its principles and measures, it will receive *my* hearty support." But it must act "boldly and fairly," get rid of the treasury surplus, and reduce the tariff. A "disturbing element," he added prophetically, would be the Pacific railroad question.

V

The Kansas-Nebraska Act

WHEN the secession decade opened, Douglas had in mind a grand strategy. To preserve the Union and his party, and as a by-product to obtain the presidency, he would consolidate the West as the balance wheel of the Republic, the upper and lower valley and the new Northwest. He had made this intent clear in the debates on the Compromise: "There is a power in this nation greater than either the North or the South — " he said, answering Calhoun as well as Webster — "a growing, increasing, swelling power, that will be able to speak the law to this nation, and to execute the law as spoken. That power is the country known as the Great West — the Valley of the Mississippi, one and indivisible from the gulf to the great lakes, and stretching on the one side and the other, to the extreme sources of the Ohio and the Misssissippi — from the Alleghenies to the Rocky Mountains. There, Sir, is the hope of this nation — the resting place of the power that is not only to control, but to save the Union. This is the mission of the great Mississippi Valley, the heart and soul of the nation and the continent."

Basic differences over slavery in that valley itself, so events proved, made the realization of this dream impossible. But the concept was sound and the nation's best hope for peace. The plan required a nice balance between the two western regions. In this lay its weakness: to retain the support of his own section the Senator could not yield too much to the Southwest, but he could not hold the Southwest if he pressed, as he must, the demands of the upper valley. Essential to his plan was the rapid territorial organization and admission of states from the new Northwest, apart from any consideration of the effect upon the location of the transcontinental railroad; this the South was able to retard. In popular sovereignty — a happy phrase which he substituted for the older "squatter sovereignty" — he was groping for a new center of gravity in politics. The Kansas-Nebraska Act, which repealed the Missouri Compromise, defined this center more specifically. Lincoln too sought a new center of gravity (one far to the left of Douglas) once he joined the Republicans after it was apparent they were going places. This is clear from his assertion in 1858 that the nation could not exist half slave and half free and that peace would not come until a crisis should be reached and passed.

In the end the Old Northwest followed Lincoln, not Douglas. In this decade that section lost much of its former homogeneity as a consequence of social and economic changes. Railroads tied it to the Northeast, whence came droves of settlers, abolitionist or morally antislavery. Increasing industrialization and commercial agriculture, as well as rivalry between its cities — chiefly Chicago and St. Louis — all sharpened the conflict between the Great Lakes region and the older Ohio Valley. This conflict was hardly less violent than the larger one between North and South. Here was a problem in the Little Giant's own back yard which would oust him from Congress. It demanded priority even over national problems.

Issues which did not pertain to slavery, but which involved it, produced conflicts between the Northwest and the Southwest. Chief of these, of course, was the location of the transcontinental railroad. The Northwest also wanted free land and opportunities for investment. Early in the 1850's the Senator from Illinois introduced a homestead bill which the southerners opposed because it would encourage free rather than slave states. The Northwest demanded Federal subsidy for internal improvements, but once again southern votes reduced appropriations in river-and-harbor bills or southern objections induced vetoes by northern "dough-face" Presidents. Since Douglas had fought the Wilmot Proviso and had insisted upon strict enforcement of the Fugitive Slave Act, he must now get action on measures desired by the West, particularly its Lakes region. When Pierce, under Davis's thumb, pushed pet southern projects, an indignant West demanded equal consideration and such action became more imperative.

In any event the decade was politically explosive. A severe depression in 1857 ended the boom and in the same year came a religious revival of more fervor than any in half a century. The nativist movement and a temperance crusade of growing intensity indicated a deep social ferment, which with depression was bound to cause parties and politicians trouble. Railroads in the older region, no less than the new, by providing for the first time a national market, acted as catalyst to an overdue industrial revolution and expanded agriculture. Industrial capitalism was forming the social pattern of the future. Already the Northeast contained an urban proletariat and the first national craft unions, like that of the printers, were established in this decade. The wealth of the new domain between the Mississippi and the Pacific, then just beginning to be suspected, increased the pressure in Washington from those who desired exploitation of natural resources and special concessions like town sites, land, franchises of all sorts, contracts for railroad construction, and so forth. As manufacturing sprang up in the West and the South, a coalition to check the trend towards lower tariffs was likely. All of these stresses were magnified by the central debate over slavery and they made a new sectional alignment likely.

Much of this Douglas recognized, some of it he sensed. By no means was he willing to become the spokesman for predatory interests, but he did wish to encourage legitimate business and to maintain the old alliance between South and West. Nationwide prosperity would check the divisive forces. The government should not, because of the danger of corruption, go into railroad building. "We can grant alternate sections of land," he wrote in 1853, "as we did for the Illinois Central but not a dollar from the National Treasury." It should, however, give liberal portions of land to the settlers migrating to the territories to drive back the wilderness. To provide capital for the necessary internal improvements, since private enterprise was hesitant because of the risk, he made a most original proposal in a letter to Governor Joel A. Matteson of Illinois. Let Congress pass a law permitting towns and cities to impose tonnage duties (the Constitution left to the states that right) to provide funds for local improvements. Thus political bargaining and jobbery in Washington would be avoided and projects kept under local control. Any town which charged excessive rates would drive commerce elsewhere. Could only one transcontinental railroad be built he logically favored a central route, with a branch to Chicago, as of most benefit to the entire nation. But he felt more than one was needed and early in 1854 introduced a bill for government aid to three roads, a southern, a central, and a northern.

To reduce the tension between North and South, Douglas pursued a cohesive and enlightened program. He would remove slavery debates from Congress by popular sovereignty so that body could get on with more vital legislation. By an aggressive foreign policy he would build a backfire and divert emotions away from divergent feelings over slavery into safer channels. He would encourage growth and prosperity by economic legislation beneficial to all sections. In this he was truly the intellectual descendant of those Young Republicans who under the leadership of Clay and Calhoun in a similar crisis after the War of 1812 had urged their American System. In both instances sectionalism triumphed over nationalism.

The genesis of the Nebraska Act lay largely in the rival sectional projects for railroads to the Pacific. Half a dozen cities, from New Orleans to Milwaukee, hoped to become the eastern terminal and each was as much opposed to its nearest as to its distant rivals. Within nation and within individual states the issue was ticklish and therefore certain, as the Senator from Illinois predicted, to prove troublesome. Since half his own state preferred St. Louis and the other half Chicago, he could not commit himself too positively; but since he was weakest in the Lakes region he had to see to it that Chicago became at least a branch terminal. Iowa competed with Missouri, and the factional politics of the latter state to a great extent determined the terms of the ultimate act organizing the territory through which a central route would pass. To the more astute it was clear that only a trunk route had a chance of passage. Indeed, in this matter the Little Giant simply repeated the tactics by which he had obtained his Illinois Central Bill. With the north-south road assured he could concentrate on a transcontinental project, in which all along he had been equally interested.

When the promoter Asa Whitney in 1844 had asked Congress for a strip of land sixty miles wide for a road from Milwaukee to the mouth of the Columbia, the new congressman from Illinois was the only member of that body to reply. He proposed instead a road from Chicago through Council Bluffs and on through the South Pass to the Pacific. With a central route in mind — of which both Chicago and St. Louis might become terminals — in 1852 he introduced for a third time a bill organizing the Nebraska Territory. Until then he had been blocked by instructions from his own legislature, which at first had directed its senators to vote for the Whitney route. Later, his colleague Breese had these instructions changed in favor of the southern route and Douglas did not obtain their repeal until 1852. When he accepted the presidency of a St. Louis railroad convention in 1849, he first insisted that a Chicago mass meeting release him from his instructions. At St. Louis he spoke for his South Pass route, with branches to St. Louis and Chicago. Severe criticism in the Missouri press caused him to resign, and the convention resolved for a trunk road with Memphis, St. Louis, and Chicago as eastern terminals. Another convention held in Memphis at the same time would have none of this; it pronounced for a southern route.

After the Compromise of 1850 the southern route had all the

advantage. Topographically it was preferable and all the territory through which it would pass was organized. With Davis as Secretary of War and intimate with the President, the chances for its selection increased when the Gila Valley was obtained by Gadsden in 1853. Advocates of a central or northern route had to block such an outcome at all costs, before they could fight out among themselves the location of an alternate route. Southerners blocked the organization of Nebraska, essential for either a central or northern route, citing the rights of the Indians who had been dumped there on the Great American Desert.

Senator William M. Gwin of California, in favor of a southern route as the cheapest and the most likely to be selected, became their ally. Upon the defeat of his Nebraska Bill in 1852, Douglas immediately proposed a measure for the protection of the emigrant route to the Pacific. This Gwin amended to include Federal aid for the construction of a railroad; a special committee approved, leaving the choice of the route to the President. To block this bill, since surely a southern route would be chosen, Senator James A. Shields of Illinois offered an amendment to the amendment that none of the money appropriated could be spent within the limits of a state. This clever ruse, in accord with the strict construction doctrine of the southerners, killed the amendment, but Douglas supported it until the end and insisted upon a roll call. For the time being the southern route was checked.

Meanwhile rivalry between Iowa and Missouri went on. Residents from both states had crossed the border and extralegally elected delegates to Congress from the Nebraska Territory. The matter was further complicated by recent political developments in Missouri, where the proslavery group led by Senator David R. Atchison had ousted from the Senate the antislavery curmudgeon Benton. The old Jacksonian fought back by demanding a Pacific Railroad and the organization of the territory of Nebraska. Since Missouri was surrounded on three sides by free soil, its proslavery party vehemently objected to the organization of Nebraska unless the prohibition upon slaveholders' taking their property there was removed.

After the Senate rejected Douglas's Nebraska Bill in 1852, Willard P. Hall of Missouri introduced a similar measure in the House. Over strong southern opposition it passed by a two-to-one vote. Referred to the Senate, it was twice defeated by a margin of several votes; all southern senators except the two from Missouri voted in the negative, since the area was free soil. Atchison, in reversal of his previous position and allegedly under the influence of wine, made the key speech. More belligerently proslavery than any of his colleagues from the Lower South, he had formerly opposed all territorial bills unless they repealed the Missouri Compromise, and he had admitted that he could see no prospect of repeal. But in this session he said he was willing to accept a territorial bill even if the Compromise was irrepealable: "We might as well agree to the admission of this Territory now as next year, or five or ten years hence." In his own speech the Little Giant never contradicted Atchison's statement about repealability and did not mention popular sovereignty. The measure was defeated by so small a margin that chances for success the next year looked good.

The Kansas-Nebraska Act passed Congress in its next session after five months of debate. It brought into existence the Republican Party, made the Whig rupture permanent, split the Democrats, and set off the chain of events which led six years later to Lincoln's election, secession, and civil war.

When the Thirty-third Congress opened, Douglas, after consulting proslavery Bright of Indiana and another northwestern senator, reported the bill on January 4, 1854, with the addition of two clauses from the Utah-New Mexico acts of 1850. These provided for the jurisdiction of the courts over slavery and stated that the territory (now enlarged to include the remainder of the Louisiana Purchase), when admitted as a state or states, would be received "with or without slavery as their constitution may prescribe at the time of admission." In a report accompanying the revised bill the committee noted that the constitutionality of the Missouri Compromise had been questioned, but said they were not prepared to commit themselves on that point.

The true intent of the bill, continued the report, was to maintain three principles established by the Compromise of 1850: the recoverability of fugitive slaves in territories as well as states, the appellate jurisdiction of the Supreme Court in cases about the freedom of and title to slaves, and the right of residents through their representatives to decide "all questions pertaining to slavery in the Territories." But Douglas's bill did not include this last principle. He needed only four additional southern votes for its passage, and his single concession to the South was the promise that the territory would not be denied admission as a state if it decided for slavery. The earlier prohibition on slavery would persist throughout the territorial stage unless the courts should rule otherwise.

Thereafter the measure went through three distinct stages of change. The first was forced upon the chairman by Atchison, president pro-tempore of the Senate, and his senatorial messmates from the South, Mason and Hunter of Virginia and Butler of South Carolina. Even though the public in their section did not demand repeal of the Missouri Compromise, as heirs of Calhoun this cabal had decided to force their party to apply the nonintervention settlement of 1850 to the older territories. Atchison recanted his previous approval and raged that he would see Nebraska "sink in hell" before he would permit it to become free soil. Later in a drunken speech he asserted that he issued an ultimatum to Douglas to eliminate the restriction on slavery or lose the chairmanship.

On January 10, a week after the bill had been reported and after it had been read twice and ordered printed, the Washington *Sentinel* explained why a new section — the twenty-first — appeared in its reprint on that day. It had been omitted from the first printing on January 7 through "clerical error." The evidence strongly indicates, however, that it was added by Douglas under pressure; the new section, hastily written in his handwriting on blue paper, had been pasted onto the first twenty sections written on white by a copyist. At any rate, the added section gave the act new meaning by inserting the key clause from the Utah-New Mexico acts explicitly empowering territorial residents to act on slavery. Furthermore, the statement previously in the report about the intent to maintain the three principles of the Compromise of 1850 was now included in the bill itself. Implicitly the Missouri prohibition was repealed; explicitly power over slavery in the territory was granted to its people and to the courts.

Even this language did not suit the southern cabal or Senator Dixon of Kentucky, who had succeeded Clay. They correctly saw that Douglas was making what could prove an empty concession. The courts might still uphold the restriction of 1820 and keep slaveholders out of Kansas; if so its residents, whenever they took formal action on slavery, would consist only of Free-Soilers. On Sunday, January 15, Dixon therefore prepared an amendment expressly repealing the Missouri prohibition of slavery in the territory north of 36° 30'. The next day he introduced it in the Senate where it instantly received southern support. Here the bill entered its second revision.

The committee chairman was perturbed by Dixon's amendment, and had the measure sent back to his committee, over which he did not have sure control. A week of high level discussions ensued. On a ride with Dixon several days later Douglas at last assented, allegedly saying "By God, sir, you are right, and I will incorporate it in my bill, though I know it will raise a hell of a storm." At the same time, to settle the Missouri-Iowa rivalry and because two delegates from the territory had already been illegally elected, provision was made for two territories, Kansas and Nebraska. The remainder of the week was taken up with considerations of strategy. By Saturday the twenty-first the full decision had been agreed upon, and on the next day the Washington *Union,* official organ of the party, reversed itself and printed a long editorial favoring the Dixon amendment. According to the final phrasing, the Missouri Compromise had been "superseded" by the Compromise of 1850 and "declared inoperative."

This second revision of the bill was thrust upon Douglas over his expressed objections. It was the combined product of a small group of men, a command decision in which he assented, though the initiative at times was taken from him. Conferences between the House and Senate Territorial Committees were certainly held; on the fateful Saturday the cabinet was in constant session. Senators Atchison, Dixon, Dodge, Hunter, and Mason, and Representatives Phillips of Alabama and Breckinridge of Kentucky were present at most of the discussions.

Once tentative agreement was reached, the chairman, recalling how Taylor's use of the patronage had defeated Clay's efforts in 1850, took the last practical step. On Sunday, a day on which Pierce habitually refused to transact business, a delegation from both houses called upon Secretary Davis to see the President. Davis's initial reluctance to disturb Pierce was overcome when it was pointed out that action was imperative as soon as Congress resumed session the next morning. First Douglas and Atchison conferred with Pierce, but soon the three joined the larger group and a long discussion followed as to the exact phraseology. At its end the chairman shrewdly insisted that the President write out the bill in his own hand. Thus it became an administration measure, even though Pierce's approval was obtained under duress and with short notice. Any Democrats who rebelled would cut themselves off from the party.

During the six weeks of Senate debate after Douglas presented the second revision on January 23, it underwent a third process of significant change by partisan and bipartisan caucuses in which southerners outvoted the chairman in several instances. At first lukewarm to repeal, the South now became aroused at charges of aggression on the part of the slave power, and Whigs from that section supported the demands of its Democrats. From the first, several factions in each party sought to play politics on the bill. The territorial chairman, as the floor leader directing passage, faithfully carried out the caucus decisions, even those which he had opposed. By one of these the Missouri Compromise was declared "void" instead of "inoperative"; by another, immigrants in the territories were denied the suffrage. But the Little Giant's most serious defeat came when he failed to induce the caucus to accept the western interpretation of popular sovereignty; that is, the power of residents to act on slavery early in the territorial stage. Fearing that this would result in most cases in the prohibition of slavery, southerners argued that territories could not act on slavery until they drew up their constitution for admission to statehood. Unable to come to an agreement, the caucus decided to leave this question to the Supreme Court.

Human motivation is ever complex, and Douglas was not the simple man he seemed. Certainly he rationalized under attack, but he felt he was acting for the good of the country and he believed that his action was enlightened and patriotic. In a letter to a St. Joseph meeting on December 17, 1853, the Senator outlined his specific objectives for the bill he was then preparing to introduce. He sought to prevent a permanent Indian barrier, extend a line of white settlement to the Pacific, organize a territory, and hasten construction of a transcontinental railroad. As for slavery he hoped the nation would "sanction and affirm the principles established by the Compromise of 1850." Such a formal political statement, while it can be accepted as a fair summary of his main purposes, naturally did not include all his various reasons.

Just back from his long trip to Europe, the Little Giant was swamped with social, business, and political matters that had accumulated during his absence. He could hardly have expected to have to make such a crucial decision so soon. When unforeseen developments occurred he acted intuitively, but he did not disregard political realities. Under the circumstances it is not surprising that he blundered in his estimate of the northern reaction to repeal of the Missouri Compromise. But his bill did pass and his party did retain the presidency in 1856.

Douglas revealed his motives in a private conversation on the day following his introduction of the finished bill. He had consented to a request from abolitionist Senators Chase and Sumner for a delay in debate until they had time to study it. That afternoon the "Appeal of the Independent Democrats" appeared in the press, which they had been engaged for days in writing with their free-soil friends. This diatribe scurrilously attacked Douglas and the South. The next night he chanced to meet, in a capital hotel, George Murray McConnel, son of a former benefactor in Illinois, to whom he poured out his heart. Walking back and forth before the fire and chewing his cigar to shreds, he let his hair down before McConnel in one of his few moments of discouragement. "Stick to the law, my boy," he told the youth, "stick to the law! Never go into politics. If you do so, no matter how sincere and earnest you may be, no matter how ardently you may devote yourself to the welfare of the country, and your whole country . . . no matter how clear it may be to you that the present is an inheritance from the past, that your hands are tied, and that you are bound to do only what you can do with loyalty to institutions fixed for you by the past, rather than what you might prefer to do if free to choose; no matter for all this or more you will be misinterpreted, vilified, traduced, and finally sacrificed to some local interest or unreasoning passion. Adams, Webster, Clay, Wright and others were victims, and I suppose I must be another."

He told McConnel that he regarded slavery *a curse beyond computation to both white and black.*" But the sword alone could destroy it and he rejected such a dangerous resort. "I am not willing to violate the Constitution to put an end to slavery," he went on, "to violate it for one purpose will lead to violating it for other purposes. To 'do evil that good may come' is false morality and worse policy, and I regard the integrity of this political Union as worth more to humanity than the whole black race. Sometime, without a doubt, slavery will be destroyed."

Douglas feared that a frontal attack upon slavery would lead to secession and war. For that reason he insisted upon a scrupulous observance of the constitutional rights of Southerners, nor would he permit, if he could help it, needless affronts to their pride or whetting of their fears. When in the future he professed an indifference to the morality or the spread of slavery, he was trying to avoid the evil of civil war.

He went on to say that he dreaded the effect of the repeal of the Compromise, that he regarded the move as politically unwise, that he had so argued in party councils, but that he had been outvoted. "All my public life I have been among party men," he continued, "For nearly twenty years I have been fighting for a place among the leaders of the party which seems to me most likely to promote the peace and prosperity of my country, and I have won it." Now that party had committed a serious error. "I must either champion the policy the party has adopted or forfeit forever all that I have fought for — must throw away my whole life and not only cease to be a leader but sink into a nobody. If I retain my leadership I may help to guide the party aright in some graver crisis. If I throw it away, I not only destroy myself but I become powerless for good forever after."

When young McConnel started to say, "But, Mr. Douglas, if you think it's right," the Senator cut him off. "Ah, my boy, I felt that way once. Felt that if I only thought anything right! But why should I or anyone oppose an individual judgment to that of a great party? Am I not at least as likely to be mistaken as the others? That is not politics, nor policy, nor wisdom. . . . I know I am politically right in keeping within the pale of the Constitution. I believe I am right as to the moral effect, and I know I am right as a party leader anxious to help in keeping his party true to the whole country. . . . No man loves his country better than I. I know she is not faultless. I see as clearly as they that she is afflicted with a dangerous tumor. But I believe she will slough it off in time, and I am not willing to risk the life of the patient by the illegal and unscientific surgery they demand. Damn them, they are traitors to freedom, not I, if there be any treason at all. We may all be overwhelmed together in the storm they are brewing, but I, at least, shall stick to the old ship while there's a plank of her afloat."

The Senator did not reopen the debate over slavery. Dixon and other southerners did that. He could not stop them; had he not yielded to them, his bill for Nebraska would probably have been defeated, but he and the nation would have become involved in a renewed debate over slavery anyway. He saw the storm which repeal of the Compromise would create, though he underestimated its intensity. He had witnessed the bitter northern attacks on Webster for his support of the Fugitive Slave Act, which was a clear confirmation of the Constitution. Repeal of the Missouri Compromise, a statute of thirty-four years' standing which Douglas himself had repeatedly pronounced a sacred compact, was bound to cause a greater furor in the North. He was certainly aware that Chase, Sumner, and Seward — particularly since the Free-Soil Party had lost so much strength in the last election and since the national solidarity of the Whigs was shattered — were waiting to pounce upon just such an incident. Why then did he believe he could sell repeal to the North, even as a bargain for Nebraska?

First of all, it was natural that a man who had recently been so successful in riding the tempest in an identical situation should believe that he could repeat his performance. But the logic of popular sovereignty, to which he had become so firmly attached for historical and practical reasons, led him to accept repeal of the Missouri Compromise as a just and compelling corollary. If the people of the territories were to decide about slavery for themselves without restriction and if equal rights of the South were to be conceded, then that statute had always been inconsistent with the principle. In this case logic was buttressed by northern self-interest. Like Clay and Webster he believed that geography had set the limits of slavery and that these limits had been reached. In his own mind close to a belief in an economic interpretation of history, Douglas was convinced that most northerners would see that no real concessions were being made to slavery and that verbal concessions were essential to the preservation of a Union from which they received much the greater economic gain. More than that, such concessions were necessary for the passage of the territorial bill.

The Senator understandingly believed that he could repeat his tactics of 1850 — compromise with southerners to get sufficient votes for his bill. These tactics had worked twice for him before, why should they not work again? Since he had won his Illinois constituents over to the Fugitive Slave Act despite their open hostility, by the same persuasive oratory he expected to win them now to repeal. After all, the new principle of popular sovereignty received its chief support from his section, and the Missouri Compromise — congressional intervention with slavery in the territories — had clearly violated it.

Certainly the Little Giant himself and his admirers exaggerated his role in the formulation of the bill, if not in its passage. To say that he had political motives is a simple truism — every senator, and particularly one who happens to be a national leader, has when he introduces a measure in Congress. But the allegation that he planned repeal and that his main purpose was to obtain support in the South for his nomination was an outright distortion. By his own testimony he laid himself open to the first charge, when he said later that he wrote the act himself in his own house. This may have been true of the bill which he reported on January 4, but that was quite a different measure from the one finally passed by Congress. By this statement he was undoubtedly trying to conceal how much southerners ultimately forced him to concede, but he was trying equally to keep their good will by proving that he accepted without mental reservations the caucus decisions.

A restatement of the chairman's position at the different stages of the bill is necessary to clarify his specific objectives. His bill of January 4 did not mention or repeal the Missouri Compromise, and a letter to the effect that he planned repeal as early as 1852 is spurious. True, the report of the committee did say the intent of the bill was to give territorial residents power over slavery, like that granted Utah and New Mexico earlier, and it implied that the Compromise of 1850 had superseded the earlier compromise. But clauses to this effect were omitted from the bill, and the statement in the report may have been a ruse by which the chairman hoped to obtain the few southern votes necessary in the Senate. The bill did give jurisdiction over slavery to the courts (a power the courts could have exercised anyway) and promised that Congress would admit the territory to statehood regardless of any provision in its constitution about slavery. The twenty-first section added on January 10 expressly granted residents power to act on slavery, thus *implicitly* repealing the Missouri prohibition. Even if his "clerical error" alibi was true, the chairman at first would go no farther than implicit repeal. By it he hoped to get enough southern votes, and he assumed he could make implicit repeal palatable to his own section. When this change did not suit certain wary southerners, he openly fought their demand for explicit repeal in party councils because he knew it would hurt the Democrats in the North. As he reluctantly yielded to their insistence, he constantly tried to tone down the language used, though ultimately the caucus declared the Missouri prohibition "void" by virtue of the legislation of 1850.

A distinction must be made between Douglas's original and his later objectives. At first the political situation in Illinois and the transcontinental railroad were his primary concern, with the presidency perhaps in the back of his mind. As for the latter, he stood strong in the South. He had failed in his bid for the nomination in 1852 because he did not carry his own Northwest, and it was in the Lakes region particularly where he was weakest. But he had recently ordered his friends to stop all speculation about his plans for 1856 — he would hardly have repeated the former error of moving too soon. Both his state and his section demanded the organization of the Nebraska Territory, which would improve the chances of a central or a northern route and of both Chicago and St. Louis as terminals. By it he avoided the charge of sacrificing the interests of either. At the same time, he could not afford to admit that by his concessions for southern votes he sought passage of a measure which indirectly would block a southern route. To protect himself further, before final action on Nebraska he introduced his bill for three roads, a northern, a central, and a southern. After six weeks of argument the Senate railroad committee, of which he was a member, rejected his proposal in favor of a single road.

From the first the Little Giant had also in mind national developments in his party. Executive leadership, it was already apparent, could not be expected from Pierce. A proslavery directory in the cabinet, led by Jefferson Davis and Caleb Cushing, were calling the plays. To save the Democrats in the North he must counteract this southern influence; at least he must get equal compensation for his own section. He realized that his own party stood in danger of the sectional split overtaking the Whigs, an event hastened by the many manifestations of the Davis-Cushing influence in the White House. The Democrats needed a quick shot of adrenalin. "The whole movement by Douglas," commented Whig Senator John Bell of Tennessee, who opposed his bill, "from the first was to get up some counterexcitement to call off public attention from the conduct of the administration."

When southern insistence upon express repeal of the Missouri Compromise produced a crisis in the party, his objectives broadened. He still pressed for his territorial bill, but unless he could work out a formula of compromise on slavery the Democrats would be hopelessly split. Apart from his own ambitions, for the party's sake a break with the southerners must be avoided. For this reason he yielded to their demands and even accepted a draw on popular sovereignty in the caucus. Later he might induce or force them over to his position; meanwhile he could read his own interpretation into the bill, as they could theirs. At the moment he may have regarded the point as only technical: were he correct about slavery having reached its geographical limits, it mattered not whether territories acted early or had to wait until they drew up a constitution. At the later date free-soilers would still be in the majority. Here he put his head in a noose. The Northwest's reaction to the bill made it clear that the right of territories to act on slavery during the territorial stage was the limit of his constituents' concession. Events in Kansas soon forced him to stand firm on this position; whereupon southern ultras turned vehemently against him.

For once Douglas was thoroughly angry at a political attack upon himself. The Chase crowd had used tactics which the Little Giant himself had employed. He had put himself out on a limb, which they were engaging to saw off, but he was incensed that they were jeopardizing peace and Union for partisan political purposes. Not for a moment did he believe them sincere.

Chase and Sumner tricked Douglas into permitting a week's delay before debate started so that their Appeal would have more time to evoke from the northern public expressions of opposition. These would either block passage in Congress or so prolong debate that Free-Soilers could make full use of that forum further to inflame northern hostility. The Appeal was mainly the work of Senator Chase, written before the Dixon repeal amendment was added. It was signed by a small group of Free-Soilers; Douglas later proved that the signatures of Seward and Ben Wade of Ohio by their own admission were forged. Full of historical inaccuracies and of false calumny of the Little Giant, it was nevertheless a clever appeal to the emotions of many northerners.

It accused the slave states of a "monstrous plot" to force slavery into all territories. "We arraign this bill," it thundered, "as a gross violation of a sacred pledge; as a criminal betrayal of precious rights, as part and parcel of an atrocious plot to exclude from a vast unoccupied region immigrants from the Old World and free laborers from our own States, and convert it into a dreary region of despotism, inhabited by masters and slaves."

The act would check the building of a Pacific railroad and make a homestead law worthless. "The dearest interests of freedom and the Union" were in imminent peril. Placing an extreme free-soil interpretation upon the origin of the Missouri Compromise, the Appeal asserted that for thirty years "this compact has been universally regarded and acted upon as inviolable American law. . . . Not a man in Congress, or out of Congress, in 1850 pretended that the Compromise measures would repeal the Missouri prohibition. Will the people permit their dearest interests to be thus made the mere hazards of a presidential game, and destroyed by false facts and false inferences?" Other phrases like "meditated bad faith" and "servile demagogues" referred unmistakably to the Senator from Illinois, who as a consequence was burned in effigy in many northern cities and excoriated by scores of editors in such epithets as the "bully of slavery." The northern public, press, pulpit, and legislatures, urged the Appeal, must join in a universal protest to stop this "enormous crime."

Douglas wished to bring the bill to a vote as soon as possible, though he would give its opponents a fair hearing. They in turn, amplifying the various charges of the Appeal, used every means of delay — particularly by amendments which would divide its northern supporters, who liked popular sovereignty but not repeal, from its southern, who liked repeal but not popular sovereignty. Actually two battles raged simultaneously, one in Congress and another among the northern public. The strategy of the Free-Soil group, like that of Lincoln in the debates a few years later, was to make Douglas pay for victory on the specific issue by loss of the larger campaign. In both cases they were successful and in the longer run not merely the Senator but the Democratic Party was the loser. In each case he had no alternative, and the dilemma was not of his own making; had he lost the battle he was certain to lose the campaign.

The bill was debated in the Senate from January 30 until it passed on March 3 by a vote of more than two-to-one. The hectic speeches on it, of which Douglas made the opening and the closing, rank with the most dramatic in the history of the Senate. Its passage through both houses, however, resulted more from the adroit management of the Chairman of the Committee on Territories. "I passed the Kansas-Nebraska Act myself," he later told his brother-in-law, Madison Cutts. "I had the authority and the power of a dictator throughout the whole controversy in both houses. The speeches were nothing. It was the marshalling and directing of men and guarding from attacks and with a ceaseless vigilance preventing surprise."

This was an overstatement; the speeches did influence public opinion and even the votes of neutrals in Congress. The bargains made in the House, however, were the decisive factor in the bill's passage, but no evidence of them has yet come to light. Having accepted repeal, the Senator made the best case possible for his party's position and took full responsibility upon himself. He could and did defend the new bill on its own merits. Since his opponents appealed to precedent he sought to refute their arguments. Popular sovereignty conformed, despite earlier congressional action to the contrary, to American tradition and experience.

Here he resorted to a *non sequitur:* the Compromise of 1850 had repealed the Missouri Compromise and the new act merely repeated the pertinent words from the later Compromise. This was the major fault in his argument. The 1850 settlement applied to new territory taken from Mexico, though parts of the Louisiana Purchase were included in Utah and New Mexico. But no one argued at the time, nor as late as 1853, not even Douglas, that the Missouri prohibition in the Louisiana Territory north of 36° 30′ had been repealed. Whig Senator Edward Everett of Massachusetts wrote in his diary that not a single man thought so in 1850, and Whig Representative Emerson Etheridge of Tennessee argued that the compromise measures would have been defeated had they been so interpreted at the time. Douglas's argument convicted him of sophistry in the minds of many northerners, but chiefly those who were predisposed to believe the worst of him anyway.

But whether his argument, in view of the ex parte interpretation of the history of congressional action on slavery by his opponents, actually lost him more votes and public support than it gained at the time is debatable. The terms of the Compromise of 1850 were highly ambiguous and more than one interpretation of them was logically tenable. That Compromise did reject the Wilmot Proviso, which would have applied the earlier prohibition of slavery in the Louisiana Territory north of 36°30′ to the new area. It could be argued that the statute of 1850 had set up a principle as much as the earlier act of 1820 and that the later principle superseded the earlier. The difference, of course, lay in the fact that the earlier principle had been followed until it was abandoned in 1848, as Douglas said, at the insistence of northern Free-Soilers. This happened to be the first instance when the principle of 1850 was to be defined.

Any impartial estimate of the debates must give Douglas a clear decision on points, for he refuted most of his opponents' contentions and individually routed their three senatorial leaders. Their thesis proclaimed the Missouri Compromise a compact, unaltered by the act of 1850. The North had kept its bargain by agreeing to the admission of Missouri and Arkansas; but the South, having accepted Iowa as a free state and Minnesota as a free territory, was now refusing to comply with fulfillment. This the Senator from Illinois denied. In the first place he insisted that it had not been the intention of the Founding Fathers to make all territories free, as Chase contended, but to divide them along a geographical line which roughly confirmed economic and climatic realties. Mainly they chose this as a pragmatic means of quieting a dangerous debate; slavery *was* permitted in the new states south of the Ohio. He proved that the North by a huge majority had voted against the Missouri Compromise of 1820 and against the admission of Missouri a year later; thus they had never approved the compact and Seward's own state of New York was one of the first to violate it. A majority of northern votes opposed the admission of Arkansas. His own bill in 1848 to extend the compromise line through California had been defeated by northerners in the House. Thus northerners had always rejected the compromise principle they now hailed as a sacred compact.

But congressional action had never conquered climate, had never made any area free. Despite the Northwest Ordinance slavery existed for years in Illinois; the residents of Iowa and Oregon themselves made those regions free, not an act of Congress, and Indians at that moment held slaves in the Nebraska Territory despite the Missouri Compromise. But slaves could no more survive there than slavery could have continued in Illinois. The popular sovereignty of 1850, and now of 1854, though forced upon the nation because Free-Soilers would no longer accept the older principle of geographical division, was actually superior in that it provided a democratic solution. Under it territorial residents would follow the dictates of nature. (The next census confirmed his argument, for in 1860 the Kansas Territory had two slaves.)

At the same time the Senator reviewed at length his own consistent and unmistakable advocacy of popular sovereignty ever since Free-Soil votes defeated his bill of 1848 to extend the Missouri line to the Pacific. He cited his contention in 1850 that the prohibition be removed from that area north of 36° 30' surrendered by Texas. He quoted from his bill in the spring of that year organizing Utah and New Mexico, which left their residents "free to decide the slavery question for themselves, *in the precise* language of the Nebraska bill now under discussion." When Clay's committee joined his bills, he reminded the Senate, and included a provision that the territorial legislatures should not pass on the subject of slavery, he led the fight against the amendment until it was finally rejected. He reiterated his stand against congressional interference in his Chicago speech that fall, and he called attention to the resolutions of the Illinois legislature both in 1851 and 1854 supporting his position. He demolished the charge of the Chase coterie that his original Nebraska Bill did not repeal the Missouri Compromise by pointing out that they had clearly stated in their Appeal that it did. That document was completed and signed before the Dixon amendment was introduced!

But the Chairman of the Committee on Territories could not hurry the Senate. The bill as originally reported had confined the right to vote and to hold office to citizens of the United States, or to those who had announced their intentions to become citizens and had in addition taken an oath to support the Constitution. Allegedly this clause would deny immigrants the franchise. To leave no doubt, Senator Clayton of Delaware introduced an amendment conferring these rights solely upon citizens. Popular with southerners, since it would reduce the Free-Soil vote and possibly the number of foreign immigrants in the territory, it passed by two votes over the opposition of Douglas and most northerners. Yet the House would not have it so, and in the final conference on the act the amendment was dropped.

The basic ambiguity about popular sovereignty remained. Other ambiguities, soon to become tragically evident in the fight over Kansas, were pointed out. Clayton observed that the bill required Congress to approve territorial laws, whereupon the Little Giant removed that section but without specifically stating that Congress surrendered its power of revision. In the modified repeal section, the key phrase, "subject only to the Constitution," left territorial residents free to regulate their own domestic institutions without interference by Congress. Until then the Constitution had been interpreted as giving Congress considerable power over territories. Chase pointed out that territorial governors, judges, and secretaries were appointed by the President; he would make all such offices elective. Douglas yielded to the extent of proposing a suspensive instead of an absolute gubernatorial veto which could be overriden by a two-thirds vote of the territorial legislature, and he asserted that other appointed officials were charged with Federal duties only. The issue was left hanging, largely because no one anticipated the difficulties shortly to arise in Kansas.

The chairman induced the Senate to agree that the vote should be taken on March 3, but it was midnight before he took the floor to make the closing speech. Because of the late hour Sam Houston proposed adjournment, to which Douglas agreed, but other Senators shouted no. Thereupon he harangued them until dawn in the most powerful speech of his long oratorical career. He proved himself beyond doubt, as he has been called, the "most formidable legislative pugilist" in congressional history. But the phrase is hardly fair; in his own mind he was not just answering premeditated slander upon himself. Cass told him on the floor of the Senate that being burnt in effigy would do him no harm. Rather he was pouring out his righteous indignation upon a group of men who he believed were seeking for political purposes to revive and to increase the agitation over slavery, regardless of the consequences for the Union.

For their full effect the portions of his speech in which he dealt with Chase, Seward, and Sumner must be read in full. He forced the Senator from New York to admit that he had "misapprehended the facts"; that his state had not agreed to or abided by the Missouri Compromise; that he was incorrect when he called the great Kentuckian the author of that compromise, for by Clay's own admission in the Senate it was the compromise act of 1821, under which Missouri actually entered as a state, that he fathered. At one point in the exchange Seward asked him to yield, "because I have never had so much respect for him as I have tonight." Douglas replied that he now saw how to command the New Yorker's respect.

But it was for Chase that he saved the full force of his contempt and sarcasm, Chase the author of the insulting epithets in the Appeal. The Ohioan ate his words and attempted a weak apology. He deplored the effigy-burnings and said he had never intended any discourtesy: "I certainly did not intend to impute to the Senator from Illinois — and I desire always to do justice — in that any improper motives. I do not think it is an unworthy ambition to desire to be a President of the United States. . . . I differ from the Senator in my judgment of the measure. . . . I do not condemn his judgment, I do not make, and I do not desire to make, any personal imputations upon him in reference to a great public question."

The pompous Sumner Douglas too reduced to silence when he sought to answer the charge that he had put his honor "up at public auction or private sale in order to procure a seat" in the Senate. "I must be permitted to remind him," thundered the Little Giant, ". . . that when he arrived here to take his seat for the first time, so firmly were senators impressed with the conviction that he had been elected by dishonorable and corrupt means, there were very few who, for a long time, could deem it consistent with personal honor to hold private intercourse with him.

So general was the impression, that for a long time he was avoided and shunned as a person unworthy of the association of gentlemen."

His triumph and his dilemma was generally recognized. "How the *Little Giant* came to put his head in such a halter," wrote a friend to Buchanan from St. Louis, "is a matter for much speculation. . . . However he got into it, or from whatever motive, he has borne himself so nobly in the contest, has stood so grim and unflinching, amidst treachery and duplicity, that his strength would give dignity even to error. He has not yielded to the storm, but has braved it nobly, whilst his allies in the measure have been tossed about like leaves before an October blast." Robert C. Winthrop of Massachusetts, who had always disagreed and continued to disagree with Douglas, told him that he admired the force of his speeches: "The effigy-burners do not seem to have consumed you yet." But for the evil already done, no amount of personal satisfaction could compensate.

The real fight came in the House, where northern sentiment was felt more directly since representation was proportional to population. The Senate bill was buried for weeks in the Committee of the Whole and defeat seemed probable, particularly since two thirds of the ninety-two northern Democrats joined the opposition because the Senate bill did not grant popular sovereignty in the territorial stage. But Douglas and his fellow Illinoisan, William A. Richardson, who took active charge of the matter, were accustomed to fighting odds. They bided their time and let executive patronage from the frightened Pierce work for them. On the eighth of May eighteen other bills were laid aside to get at the measure. Richardson, as Chairman of the Committee on Territories, tried to restrict debate to four days, but the House argued for two weeks. Some of the northern rebels changed sides, but a majority was obtained only with the affirmative vote of thirteen southern Whigs. In the stretch the parliamentary skill of Georgian Alexander Stephens proved invaluable. On May 22 the act, minus the Clayton amendment, passed by a vote of 113 to 100 and shortly the Senate concurred.

In its final form the bill was as much the southerners' as it was Douglas's. He had yielded much — as it turned out, too much. In the prelude to most wars there comes a point when efforts at compromise, usually efficacious, defeat their purposes; instead they actually increase the rigidity of extremists on both sides. Such, in retrospect, was the consequence of the Nebraska Act. "The great volcano of American politics was in a state of eruption," writes Roy Nichols. "When the flow subsided, old landmarks were found to be either greatly altered or obliterated. Two new masses were prominent on the political landscape, the Republican Party and the Solid South. Douglas had disappeared."

The last sentence is inaccurate, for Douglas remained a leading actor until his death in 1861. In times of crisis men cannot foresee even the immediate future, nor can they afford to yield to pessimism. Having made his decision, the Little Giant acted upon it with confidence that he had at least an even chance of winning in the end.

V I
Who Sows the Wind

THE 1850's, in retrospect, formed one of those critical periods in the destiny of a nation full of grand drama that was to end in stark tragedy. Of this the men living in it had no way of knowing, though some — like Douglas — feared the grinding of the fates. The repeal of the Missouri Compromise began a political revolution and evoked an immediate reaction which rocked the Democratic Party. In the fall elections it lost 350,000 votes and all but two of the northern states that held elections that year; only seven of the forty-two northern Democrats who voted for the Nebraska Bill retained their seats. The opposition ticket in most states consisted of anti-Nebraska Democrats, old Whigs and old Free-Soilers, Know-Nothings, Prohibitionists, and a new group calling themselves Republicans. Yet fusionists were united only in opposition to the Democrats and could not be unified into one party.

For more than a year the political situation was muddled while the Democrats fought back as best they could and sought to ride out the storm. Seward, oldest in point of time of the antisouthern leaders, swore that he would die a Whig; Chase, the new leader, and his journalistic counterpart in vituperation, Horace Greeley of the New York *Tribune,* urged launching the Republican Party — Free-Soilers with a new name. But the emerging nativist party, called Americans or Know-Nothings, seemed potentially to have as much popular appeal, and many anti-Nebraska Democrats refused to go over to their old enemies the Whigs or to join either of the new parties. The old Blair-Benton Democrats, loud opponents of the "slave power" disaffected since Polk's administration, attempted to regain control by pressing the candidacy of Sam Houston, who had fought the Nebraska Bill until the end. The situation was reflected in the composition of the House of Representatives at the end of 1855, when new congressmen chosen in 1854 sat for the first time; according to one estimate there were one hundred and eight Republicans and anti-Nebraska Democrats, eighty-three regular Democrats, and forty-three Know-Nothings. Probably many of the Republicans and anti-Nebraska Democrats were secretly Know-Nothings, for it was still a secret order and not a formal party.

Such a consequence was largely, but not exclusively, the result of the repeal of the compromise. A generation earlier a majority of northerners, for varied reasons, had tried to prohibit slavery in the Louisiana Territory. Less than a decade before a large northern majority had voted to exclude slavery from the new territory taken from Mexico, and the precedent followed since 1820 of maintaining a balance between slave and free states in the Senate had been formally abandoned. Thus slavery had been checked even though the Wilmot Proviso had been rejected. Now it was back on the offensive and had regained a large area closed to the pernicious institution for thirty-four years. The inevitable popular protest found leaders, sincere and otherwise. Whigs were bound to use their advantage, as were all other frustrated or politically hopeful groups and individuals. Under the circumstances the false charge that the act resulted from a southern plot to force slavery upon the entire nation was credible, and too useful to be ignored. But at first only the northern public was aroused.

Tutored by editors and politicians who read what they wished into the Nebraska Act, the common man of the North moved to a new attitude towards slavery which won him to abolitionist objectives without converting him to orthodox abolitionist doctrine. Particularly was this so in the Northwest. Fusionists or Republicans carried every state, and even in Illinois the Democrats retained only four of the nine congressional seats. Slavery was no longer an abstract matter; it was a practical obstruction to progress and conflicted with the moral concepts of American democracy. Slavery extension became *the* slavery issue. Whether or not citizens thought of moving to the western area, they would have no Negroes there, slave or free, and no aristocrats. Kansas, it should be remembered, was much larger than the ultimate state and included fully a third of the northern part of the Louisiana Purchase. Northern men were unconvinced by Douglas's insistence that nature had foreordained it for freedom. Slavery existed in Missouri, why should it not spread westward? Indeed, if history repeated itself emigrants from the state immediately to the eastward would be in the majority and thus would settle the question.

As in earlier antislavery attitudes, it cannot be said that the central drive stemmed purely, and perhaps it did not even spring mainly, from moral impulses. Anti-Negro sentiment, philosophically the reverse, was so strong that both Douglas and Lincoln appealed cogently to it. Antisouthern sentiment — sectional opposition to southern control of the national administration — was if anything greater than ever. The timing of the Nebraska Act had been most unfortunate. Pierce had just obtained the Gadsden Purchase for the South and his ministers were shortly to attempt to take Cuba from Spain. Southern votes soon defeated a homestead act and the President later vetoed a rivers-and-harbors bill. When the fight over Kansas began he took the extreme position demanded by southern ultras. These actions, seized upon by the Democrats' opponents, kept the excitement over Nebraska from subsiding.

In the South, prior to the introduction of the act, no general sentiment for repeal existed. Accepting Calhoun's arguments, a majority believed the Missouri Compromise unconstitutional. Yet they did not believe that slavery would spread to Kansas; only two of the more than fifty southern congressmen who had spoken in the debates had any confidence that it would. But they voted for it as a just recognition of their rights in the territories. Only a few saw the harm which would result. Do not stir up the North by a measure from which the South would gain nothing, pleaded Sam Houston; the South had not asked for repeal. "I, as the most extreme Southern Senator upon this floor, do not desire it. . . . I reject it. . . . *Maintain the Missouri Compromise!* Stir not up agitation! Give us peace!"

Events which followed repeal, however, produced a southern excitement which became in time as shrill as that in the North. So great was northern resistance to the Fugitive Slave Act, once the Nebraska Bill passed, that the measure became ineffective. Here *was* a right that mattered! Another right was violated when the Emigrant Aid Society, subsidized by northern funds, took action in Kansas to deny proslavery Missourians who emigrated there the privilege of popular sovereignty. Sumner's scurrilous attack upon the South, in his Senate speech on the "Crime against Kansas," infuriated its citizens and many of them approved when Carolinian Preston Brooks beat him into insensibility. The success of a sectional party advocating the Wilmot Proviso, which carried most of the North in 1856, aroused their old fears and a minority talked openly of secession in the event of a Frémont victory. Southern radicalism had been revived as much as northern.

Judging by the situation in Chicago, where he was howled down by a nativist mob, but indulging also in wishful thinking, the Little Giant insisted that Democratic losses were the work of the Know-Nothings. In a set-to with Ohio Senator Wade he argued that the opposition in the free states had been a "crucible into which they poured Abolitionism, Maine liquor-lawism, and what there was left of Northern Whiggism, and then the Protestant feeling against the Catholic and the native feeling against the foreigner." He challenged Wade to name a single anti-Nebraska congressman who had not been elected by Know-Nothing votes. "Look all over the recent elections," he continued, "and wherever you will show me one Nebraska member of the

House cut down, I will show you, I think, nearly two for one anti-Nebraska men defeated at the same election by the same causes. Was it the Nebraska issue, then, that administered this rebuke, or was it caused by your secret conclaves . . . ?"

He urged senators to give no credence to Wade's distortion of the issue; the North had intended no affront to the South, for "the North are Union people, a law-abiding people, a people loyal to the Constitution and willing to perform its obligations." Under unusual circumstances a temporary combination of factions might elect a man "misrepresentative of the Sentiment of the North [but such men had no right] to speak in the name of the North or for the North. This Abolition faction, this disunion cabal, this set of men who make their reputation by slandering better men than themselves, have never been the true representatives of the North. They always come here by a bargain, and they go out at the end of the term at which they arrive."

These words were spoken early in 1855 and at the time they may have seemed warranted. At any rate they were good tactics, for the sooner the Nebraska business was forgotten the better for the Democrats and the nation. As experienced a campaigner as Secretary William L. Marcy agreed completely with Douglas's estimate. The Know-Nothings had actually captured some northeastern states. The Little Giant in a Philadelphia speech the previous summer had been the first prominent national statesman to defy them. When they tried to take the South, the Democrats held the line and elected Governors Henry A. Wise in Virginia and Andrew Johnson in Tennessee, both of whom defied the secret order. Douglas went to Virginia and spoke several times for Wise. When the Grand Council of the order came out strongly for the Nebraska Act in what was actually a national convention of the party in the summer of 1855, the northern wing withdrew. The next year, with considerable support from the Whigs, they polled a sizable vote for ex-President Fillmore, but it was clear they were finished as a national party. In the interim they had proved quite useful to the Republicans, for they had forced the Democrats to expend ammunition and they served as a bridge which made it easier for both northern Democrats and Whigs to abandon old loyalties and transfer their allegiance to a new third party.

Democratic victories in the North during 1855, by which they regained much lost ground, gave Douglas and Pierce a false optimism. The former wrote his Georgia friend Howell Cobb that "the tide is now completely turned. The torrent of fanaticism has been rolled back almost everywhere." A year later he must have been aware that he was wrong. At first Whigs like Seward and Lincoln bided their time, waiting to see whether their party could be maintained or, if not, which of the two new parties should be chosen for fusion. Never was a third party so lucky in the breaks as the Republicans. They held a majority in the House and did not "want the Kansas question settled," observed the *Kansas Weekly Herald*. "They want to keep up the cry of 'bleeding Kansas' and delude the ignorant into the embraces of black republicanism." The Sumner-Brooks affair perfectly fitted their strategy. To the more astute observers it was evident that the Know-Nothings were on the wane, and the Whigs began to come over. But in no instance was the opportunism of the new party so evident as when its convention passed over its congressional leaders and chose General John Frémont as candidate.

Clearly the anti-Nebraska sentiment had not subsided. The new party received 1,341,000 votes to the Democrats' 1,838,000 (Fillmore got 874,000), and won all northern states but five. Could it gain part of the Fillmore votes and entice more Democrats before 1860, it would sweep the section. In Illinois Douglas was beaten when anti-Nebraska Democrat Lyman Trumbull was chosen senator over his friend Shields in 1855, and again the next year his lieutenant Richardson was defeated for governor by the Republican candidate. Even though Buchanan carried the state, he received only a plurality, not a majority.

Rarely has a statesman been subjected to the abuse which the Little Giant received for his defense of the Nebraska Act. He could travel from Boston to Chicago, he freely admitted, by the light of his own effigies. Preachers and editors called him "Arnold" and "Judas"; a group of women in Ohio presented him with thirty pieces of silver. One writer suggested that the recent death of his wife was divine punishment and the charge that he owned slaves was widely revived, particularly in the Senate.

Abolitionists were behind much of this, but Douglas had added the American clergy to the ranks of his enemies. When three thousand New England clergymen submitted a resolution protesting the immorality of the bill, he carried the fight to them on the floor of the Senate for claiming "to speak in the name of the Almighty upon a political question pending in the Congress of the United States. I deny their authority." The petition was evidence of "a deliberate attempt to organize the clergy of this country into a great political, sectional party for Abolition schemes." Later he presented a similar appeal from twenty-five Chicago preachers and another five hundred of their northwestern brethren, but this time replied by a public letter in which he attempted to reason with them. "If you should remove to Nebraska," he asked, "with a view of making it your permanent home, would you be any less competent to decide it [the question of slavery] when you should have arrived in the country?" But the ministry continued to attack him as an Apocalyptic beast.

Then in the summer, when the Senator spoke in defense of the bill at Independence Hall in Philadelphia where the city election had just been won by the Know-Nothings, he defied that secret order which seemed to be taking the nation. "To proscribe a man in this country," he said in an address which won praise from some courageous editors, "on account of his birthplace or religious faith is subversive of all our ideas of civil and religious freedom. It is revolting to our sense of justice and right." At the same time he fought the temperance crusade as another manifestation of intolerance and led a successful fight the next year in Illinois to defeat a prohibition law, submitted by the legislature to a popular referendum. All along, of course, he had been denouncing his congressional opponents as "pure, unadulterated representatives of Abolitionism, Free-Soilism, Niggerism in the Congress of the United States." Douglas was fighting mad, but no mere politician currying popular favor would have taken on such a host of enemies at once. In these various actions there was a clear intellectual and moral consistency; he was striking back at intolerance in all of its current forms, striking back at all those who on their assumption of superior moral rectitude and judgment were bent on removing motes from the eyes of their brothers.

When he returned to Chicago at the end of the summer upon the adjournment of Congress, he announced that he would speak to his fellow citizens about the bill on the evening of September 1. Every paper in the city had turned against him, so a few weeks before he had helped set up the *Times,* with James Sheehan of Washington as editor. Revolt in his own party in Illinois was open; for months Old Line Whigs and abolitionists had been arraigning him. Chicago Know-Nothings had promised to mob him, the local clergy had attacked him in their sermons, and even the German immigrants had turned against him, though he had voted against the Clayton amendment. With his friends, including the loyal Irish, preparing to insure a hearing for him by force if necessary, the situation was ugly and a riot might have resulted had he permitted it. As a showman he used the drama of the moment to his own advantage.

On the afternoon of the scheduled speech flags were lowered on ships at the docks. As dark approached church bells began to toll and continued to do so until the hour of his speech. The night was hot and the crowd armed, but he assured his friends that he could handle the mob. He began by saying that the Nebraska bill, for which the local press had vilified him, had never been printed by it until that very morning. When the mob refused to let him speak he proceeded to attack the Chicago *Tribune* as responsible for the melee, and he boldly denounced the Know-Nothings. Undoubtedly he lost his temper. After several hours it became apparent that he could not calm the tumult. He pulled out his watch and during a moment's lull waved his fist and shouted: "Abolitionists of Chicago! It is now Sunday morning. I'll go to church and you may go to hell!" The outcome contrasted

sharply with his success in the city four years before, and only a
man of his magnetism and courage could have escaped without
physical injury.

In Chicago and in northern Illinois the Little Giant knew he
was in enemy country; he was taking the offensive deliberately.
But for the force of his personality, so suited for that type of campaign, his party might have been completely routed instead of
losing only half the congressional seats that fall. Old-Line Whigs
and abolitionists were bound to take advantage of his discom-
fort, but there was reason at first for his belief that the Know-
Nothings were the strength of the fusionists. The more serious
trouble, schism in his own party, he for some time regarded as
only temporary. But many Democratic leaders in the state deserted him, either because of their own feelings about the Nebraska Act or because they thought he had committed a fatal
strategic error in supporting it. When he insisted upon unqualified acceptance of the act as a test of party loyalty, many of his
friends bolted or became disaffected: editor "Long John" Went-
worth, Lyman Trumbull, John M. Palmer, and even his faithful
lieutenant, McLernand.

Speaking in the north after the Chicago meeting, he continued
to find audiences hostile; but the situation changed when he
reached the center of the state. He hammered on the main points
of his closing Senate address: the virtue of popular sovereignty,
the change effected by the Compromise of 1850, and the impossibility of slavery in the West. Usually he closed with an appeal
for the Constitution, the Union, and the Democratic Party as a
national institution. The opposition put their own speakers on
his trail and asked him to divide time with them. The Senator
refused. "I won't do it," he said, when efforts were made for a
joint debate with Lincoln (no one could think that a man with
his record was afraid). "I come to Chicago, I am met by an Abolitionist; I come to the center of the state and am met by an Old-
Line Whig; I come to the South and am met by a Democrat. I
can't hold the Abolitionist responsible for what the Whig says; I
can't hold the Whig responsible for what the Abolitionist says,

and I can't hold either responsible for what the Democrat says. It looks like 'dogging' a man over the State. This is my meeting. The people came here to hear me, and I want to talk to them." Usually opponents held their own meeting in a town a few hours after his speech. They gave him considerable trouble, particularly since he was seriously bothered on the tour with a hoarseness that a year later resulted in a long illness and a throat operation.

Early in October Douglas gave his usual speech at Springfield, the state capital, to an enthusiastic audience. At its close Lincoln, who had been following his words attentively, announced that Trumbull would reply on the next day; but if the anti-Nebraska Democrat was unable to appear, he himself would speak. So it was; here at Springfield he gave his "Peoria" speech (so-called because he repeated it in that city a few days later), which he had been practicing and polishing for two months. This was the speech which launched him — until then a frustrated local politician — on the road to the White House.

Unlike Sumner, Wade, and Seward, Lincoln attacked neither the South nor Douglas. He did not "wish to question patriotism or to assail the motives of any man or class of men [but] to be . . . national in all the positions I may take." He did intend "to make and keep the distinction between the existing institution and the extension of it." The Little Giant's "declared indifference" to whether the territories chose slavery or not he hated "because of the monstrous injustice of slavery itself." (This was the first time in Lincoln's life that he ever publicly denounced slavery, though privately he had always been perturbed about it.) He did not blame slaveholders — "they are just what we would be in their situation." He recognized their constitutional rights, "not grudgingly, but fully and fairly," and favored any fugitive slave legislation "which should not in its stringency be more likely to carry a free man into slavery than our ordinary criminal laws are to hang an innocent one."

He frankly admitted that "if all earthly power were given me, I should not know what to do as to the existing institution." Like Jefferson he considered colonization, but that could work, if at all, only "in the long run." He hoped for gradual emancipation, yet saw the dilemma: "What next? Free them, and make them politically and socially our equals? *My own feelings will not admit of this,* and if mine would, we well know that those of the great mass of whites will not. Whether this feeling accords with justice and sound judgment is not the sole question, if indeed it is any part of it. A universal feeling, whether well or ill founded, cannot be safely disregarded." Of one thing he was sure: he would not consent to the introduction of the institution into territories already free. "The great mass of mankind consider slavery a great moral wrong. [This belief] lies at the very foundation of their sense of justice, and it cannot be trifled with. . . . No statesman can safely disregard it."

He admitted that justice compelled protection for the property of southerners in the territories "if there is no difference between hogs and Negroes." As for popular sovereignty, he denied that the question was the exclusive concern of territorial residents: "Is not Nebraska, while a Territory, a part of us? Do we not own the country? And if we surrender control of it, do we not surrender the right of self-government? . . . You say this question should be left to the people of Nebraska. . . . What better moral right have thirty-one citizens of Nebraska to say that the thirty-second shall not hold slaves than the people of the thirty-one States have to say that slavery shall not go to the thirty-second State at all?" The decision vitally affected every American citizen: "The whole nation is interested that the best use shall be made of these Territories. *We want them for homes of free white people. This they cannot be, to any considerable extent, if slavery shall be planted within them.* Slave States are places for poor white people to remove from, not to remove to. New free States are the places for poor people to go to, and better their condition. For this use the nation needs these Territories."

Repeal of the Missouri Compromise, he categorically asserted, had been unnecessary to the passage of the act organizing the Nebraska Territory. Repeal was "wrong — wrong in its direct effect, letting slavery into Kansas and Nebraska, and wrong in its prospective principle, allowing it to spread to every other part of the wide world where men can be found inclined to take it." Earlier he had said that "no man is good enough to govern another man, without that man's consent."

In all of this the politician spoke as much as the philosopher. Like Tom Paine's *Common Sense* in the revolutionary crisis, in the current state of northern public opinion the speech was amazingly clever. Even Douglas was aware that Lincoln was striking body blows. He sprang to the platform and for an hour and a half sought to refute Lincoln's arguments. The Nebraska Act had not been designed to increase the area of slavery, and it would not do so. Congressional action had never prevented — but local self-government had and would prevent — the spread of slavery.

The logical inconsistencies in Lincoln's argument — if they mattered — can easily be pointed out. Having admitted that the problem was insoluble, he proceeded to propose his own solution: the pragmatic one of confining the institution to the area where it already existed. The great virtue of his remarks was the degree to which they expressed the confusion in the minds of northern moderates; but not less did his words please the radicals, for he pronounced slavery immoral and expressed hope for its extinction. He appealed pointedly to the material interests of northern whites who expected to find a utopia in the West. He gave the Republican Party (which he was careful not to join for two years) an eclectic platform on which it, unlike the earlier Free-Soilers, could ride to power. He won both the Negrophobes and the humanitarians, the moderates and the radicals.

Lincoln and Douglas were politicians, the one as much as the other. If the worse interpretation be placed on the motives of the one, so must they be placed on those of the other. If they are judged on the basis of hindsight, however, one conclusion is unchallengeable. Lincoln seized upon the key vulnerability in his rival's position: the Little Giant's repeated statement that he did not care whether the territories voted slavery up or down. Such was not the Senator's true feeling.

He made the statement because of his own conviction that, in view of increasing southern sensitivities, northern attacks upon the immorality of slavery must cease if the Union and the Democratic Party were to survive. In short, he was setting an example and seeking to counteract the effect upon the South of attacks by northern radicals. His action, as he saw it, could in no way encourage the spread of slavery. Lincoln, for all his seeming moderation, was making an even more insidious attack on the South than the radicals. By so doing he won the North and the presidency, whereupon the South seceded and war began. The inconsistency of the stand of Lincoln and his more vituperative Republican fellows against Douglas's popular sovereignty — the northern moderate position — is manifested by their action in 1861 when the southern states seceded: these same Republicans organized the territories of Colorado, Nevada, and Dakota without prohibiting slavery therein. Having beaten Douglas on the issue, they adopted in full his territorial policy they had fought for a decade.

Even before the ballots were cast in the fall of 1854, it was obvious to most Democratic Regulars in Illinois that they would lose the election. Compared to the disaster in other states, they were fortunate in winning four out of the nine congressional seats. Some talk arose of ousting the Little Giant from leadership, and even he admitted, at a testimonial banquet in Chicago given him by his loyal friends on the night after the election, that "the skies were partially overcast." The campaign for the legislature was actually more crucial than that for Congress, since Douglas's friend and colleague Senator Shields had to stand for re-election early in the new year. Lincoln had this goal in mind, and shortly resigned the seat in the legislature, to which he had just been elected, to begin an active senatorial campaign. While the fusionists controlled a joint caucus of both houses, the Regular Democrats hoped for a small majority in the upper and they saw that it would be difficult for the Whigs to induce former Democrats to support their old foe Lincoln. Since Douglas and Shields had to return to Washington for the short session, they left the campaign in the hands of their lieutenants, Charles H. Lanphier, editor of the *State Register,* and Thomas L. Harris.

A defeat of Shields would amount to a repudiation of the senior senator. Some party leaders proposed, therefore, that Shields — vulnerable because of his active support of the Nebraska Act — be dropped in favor of the popular governor, Joel A. Matteson, who had been noncommittal on the issue. In the face of this logic the Little Giant refused to desert his friend and he repeatedly wrote so in strong terms: "Our friends must stand by Shields, and throw the responsibility on the Whigs of beating him *because he was born in Ireland.* The Nebraska fight is over and Know-Nothingism has taken its place as the chief issue in the future." Should he be beaten the reasons would be clear; there must be no compromise on issues, no bargains, no alliances. Douglas seemed to think that disunity among the fusionists would lead at worse to a postponement of the election, but time soon proved the price he paid for his loyalty to his friend. Perhaps he was consciously, for political reasons, trying to shift the issue from the Nebraska Act to nativism.

When the legislature got around to voting in February, after a month of sparring, both Harris and Sheehan had been writing Douglas without success to win him over to the Matteson swap. On the first ballot Shields received 41 votes, Lincoln 45, Trumbull 5, and the rest were scattered. For several ballots Lincoln dropped and Shields gained slightly, but without ever reaching the required majority. Then Harris, acting on his own, made the change to Matteson, who at once received 46 votes, five short of victory. At this point Lincoln had dropped to 27 and Trumbull, the anti-Nebraska Democrat, had climbed to 18. When the shift continued the Whigs induced Lincoln to drop out and threw their full support to Trumbull, who on the tenth ballot reached a bare majority. Lincoln took what consolation he could from the fact that the Nebraska crowd was "worse whipped than I am."

Had the Matteson candidacy been attempted by the regulars from the start, it might well have succeeded.

Like Seward and Lincoln, Lyman Trumbull later went over to the Republicans. Upon his arrival in Washington Douglas refuted the new senator's claim to any affiliation with the Democrats. "That fact will be news to the Democracy of Illinois," he thundered. "Such a statement is a libel upon the Democracy of that State. When he was elected he received every Abolition vote in the legislature of Illinois. He received every Know-Nothing vote in the Legislature of Illinois. . . . He came here as the Know-Nothing-Abolition candidate, in opposition to the united Democracy of his state and to its candidate." The senior senator continued to make the issue between them a personal one and later proposed that both resign and stand for re-election. The hostility between the Illinois regulars and the bolters was that of the true believers and the heretics, shared by the two Senators who were their respective champions.

With an old party dying and two new ones scrambling for its place, and in the midst of emotional movements of such fervor as those of prohibition, nativism, and abolitionism, the wisest politicians could not predict the future with any confidence. Douglas was subject to this uncertainty no less than Seward and Lincoln, who so long hesitated to commit themselves. In those days little uniformity existed among the states as to the times of elections; some states were holding congressional elections every year and in every month of the year except four. Campaigning was therefore incessant. As the congressional leader of the party in power and the author of the act which was producing so much furor, the Little Giant was in a difficult position. The intense physical and emotional strain under which he was operating — as a result of his wife's death, the unprecedented personal abuse and vilification to which he was subjected, his strenuous oratorical efforts in Washington and on the stump in defense of his party and its course, and his own awareness that the Union hung in the balance — may have clouded his judgment. The Illinoisan's initial belief that the Know-Nothing rage was the root of the troubles appeared for a while a logical analysis, and the accuracy of his prediction that it would soon wane may have confirmed his confidence in his own judgment. But after Trumbull's election he must have realized that the Nebraska question was serious and that heavy weather lay ahead of him in Washington and in his own state.

Thus, by his attack upon prohibition and nativism, he could have been trying to turn attention away from the more dangerous question, to confuse the issues, and at the same time to boost party morale by conquest of easier opponents. Party loyalty, he knew, was a deep habit, and parties in power had frequently lost the lower house in by-elections without permanent damage. Temperamentally and intellectually he was inclined to action. His conversation with young McConnel reveals that he had considered the full complexities of the situation and had concluded that his course was the best of the alternatives. As soon as Congress adjourned in the spring of 1855, therefore, he took the stump again, speaking in Indiana, Kentucky, and Illinois. In his own state he successfully led the fight against the prohibition law, then engaged the whole fusionist group in debate, though no election was pending. His official optimism at Democratic victories elsewhere in the nation, quoted above in his letter to Cobb, was largely for its effect upon the party. Persistence had won many victories for him and for his party when the tide seemed strong against them; in politics as in war, group morale and a stubborn holding of the line often turned the issue in the midst of battle when the outcome was uncertain. Whatever doubts he must have felt as he faced the crucial election of the next year, Douglas gave no hint of them to his following.

Even a man of his amazing vigor could not stand the pace at which he had been going and the complete disregard of the fundamental rules of health. Since his wife's death he had taken to drinking again. In October, while still on the stump, he had to cancel a speech because of hoarseness. He was immediately hospitalized by his friends, who for a time feared for his life. A month later he was taken to Cleveland for the removal of his tonsils and lower palate by that city's leading surgeon. Even there he was not safe from attack, for a local paper reported that his illness was actually delirium tremens. Convalescence was slow, but it gave him time for contemplation of recent events, and confidential friends gathered around him. The long rest revived his spirits, and when he left for the Senate in February, 1856, he had about made up his mind to try a second time for the presidency.

Public opinion and the course of events in Illinois and the nation were influenced chiefly by current developments in Kansas, where the efficacy of popular sovereignty was being tested. Distance and the difficulties of determining the true facts, and particularly the deliberate distortion of the antislavery press and leaders seeking grist for agitation, created the utmost confusion. Kansas became a symbol. When civil war broke out between its proslavery and antislavery settlers, public opinion rose to a new heat, to the profit of extremist groups North and South. The Pierce and Buchanan administrations bungled the situation, but so great were the inherent difficulties that even the wisest statesmen must have stumbled. In a short time two territorial governments emerged which fought each other and Washington; over their recognition Congress and the Executive wrangled for several years.

In the past territories had been settled largely by squatters, and organized government came in time from Congress. Fact and legal theory had always conflicted, but the nation bothered little; somehow territories "just growed" like Topsy. That the powers of the national government were ill-defined, that an army would have been required to coerce stubborn territorials, and that executive orders were frequently ignored were facts that had gone unnoticed. Iowans did in Nebraska pretty much what Missourians were doing in Kansas, and the current experiences of the northern territory were in many ways much the same as those of the southern. But the South let Nebraska go without a struggle and its local affairs did not make the front page in the eastern press. Kansas and Nebraska were different from earlier territories in that they were the first such areas to be settled *after* a territorial act was passed. Indians were just beginning to be removed, land surveys took time to run, and many settlers temporarily returned eastward after staking their claims. Under such circumstances, how could a bona fide resident be differentiated for franchise purposes from a man who crossed the border only to vote? These difficulties, of course, were inherent in popular sovereignty and doomed it as a peaceful solution.

"Some of the disorder," writes Avery Craven in regard to the Kansas turmoil, "went with the frontier as such, some of it grew out of conflicting land titles and rivalry between localities for political and railroad advantages, some of it existed only in the reports which newspaper correspondents sent back east." Control of local government was a practical, pecuniary matter to settlers, the difference between survival and failure, between large and moderate profits. With it went the power to determine areas of settlement, locations of county seats and capitals, and the routes of railroads. Politicians who failed back east might recoup in the new areas where competition was not as great. "The Kansas struggle was, to some extent, a conflict between two rival groups for just such advantages. Slavery differences aggravated but did not produce the interests involved. Disputes over land contributed even more to the struggle. . . . Genuine free-state and proslavery attitudes contributed to the troubles of the new territory, but a surprising number of personal and interest difficulties were elevated to the dignity of battles for principle. Unquestionably also many men made the slavery issue a pretext for violence in the interest of personal gain."

Left to herself Kansas would in time have settled such troubles, but as Lincoln said the other thirty-one states very much regarded the matter as their concern. Missourians, directly to the east and therefore on the defensive as slaveholders, and the Republican Party cared most. The Emigrant Aid Society, started as a financial enterprise to send settlers to Kansas to prove the superiority of free labor, cared too. Rather early the general idea arose that the North and the South would battle for Kansas, with the latter

in the strong position of making a deal of slave Kansas for free
Nebraska as states. It is bootless to argue whether the "border
ruffians" of Missouri or the New Englanders first resorted to
violence. Both continued the strife once it began; both resorted
to loud charges and appeals for assistance from the aroused sections back east, who regarded the respective belligerents as their
representatives in trial-by-combat. At first proslavery settlers were
in the majority, as might be expected, and they would have
controlled the first territorial government even if Missourians
had not crossed the border and voted illegally. But in time free-
state emigrants were bound to outnumber the southerners, who
preferred Arkansas and Texas and who would hardly have risked
valuable slave property in such a dubious region. Such, in fact,
was the outcome.

President Pierce selected for Governor Andrew H. Reeder, a
Pennsylvania lawyer who had never held office, and as chief
justice an intemperate, partisan Marylander, Samuel D. Le-
compte. Reeder at once engaged in heavy land speculation,
catered to the proslavery majority, and in the winter of 1854-1855
held elections for a congressional delegate and a territorial legislature. Proslavery forces won both but Missourians committed
flagrant frauds, so Reeder ordered new elections in eight districts.
He then sent a certification of the returns to Washington without
mention of the irregularities. The legislature was forced to meet
at Pawnee, his own townsite, more than one hundred miles in
the interior. There it assembled, but at once moved itself to
Shawnee Mission, where it proceeded to ask Pierce for Reeder's
removal and to adopt the laws of Missouri, with numerous addi-
tions in regard to slavery of exceptional severity. The President
had already urged the Governor to resign when he came to Washington to make a personal report in the spring, but had weakly
allowed him to return to his duties. Pierce subsequently dismissed
Reeder because of his land deals, before receiving the petition
from the legislature. William Shannon, who had served two terms
as governor of Ohio, was named his successor.

Meanwhile the Emigrant Aid Settlers had founded Lawrence,

at first a safe distance from proslavery settlements. Aroused by the actions and the threats of Missourians, who had organized themselves into "Blue Lodges," settlers from free states took formal steps for self-defense. The open fraud of the first election gave them grounds for boycotting the territorial legislature, which moved the capital to Lecompton. In the fall of 1855 free-staters held a convention of their own at Topeka, drew up a constitution which prohibited the immigration of both slaves and free Negroes, and asked Congress for direct admission as a state. In the interim they elected Reeder (who had deserted to them) as congressional delegate and Charles Robinson, a Californian forty-niner who headed the Emigrant Aid migration, as governor. At the same time they called an election for a legislature of their own.

Technically such action was revolutionary. But the free-staters found a convenient precedent in the fact that California had drawn up its constitution without congressional authority and had actually been admitted without passing through a formal territorial stage. Thus Governor Shannon upon his arrival faced the open threat of civil war, for by this time the rival legislatures were ready and eager to fight. At this point the initiative seems to have been taken by John Calhoun, Douglas's Illinois friend whom he had induced the President to appoint surveyor-general. Instructed no doubt to exert every effort to make Kansas a Democratic state, Calhoun somehow persuaded the Lecompton crowd to accept a modification of their extreme slavery regulations, in a move to win the support of those conservative free-staters who saw the need for law and order. Yet the Topeka forces continued their defiance and Shannon set off the "Wakarusa War" by calling out a posse to make an arrest in their area. Violence was avoided when he arranged what he thought was a truce.

This was the situation when President Pierce sent his message to Congress in January, 1856. In it he recognized Lecompton as the legal legislature. By formal proclamation he ordered its Topeka rival to disband, and authorized Shannon to use militia and Federal troops if necessary to put down resistance. Topeka leaders were shortly indicted for treason in a Federal district court; writs were issued against Lawrence's two abolitionist newspapers. Once again Shannon called for a posse; Missourians responded to his call, and the "Sack of Lawrence" followed. The drunken posse got out of hand, destroyed the two newspapers and a hotel, looted the town, but did not physically harm the inhabitants. The free-state leaders escaped before the attack. Partly in revenge for this action, John Brown and his sons in cold blood killed five proslavery settlers. Civil war of such intensity then began that the frightened Shannon resigned. In his place Pierce appointed John W. Geary, an able officer with experience in the Mexican War. By tact and firmness Geary at length checked the Kansas fighting, in time for the Democrats to claim credit on the eve of the presidential election.

During the winter and spring Congress hotly debated the Kansas issue. Whatever chance existed for a solution was nullified by the approaching election, for the Republicans saw their advantage in keeping the blood of Kansas flowing. The lower house balloted endlessly for two months, but finally the new party elected Nathaniel P. Banks of Massachusetts as speaker over William Aiken of South Carolina by a vote of 103 to 100. Faced with the choice between the two delegates from Kansas, it sent its own investigating committee to the territory, sensing that the report would make excellent campaign material for the Republicans. The Senate was forced to wait until March for the ailing Douglas's return, and on the twelfth of that month he reported for his committee. Thereafter he found himself engaged in a series of verbal encounters, chiefly with Seward, Sumner, and Trumbull, not unlike those on the Nebraska Bill two years before. The crux of the matter, as in the controversy prior to the adoption of the Compromise of 1850, was that the two houses could not come to an agreement.

The Republicans charged that the Kansas troubles were the result of a plot on the part of the slave states, the prosouthern bias of the Pierce administration, and the unworkability of popular sovereignty. Douglas more than Pierce was their target, since he was the champion of that doctrine and the author of the specific act responsible for the situation. In one of his more fiery speeches he took the same position the President had in his January message. Fraud had occurred in the elections, he admitted, but Lecompton was the legal government of Kansas and the choice of a clear majority of its residents even if the challenged votes were thrown out. The organic act under which it was established, that is, the Kansas-Nebraska Act, derived from the power of Congress to take necessary steps to admit new states. Beyond that Congress could not go. A "vast moneyed corporation" — the Emigrant Aid Society — consisting of the same abolitionist groups which had fought the original act, were now causing trouble by interfering with the sovereign rights of the citizens of the territory. To prove his point he cited the peaceful history of Nebraska, where no such interference was attempted. The Missourians had resorted to violence only in self-defense.

The chairman's arguments were technically valid, despite minor inconsistencies. What he attempted was a defense of popular sovereignty; he was not trying to make Kansas a slave state, nor to do injustice to its free-state settlers. His motives were vindicated by his later break with Buchanan over the Lecompton Constitution, when it became clear that a majority of the territorial residents were then opposed to slavery. Such was definitely not apparent at the beginning of 1856. Mrs. Harriet Beecher Stowe, an unfriendly critic, heard his reply to Trumbull and called him "the very ideal of vitality. . . . His forte in debating is his power of mystifying the point. With the most off-hand assured airs in the world, and a certain appearance of honest superiority, like one who has a regard for you and wishes to set you right on one or two little matters, he proceeds to set up some point which is *not* that in question, but only a family connection of it, and this point he attacks with the very best of logic and language; he charges upon it horse and foot, runs it down, tramples it in the dust, and then turns upon you with — 'Sir, there is your argument! Did I not tell you so? You see it is all stuff;' and if you have allowed yourself to be so dazzled by his quickness as to forget that the routed point is not, after all, the one in question, you suppose all is over with it.''

As his solution Douglas introduced a bill which provided that when the population of Kansas reached the required number for a representative in Congress (93,000), it should draw up a constitution and be admitted to the Union. Seward countered for the Republicans with a bill which would admit it at once as a free state under the Topeka Constitution. Objection arose to the Douglas plan because it gave the governor power to take the census and the legislature power to control elections. Since a biased administration in Washington could influence both, no assurance existed that the election would be fair or that justice would be done to free-state settlers. Furthermore, the admission of Kansas would be delayed several years, since its population in 1856 amounted probably to no more than thirty thousand. Meanwhile the Lecompton regime would continue in power.

But events in Kansas and their propaganda advantage to the Republicans made the Senator realize the need for haste, and he soon receded from this position. After many conferences his committee reported the Toombs Bill, which made definite concessions to the free-staters. Five commissioners appointed by the President would conduct a new census and registration of voters, who would choose delegates for a constitutional convention the next November. The following month this convention would meet to draw up a constitution for admission to the Union. Backed by the Democrats as a party measure, the bill passed the Senate but the Republican House rejected it, even though it provided that all bona fide residents who had been driven from the territory could vote if they returned by October. (This answered the objection that most of the settlers driven away by violence had been free-staters.) The Republicans feared that the proslavery Pierce administration would rig the registration just as the Lecompton legislature had done, but their major motive in rejecting it was partisan. "An angel from Heaven," retorted the territorial chairman, "could not write a bill to restore peace in Kansas that would be acceptable to the Abolition Republican Party previous to the presidential election."

By this time the Little Giant, to Pierce's great chagrin, had decided to enter the presidential race, and in his speeches he too played politics. He summarized the Republican platform: No more slave states, repeal of the Fugitive Slave Act, abolition of the internal slave trade between states and of slavery in the District of Columbia, restoration of the Missouri Compromise, and the Wilmot Proviso for any additional territory. He hoped the Republicans would not evade the issue: "Let us have a fair bold fight before the people." When Seward assured him the Democrats would get one, Douglas referred to rumors that the new party was about to pass over its previous leaders and pick a safe candidate. "Are the offices and the patronage of the government," he asked, "so much more important to you than your principles, that you feel it your duty to sacrifice your creed, and the men identified with it in order to get power [and] for the purpose of cheating somebody by getting votes from all sorts of men?"

The climax of the running debate came when Sumner delivered his speech, the "Crime against Kansas," which the veteran Cass at once pronounced "the most un-American and unpatriotic that ever grated on the ears of the members of this high body." Its unprecedented vulgarity and personal vilifications were deliberate; as the Little Giant said, the Massachusetts Senator had practiced it for weeks. What made it more inexcusable was the fact that it was delivered before news of the Sack of Lawrence. Its most outrageous passages heaped insults upon the states of South Carolina and Virginia, their two Senators, Mason and Butler, and upon Douglas. Sumner referred to the highly respected Butler (absent because of a stroke) as a knight who had chosen as a mistress "the harlot slavery." The Senator from Illinois was "the squire of slavery, its very Sancho Panza — ready to do all its humiliating offices." While he was speaking Douglas, pacing across the rear of the Senate in irritation, remarked under his breath to a colleague: "That damn fool will get himself killed by some other damn fool."

Sumner was paying off past debts and dramatizing himself in his neurotic manner. Naturally the Little Giant was among the many who rose to rebuke him. What was his opponent trying to do, Douglas asked, turn the Senate "into a bear garden?" Did he wish "to provoke some of us to kick him as we would a dog, that he may get sympathy upon the just chastisement?"

In reply Sumner told him to "remember hereafter that the bowie-knife and the bludgeon are not the proper emblems of senatorial debate. . . . No person with the upright form of a man can be allowed, without violation of all decency, to switch out from his tongue the perpetual stench of offensive personality. Sir, this is not a proper weapon of debate, at least, not on this floor. The noisome, squat, and nameless animal, to which I refer, is not a proper model for an American Senator. Will the Senator from Illinois take notice?" After further interchange, Douglas had the last word: "I will only say that a man who has been branded by me in the Senate, and convicted by the Senate of falsehood, cannot use language requiring reply."

Two days later Representative Preston Brooks, brooding over the insults to his kinsman and his state, walked up to Sumner's desk in the Senate when it was not in session and assaulted him with a cane. Douglas later told the Senate that, hearing the commotion from the anteroom, he went to the door and saw Sumner being attacked. Acting upon impulse he made no move to intervene for fear that he would be charged with being a party to it, in view of the bad blood between them. He did not enter the chamber until a crowd gathered, but he had no foreknowledge of Brooks's intent.

The incident inflamed the nation more than all the outrages in Kansas. Brooks, who in vain challenged northern congressmen to duels, and Sumner, who was absent himself from the Senate for years because of his injury, became champions in another trial-by-combat between the sections.

V I I
Break with Buchanan

Soon after the election of 1852, Douglas warned his friends against any talk about his candidacy in the next contest. He was not sure he would want the nomination in 1856, but he intended to maintain his freedom of action. Upon the Democrats' defeat in Illinois in the fall and winter of 1854, he asked Beverly Tucker, publisher of the Washington *Sentinel,* to print a card stating that he was not a candidate. Then he asked Sheehan in Chicago to repeat the statement and add that his "determination not to be a candidate" had been known since the nomination of General Pierce and would be "resolutely adhered to." The Little Giant thus put himself on record as unavailable more than a year before the party convention met. At the same time Pierce wrote Buchanan in England that the ambassador was the only Democrat who could win against the Republicans, since he shared none of the responsibility for the Nebraska business.

When the Know-Nothing threat was checked the next year in the South, the President changed his mind. At once he began to cultivate the Little Giant. Democratic successes in 1855 had cheered them both, and Douglas knew that his own friends hoped to draft him later. The Senator was sure that Pierce had no chance of renomination, but made no move against him. For the moment he was much more concerned with the party's platform. He wanted the party organization to be "consolidated and placed immovably upon a sound national, constitutional platform . . . bold, unequivocal, and specific on all contraverted points. There must be no general, high-sounding phrases meaning nothing — no equivocal terms — no doubtful meaning — no double dealing for the benefit of timid and tricky politicians. We must make the next fight a fight for principles. . . . The new administration must not be a coalition of discordant materials . . . but it must be . . . composed of men who are identified and bound by every tie to carry out those principles in their appointments as well as by their measures."

By this the Senator probably meant that he wanted a positive definition of popular sovereignty in the next party platform. The triumph of his cause over the factions who opposed it, he assured his friend Cobb, would be full personal reward. "From what I have said," he continued, "you will perceive that if my name be connected with the presidential election, it must be by the voluntary act of our friends, prompted by the eye single to the success of the cause and the permanent triumph of our Principles, without any reference to my personal wishes or aggrandizement, and especially without any agency on my part, directly or indirectly, by word or deed."

Four months later, after an operation and a long convalescence, he yielded to the persuasion of his friends. The much-needed rest had improved his spirits and long conversation with intimates convinced him that his previous estimate of his prospects was too pessimistic. Ambition and wishful thinking played a minor part in his decision. Were the presidency his main objective, young as he was he would have waited until 1860 if serious doubt existed about his chances in 1856. Failure in 1856 might eliminate him from the race four years later; by the later date the Nebraska furor might be forgotten. After much talk and contemplation, however, he realized that by 1860 there might be no party or country left. Both the party and popular sovereignty needed strong leadership immediately. Pierce had failed abysmally and Buchanan would prove little better. Thus Douglas felt compelled to let friends "use his name or be driven to ignore the great act of his life." Had his party nominated him when it adopted his platform, the Union might have been preserved without civil war.

At first the Little Giant left the campaign in the hands of his friends, but under his active direction. Letters were sent to key men, like that to Breckinridge of Kentucky, informing him that the Senator had "more confidence in your friendship, sagacity, and ability than that of any man living." Senator Slidell of Louisiana, Buchanan's campaign manager, feared the competition of Douglas much more than that of Pierce and thought at first that he had persuaded him not to enter the race. The Illinoisan's Young American friends like Sanders, for various reasons, had deserted him for the Pennsylvanian. In their places he selected as confidential advisors General James W. Singleton, formerly a Virginia Whig, and D. T. Disney, an able Ohio Congressman. After his report of March 12 on Kansas it was openly known that he was in the contest. Events would prove that, in contrast to 1852 when he began his canvass too soon, now he became an active candidate too late, for the Buchanan managers had already obtained commitments in the South and in the Northwest from important men who would have preferred Douglas. His friend Cobb was one of them.

At first the effect of delay was not evident. Douglas's strategy was simple: unite the Northwest with the support of at least one of the New York factions, and the South (which would back Pierce as long as he was a candidate) would swing to him as its second choice when the President withdrew. The victory of his ticket in a Chicago election on March 4 induced the Little Giant to admit his active candidacy. He felt certain of Illinois, Ohio, and Iowa, but he counted chiefly on the support of Bright in Indiana, against whom Yulee had warned him four years before. Recently the slaveholding Bright had fawned upon him, and the Senator had even included him in the Superior land speculation. The strategy was sound; if the South would unite behind the candidate chosen by the northern Democracy, victory was certain even though he failed, as Buchanan actually did, to win most of the northern states.

Douglas did not receive the party's nomination because, as in 1852, he could not win the Democrats in his own section, the Northwest. Little national party organization existed in those days. Thirty-one separate state machines, wielding great power because of patronage and senatorial courtesy, had to be dealt with individually. The general popularity which Douglas enjoyed with the rank-and-file, even after the Nebraska fight, was not sufficient to compel his choice. A candidate could obtain the nomination only if, in states with enough electoral votes, he gained the backing of politicians by deals or agreements about legislation. The two-thirds rule of the Democrats made this more difficult, since it gave minorities greater bargaining strength. Powerful leaders in crucial states, chiefly Slidell in Louisiana and Bright in Indiana, blocked the nomination of the Little Giant in 1856. Personal jealousy in many instances was a factor, but in addition the Senator from Illinois had dictatorially enforced party discipline in the battle over Nebraska, and even those who admitted the necessity for it were not happy. Most of all, inclined from long experience to play it safe, these leaders doubted that Douglas could overcome the handicap of the personal opprobrium he had recently provoked throughout the North. A candidate who had been defeated in his own state, as he had by the election of Trumbull in 1855, could hardly hold the confidence of his party. In his own sectiton he was opposed by Cass, who had never forgiven him for his rivalry in 1852, and by Bright, who had sold out to the Buchananites in return for the control of patronage in the Northwest.

When the Democratic convention met in Cincinnati on June 2, a senatorial cabal consisting of Slidell and Judah P. Benjamin of Louisiana, James A. Bayard of Delaware, and Bright had already been on the scene for two weeks working to elect Buchanan. They had passed over Pierce, who could not carry sufficient northern states. Buchanan had become their choice because of his long, if undistinguished, service in public office, his conservatism, his southern sympathies, and his "availability" as a result of his residence in England during the past four years as American Ambassador. He was untainted with the Nebraska Act. The practical politicos had few illusions; they recognized the strength and the weakness of their party's position. With the opposition divided between the Republicans and Know-Nothings, whose northern wing had deserted, theirs was the only national party. Real danger lay in the fact that the Republicans could concentrate on the North and the Know-Nothings on the South, while the Democrats must hedge in both sections to get votes. In the face of this dilemma the cabal had fallen back on the second-rater from Pennsylvania.

Rumors abounded that the Little Giant planned to withdraw. Pierce supporters hated Buchanan, and with the support of the Douglas following they could block the Pennsylvanian's selection. But the Senator from Illinois, knowing that anything could happen, counted on the Pierce votes in the later ballots. On the first ballot Buchanan received 131½, Pierce 118½, and Douglas 33. Since Indiana, Ohio, and Michigan went against him, Douglas's lieutenants wished him to withdraw at once. On the seventh the shift from Pierce to the Senator began; on the fourteenth the count stood Buchanan 152½, Pierce 75, and Douglas 63. Apparently that night the Pierce and Douglas leaders came to some sort of agreement, for the next day the Little Giant jumped to 118, though Tennessee deserted him. Two roll calls later Douglas had gained four more votes and Buchanan was still short of the required two-thirds majority. The votes in this sixteenth ballot (168 to 122) showed that Douglas's weakness lay in the North. In the slave states he received 73 votes to Buchanan's 47; in New England only 13 to Buchanan's 28; and in the Northwest only 19 to Buchanan's 41.

At this point Douglas's lieutenant Richardson rose to read a telegram from the Senator in Washington: "If the withdrawal of my name will contribute to the harmony of our party or the success of our cause, I hope you will not hesitate to take the step. . . . If Mr. Pierce or Mr. Buchanan, or any other statesman who is faithful to the great issues involved in the contest, shall receive a majority of the convention, I earnestly hope that all my friends will unite in insuring him the two-thirds, and then making his nomination unanimous." Buchanan was then nominated by acclamation, but Douglas's candidate, John C. Breckinridge of Kentucky, was chosen for the vice-presidency.

Unity between the Douglas and Pierce forces could have blocked Buchanan and have compelled the choice of a dark horse as in 1852. Once again the Senator from Illinois acted from enlightened self-interest and for the good of the party. He preferred the chance of the faithful execution of his popular sovereignty platform by Buchanan to the selection of a weak compromise candidate. Since party unity was essential, he wished to avoid a prolonged contest over the candidate. For the same reason he permitted a southern construction on popular sovereignty in the platform. His prospects for 1860 were good, for by his withdrawal he had put the party in his debt a second time. "It was unmistakable," wrote one of the Illinois delegates with little exaggeration, "that there was a deep undercurrent of feeling in your favor running through the entire convention, and had it not been for the eternal cry of 'availability', 'Pennsylvania's last chance', 'safe man', 'prudent politic statesman', 'can carry the doubtful states', and all such stuff, echoed and re-echoed from ten thousand voices from the South, I firmly believe you would have received the nomination."

From a longer perspective Douglas had little chance for the presidency. Strong congressional leaders made more enemies than friends; professional politicians did not want them in the White House. Webster and Calhoun had never been nominated and Clay had never won when nominated. Buchanan's congressional service was in the distant past. Generals and governors had all the advantage over leaders in Congress. The Democrats had not nominated a strong leader since Jackson, and whenever the Whigs did so they lost.

When Congress adjourned in midsummer of 1856, news from party friends that the Illinois situation was desperate forced the Little Giant to hurry home rather than stump other states as he had planned. Indeed, the prospect was critical, for the state held its gubernatorial election a month before the presidential voting in November. A defeat in the earlier race might influence the outcome of the later. In the Senate contest a year before the legislature had rejected Douglas's candidate Shields; now William Richardson, even more closely associated with him and the Kansas-Nebraska Act, was running for governor. Defeat of either Richardson or Buchanan would affect the Senator's own chances for re-election in 1858, as well as his own presidential prospects in 1860.

In August and September, therefore, he spoke throughout Illinois. But the Republican candidate, William H. Bissell, an anti-Nebraska Democrat supported by many of the Know-Nothings, proved so popular that even before the election the Little Giant foresaw the outcome. Early in October he advised editor Sheehan that it might be wise "to prepare the minds of your readers for losing the State elections. . . . Buchanan's friends expect to lose it then, but carry the State by 20,000 in November. We may have to fight against wind and tide after the 14th."

Already it was apparent that Frémont would probably carry New England and New York, and Buchanan the South, thus leaving the outcome with the states between. Democratic strategy, determined during the hectic months of the campaign largely through correspondence between the Little Giant, Buchanan, and other state leaders, called for concentration upon Illinois, Indiana, and Pennsylvania. While the Senator from Illinois devoted his energies more to his own state than in previous campaigns, he spoke several times in Indiana and contributed heavily to Buchanan's cause when it appeared that only money could win the nominee's home state. Sheehan's claim that the amount was eighty thousand dollars is undoubtedly an exaggeration, but it is probable that Douglas spent in one way or another a total of one hundred thousand dollars on the election, obtained by the sale of some of his Chicago real estate. Once again the party was heavily in his debt; he had not sulked in his tent. Rather he had given as unstintedly of time and money as if he himself were a candidate.

Superior organization and more funds, thanks to the fear of most business interests that secession would follow a Frémont victory, kept the Democrats in office for another four years. Most ex-Whigs voted for Buchanan or Fillmore. But the victors had carried only five northern states and the Republicans could claim a moral victory. Should the drift of northern Whigs, Democrats, and Know-Nothings into their ranks continue, they could win in 1860 without a single southern vote.

Douglas's party had lost the popular vote of the North. It had four years in which to recoup its losses. But in his own state, instead of the larger majority he had recently predicted in debate with Trumbull, Buchanan's plurality was less than 10,000 and the Democratic candidate for governor had lost by 5000.

	Democratic	Republican	Know-Nothing
Illinois: Gubernatorial	106,769	111,466	19,088
Presidential	105,528	96,278	37,351

Obviously many Know-Nothings voted locally for the Republican Bissell, but not for Frémont later. The Little Giant was slipping, for Illinois had now twice voted against his candidate and in favor of former Democrats who had openly broken with him and his policies. Victory in the national election was scant compensation for this unmistakable personal defeat in his own constituency. In the remaining four years of his life, therefore, his actions were influenced chiefly by the harsh realities of politics in Illinois. Defeat there would end his career and his opportunity for national leadership; success would at least keep the road open.

These very realities, in fact, compelled his subsequent break with the President, a break on a matter of principle and national policy. Buchanan's treatment of him during and after the election, motivated essentially by jealousy, was both unjustified and impolitic. As Pierce had done four years before, the President proceeded to ignore the Illinois leader on cabinet appointments. The fact that Federal patronage in the Northwest had been promised Bright was certain to provoke deep resentment from the Little Giant, who shortly found conclusive evidence of his betrayal. The Indianian wanted a cabinet post himself in case he failed of re-election to the Senate. Buchanan did not help matters by addressing one of his few letters to his late rival as the "Hon. *Samuel* A. Douglas." Douglas pressed in vain for cabinet posts for the defeated Richardson and his Missouri friend, Judge Samuel Treat.

The Bright-Douglas feud was typical — similar conflicts existed in many sections. The President naturally had to reward the South for its support, but with a party divided as badly as his the difficult job of distributing cabinet appointments between sections and interests proved more troublesome than usual. The Georgian Howell Cobb, who had contributed so much to Democratic success, was the logical choice for secretary of state, but he was disliked by southern ultras. Instead they and Douglas urged the selection of Robert J. Walker of Mississippi. Buchanan finally solved his dilemma (after Bright won re-election) by choosing the aging Cass for the state department, thus recognizing the claims of the Northwest, and by inducing the none-too-enthusiastic Cobb to take the treasury. Most of the other posts went to southerners and the rest to northerners acceptable to the South.

Douglas, who usually subordinated personal feeling to party harmony, was bitter. "If . . . I am the object of attack," he wrote confidentially to Treat, "I shall fight all my enemies and neither ask nor give quarter. . . . At present I am an outsider. My advice is not invited. . . . I ask nothing for myself. I want only a fair share for my friends." His anger at repeated slights reached a climax when he learned that the President had appointed James M. Cutts, the Senator's father-in-law, as auditor in the treasury department. When Douglas protested that this appointment exposed him to the charge of nepotism, the chief executive told him to mind his own business. This incident and Buchanan's subsequent betrayal of Governor Walker in Kansas reportedly led the Little Giant to exclaim: "By God, Sir, I made Mr. James Buchanan, and by God, Sir, I will unmake him."

In contrast to his political vicissitudes, the Senator's personal life at this point took a decided turn for the better, though his operation did not save him from occasional severe illness. So great was the increase in the value of his Chicago real estate that he found himself a rich man, at least until the depression of 1857. Most important of all, soon after the presidential election he married his second wife, Adele Cutts, grandniece of Dolly Madison and unquestionably a leading belle of the capital city. As a man of affluence and the father of two young motherless boys, Douglas had good reasons for a second matrimonial venture; but apparently this was a genuine affair of the heart, for the couple became engaged a few weeks after they met. Adele, a member of an impecunious Maryland Catholic family, had been educated in a nunnery. Charming, intelligent, and well-liked by both sexes, she proved in almost every way an ideal wife, traveling with her husband on his political tours, managing her salon with tact and poise, and giving him again a normal home life.

After one miscarriage she gave birth in the fall of 1859 to a baby girl that died ten weeks later, and puerperal fever endangered the life of the mother for more than a month. During her illness her husband dropped all political duties and stayed by her bedside, until he too came down with a violent attack of rheumatism. In their new home on Minnesota Row the Douglases soon became leaders in the gay social life of the capital, the Senator even sporting a full beard. When he broke with the President over the Lecompton Bill, the lovely Adele dutifully carried on a social feud with Harriet Lane, Buchanan's niece and hostess, which reached a point of extreme bitterness by 1860. The Senator permitted his wife to send his sons to a Catholic school, and began to drop many of the wild habits he had resumed during his widowerhood. Certainly this second marriage had a salubrious effect upon both his health and his spirits, and gave him a certain philosophical calm with which to meet the growing national crisis.

The main issue over which Democrats and Republicans battled in the campaigns of 1856 and 1860, and the one over which Douglas and Buchanan broke, was the status of slavery in the territories, particularly in Kansas. The Senator had argued that Congress, implicitly by the legislation of 1850 and explicitly by the Kansas-Nebraska Act four years later, had adopted the principle of popular sovereignty. This the Republicans denied, and they opposed the principle on its own merits. The Democratic platform of 1856 in strong language endorsed Douglas's doctrine of congressional noninterference with slavery in the territories. It recognized the "right of all the territories . . . acting through the legally and fairly expressed will of a majority of actual residents . . . to form a Constitution, with or without domestic slavery, and be admitted into the Union upon terms of perfect equality with the other states."

But the rub was that northern and southern Democrats did not agree on one central point, which as recently as the Nebraska Act they had decided in caucus to leave to the Supreme Court; namely, exactly when could the residents of a territory pass upon slavery. Southerners said not until the statehood stage; that is, when the territory drew up a constitution for admission into the Union. Until then slaves could be taken freely into the territory. Northern Democrats argued on the contrary that territorial residents could decide the question at a much earlier stage, and thus by preventing the transport of slaves into their territory actually remove all chances that the ultimate constitution of the state might permit slavery. The consideration was highly practical as well as theoretical; the platform of 1856 seemed to confirm the southern position. The fact that Douglas accepted its wording indicated that he realized how divided the party remained, and he would not risk a fight. Nevertheless, he continued to defend the contrary interpretation which he had already advanced in Congress.

Buchanan hedged during the campaign, at one time supporting one interpretation, at another time the other. Prosouthern in his sympathies from the outset, owing both his nomination
and his election to that section, he eventually went completely
over to its position. Politician enough to realize, however, that
the five northern states which had remained loyal had been the
margin of his victory, he was aware of the consequences to himself and to the Union of the fatal split in the party to which its
fundamental disagreement was leading. Dodging the issue for the
moment was imperative; it struck him that he could remain
overtly noncommittal by passing the decision on to the Supreme
Court, which was then reviewing the Dred Scott case. Such a
tactic might remove the debate over slavery from the halls of
Congress. Douglas's popular sovereignty had definitely not
done so. Thus in his inaugural the President stated simply that
the territorial question would be "speedily and finally" decided
by the Court; "to their decision, in common with all good citizens
I shall cheerfully submit, whatever this may be." His "individual
opinion" had always been — he added to the satisfaction of his
southern friends — "that residents of a territory could not pass
upon slavery until they were numerous enough for statehood."

When he made this statement Buchanan had been for two
months in highly confidential correspondence with two associate
justices about the pending Dred Scott case. He knew that it
would soon be decided, and he knew also that the decision would
deny the power of Congress to prohibit slavery in the territories.
He had even gone so far as to influence the concurrence of one
northern judge in the *dictum* of his southern colleagues to that
effect. At first, through several letters to his friend Judge John
Catron of Tennessee, he had sought to induce the court to make
its decision before the inauguration, but the death of a justice's
wife and internal dissensions within the group made this impossible. Knowing of this dissension he then wrote his fellow-Penn-
sylvanian Judge Robert C. Grier, urging the importance of a
positive, majority decision.

Dred Scott had been taken by his master to a free state and

then to a territory made free by the Missouri Compromise. Brought back to Missouri, he began his suit for freedom in 1846. When the case reached the Supreme Court, seven of whose justices were Democrats and five of whom were southerners, it had been inclined to dismiss the case on grounds of lack of jurisdiction. By Missouri law a slave was not a citizen and therefore could not sue; so a majority finally ruled. But the two Republican judges made it clear that they would file a dissent asserting that residence in a free territory had made Scott free. Thereupon the Democratic majority, divided among themselves on the several issues, decided to pass on the territorial question.

In the end, six judges — five from the South and one from the North — agreed that the Missouri Compromise had been unconstitutional. Yet one of the southerners — Catron of Tennessee — held that Congress had some power over the territories (the key argument of the Republicans); in his opinion the Compromise of 1820 was unconstitutional only because the Louisiana Purchase Treaty had guaranteed slavery. Thus only five judges actually accepted the southern contention that congressional discrimination against slave property in the territories violated the due process clause in the fifth amendment (since the Constitution recognized slaves as property, a Virginian could take his Negro to a territory if a New Yorker could take his mule). Buchanan's pressure upon Grier produced a majority of six, which by his concurrence was not exclusively southern. Only a minority agreed with Chief Justice Taney that Negroes had not been and could not be citizens of a state.

Douglas supported the decision because the court, strictly speaking, had only thrown out congressional interference with slavery in the territories, thus confirming his Kansas-Nebraska Act. It had not passed directly upon popular sovereignty — no act of a territorial legislature prohibiting slavery was before it. Indeed the court might never do so, since it had taken thirty-seven years for the act of 1820 to reach it. Should Douglas become President, as he might shortly, he could appoint judges who shared his views on that issue when vacancies occurred. Had he not supported the decision he would thereby have broken with the administration and at the same time lost his popularity in the South. Already he had yielded much to that section for the sake of party harmony. But as a former judge and a political realist he surely saw that southerners would argue that the decision denied territorial as well as congressional interference with slavery in the territories; that is, when the court denied the power of Congress to control slavery there, this struck not only at the power to legislate but at the power to delegate control to local territorial legislatures (popular sovereignty as construed by the North). In this dilemma he played for time. First he must defend the decision in the North, but at the same time he must take a safe position for a possible fight with southerners over the effect of the decision on the meaning of popular sovereignty.

Contrary to the hopes of the President and the court, the Dred Scott decision soon added fuel to the raging controversy. The Republican Party, bound to lose Kansas as its most popular issue in the North as soon as Congress disposed of the matter, found a new charge and one much easier to substantiate. The southern minority, the Republicans now said, having entrenched itself in power, controlled the nation. Through its influence over the Senate and the executive it had packed the court which handed down this unjust decision. The lower house of Congress, which the northern majority could dominate if united — and properly so if democracy meant majority rule as most northerners were inclined to believe — was helpless. A plot of the slavocracy was evident; the territories had been lost to freedom, and the next attack would seek to force slavery upon the free states themselves. Soon Lincoln would predict in his famous "House Divided" speech that the nation would — and *must* — become all slave or all free.

The decision forced Douglas and Lincoln, leaders of their respective parties in Illinois, to review the conflicting arguments of the judges in long speeches to their constituents. They did so chiefly with their approaching contest for the Senate in mind, and before the struggle over Kansas reached its climax. Their speeches contained practically everything that each had to say about equality, the Declaration, the Constitution, and the court. Indeed, the more famous debates between them the following year were but forensic repetitions of the points they had already made and had attempted to refute. As might be expected, the Democrat echoed the arguments of Chief Justice Taney and the Republican those of the minority opinion.

Douglas spoke extemporaneously on June 12, 1857, to an overflow crowd in the Hall of Representatives in Springfield. (Later he wrote out his speech for publication.) Lincoln replied in the same chamber two weeks later. The political situation was quite different from that of the joint debates a year later, which occurred after the Senator had broken with the administration. The Little Giant hailed the decision as a vindication of popular sovereignty. The court was properly the expounder of the "higher law" of the Constitution; it had been legally and morally right in deciding the main questions involved. Had it refused to do so it would have subjected itself to even more virulent attack from dissenters, and the consequences would have been much worse. Now that the Supreme Court had spoken, resistance to its decision would be "a deadly blow to our whole republican system of government." In this speech he resolved his potential dilemma by arguing that the decision eliminated congressional legislation, but left the territories free to choose between making slavery possible through positive local legislation, or making it impossible by omitting such legislation. The right of a master to take slaves into a territory, he asserted, would remain a "barren and worthless right, unless sustained, protected, and enforced by appropriate police regulations and local legislation." Here he proclaimed what later was to become known as his Freeport Doctrine. Popular sovereignty did not inhere in the power of Congress to exclude slavery and therefore was not impaired by the Supreme Court's decision. It derived from the basic sovereignty of territories over their domestic institutions, which he would soon contend was equal to that of the states themselves.

Challenging the Republican's interpretation of the Declaration of Independence, he charged them with advocating the equality of the black and white races, which in essence meant amalgamation. Emancipation and political equality could lead only to full social equality. The United States, he insisted, was a white man's country. The framers of the Declaration had intended it only for white men; they regarded Negroes as an inferior race. No state had abolished slavery during the Revolution, and no state since had placed Negroes on a full equality with whites. Inferiority did not doom the blacks to slavery, however, but to certain limitations upon their rights "consistent with the welfare of the community where they reside," the extent of such limitation to be decided by the people of each state and territory. The founding fathers, in his opinion, did not regard uniformity in social legislation among the states as either possible or desirable.

In his reply Lincoln was quite as partisan as Douglas in defending his party. In contrast to his later speeches, his position was still extremely moderate, probably because he realized the influence which the vote of the ex-Whigs would have in the coming senatorial contest. He made no charge as yet of a "plot of the slavocracy," though he did call popular sovereignty a "mere deceitful pretense for the benefit of slavery." His party would not resist the Dred Scott decision, but it did regard the decision as erroneous and would seek its reversal. This was proper, Lincoln insisted, in view of the fact that the judges had been so closely divided on the constitutional question. Other branches of the national government were not bound by decisions of the court; each could determine constitution for itself. Here he emphasized the inconsistency of Douglas and the Democrats, since their hero Jackson had defied Chief Justice Marshall's decisions on the bank and the Indians.

The Little Giant had appealed to northern Negrophobia by charging the Republicans with favoring amalgamation of the races. This Lincoln hotly denied: "I protest against the counterfeit logic which concludes that, because I do not want a black woman for a *slave* I must necessarily want her for a wife. I need not have her for either." Segregation of the races, ultimately by colonization but temporarily by keeping Negroes out of the territories, was the solution proposed by his party. In an extended argument he sought to refute the Senator's interpretation of the Declaration. The fathers did intend that *all men*, black and white, should enjoy "certain inalienable rights," but they did not declare even all white men equal in all respects. "They meant to set up a standard maxim for free society . . . constantly looked to, constantly labored for, and even though never perfectly attained, constantly approximated." The Republicans believed the Negro was a man, that "his bondage is cruelly wrong," and they therefore opposed the extension of slavery which the Democrats would permit.

The Dred Scott decision, supported both by northern and southern Democrats, made the position of their party in the North even more precarious; Buchanan's subsequent repudiation of popular sovereignty in Kansas doomed it. But the court's decision had no effect upon the Kansas issue in 1857, for Congress had already repealed the prohibition on slavery in that area. Neither was the disputed question of the right of the territory to act on slavery involved; the Lecompton legislature had passed stringent laws protecting slavery which the southerners had applauded. Instead the issue — anticipated by no one in 1854 — was whether a majority of the territorial residents wished to enter the Union under a constitution which permitted slavery or under one which rejected it.

The sequence of events which produced the final Kansas climax was so confusing that contemporary Americans, North and South, came with assurance to opposite views about the territory. The Covode Report, published by the House after an extensive investigation several years later, did not clarify the matter. This same confusion produced the open break between Douglas and Buchanan that resulted in a fatal schism in the Democratic Party and victory for the Republican in 1860.

Two governments existed in the territory of Kansas: the official proslavery one of Lecompton and the technically extralegal free-state one of Topeka. Probably in the majority by the end of 1856, free-state settlers soon predominated, but most were denied the franchise by the Lecompton group which controlled the election machinery and had the backing of Washington. Free-staters therefore boycotted the official territorial government, knowing that they were counted out in advance, but the Topeka organization survived because it had its own militia and ultimately the support of the majority of settlers. It wisely avoided open conflict with Federal officials. Both Governor Geary and his successor Robert J. Walker, Buchanan's appointee, pursued a conciliatory course and sought to persuade Topeka free-staters to participate in official elections. This they refused to do, until October, 1857, because the Lecompton legislature continued its various discriminatory acts and wholesale fraud. Actually John Calhoun, territorial surveyor-general, through control of the legislature blocked both governors' efforts towards peace and forced their resignations. Originally an unofficial agent of Douglas instructed to work for a compromise, Calhoun betrayed his chief to promote his own financial interests. He seems to have done so largely by the secret support of the prosouthern clique in Buchanan's cabinet determined to make Kansas a slave state. To its wishes he yielded, and in turn this clique bent the President at will.

Several territorial elections took place during the fateful year of 1857. In February the Lecompton legislature — over Geary's vote — called for an election of delegates to a constitutional convention in June, but did not provide that the document be presented to the electorate for ratification. Walker, appointed by Buchanan in March to succeed Geary, failed in his efforts to induce the free-state men to take part in the June election; only 2200 residents out of a total registration of 9200 (half the adult males in the territory) voted. The stanchly proslavery convention thus selected met in September under Calhoun's presidency, and promptly adjourned until after the October election for the territorial legislature. In this latter election the free-staters voted for the first time, despite legal discrimination placed upon them. They elected their candidate for congressional delegate (a Republican) by a 4000 majority, but by first returns the Lecompton forces maintained their majority in the legislature. (The Territory had been effectively gerrymandered.) When Governor Walker discovered that two counties with a little over a hundred voters had reported over 2800 proslavery votes, he threw out the obviously fraudulent returns, giving control of the legislature also to the free-staters.

As a consequence the Kansas constitutional convention was proslavery, the legislature free-state; but by any objective test the convention had been repudiated before it sat. Nevertheless, immediately after this election, it drew up a constitution protecting slave property in the territory. (By inference from the document's oblique wording, no amendment on slavery could be passed before 1864.) A provisional government under "regent" Calhoun, replacing the Walker regime, would hold a referendum for ratification. But the voters would pass, not on the whole constitution, but only on the constitution "with slavery" or "without slavery"; that is, they could vote only for or against subsequent introduction of slaves. They could not vote for any other provision of the constitution; that is, on requirements for voting and office-holding, or on regulations about banking and taxation. In this referendum, held in December and boycotted by the irate free-staters, the document carried by a vote of 6243 to 569. But in a second referendum on January 4, ordered by the new Republican legislature which acting-Governor Stanton had called into special session and which for that reason was boycotted by Lecompton supporters, the constitution in its entirety was defeated 10,266 to 162. These returns indicated that the free-staters in Kansas outnumbered proslavery residents almost two-to-one. At this point the battle moved to Washington.

Against this background the courses of Douglas and Buchanan must now be traced in some detail. The Senator had been in the center of fire for several years, inevitably so since he was the author of the Kansas-Nebraska Act, spokesman for popular sovereignty, and chairman of the Senate Committee on Territories. From the first he had predicted that climate would make Kansas a free state, and he never made or supported any move to block the will of what seemed to be the majority of its residents. He knew the sentiments of Illinois and the Northwest too well to take any other position. But his course did change as events unfolded in the territory, or rather as they were reported in the East.

In 1855 he backed Pierce in denouncing the Topeka move as revolutionary and blaming the trouble on the Emigrant Aid Society and the Republicans. Even if the admittedly fraudulent votes in the early elections were thrown out, he argued, a majority of settlers definitely favored slavery. At the time, they probably did, for in previous territories the first wave of settlers had come from the state immediately to the east, in this instance Missouri. But he instructed Calhoun to work for the repeal of the more extreme Lecompton laws on slavery and to weld free-state and slavery Democrats into one party. From long instinct he sought an acceptable compromise which would hasten admission as a state. At first he favored delay in admission until the territory attained the population required for a representative in Congress, but when strife arose he saw the necessity for speed. Accordingly, his committee reported the Toombs Act, which would set up a presidential commission to take a new census and registration and to hold an election for delegates to a constitutional convention in the fall of 1856. Having passed the House, this measure failed in the Republican Senate early in the election year.

Fully aware that the new President might side with the southerners should a fight develop over the effect of the Dred Scott decision upon popular sovereignty, nevertheless the Senator from Illinois in the spring of 1857 co-operated fully with him in his policy on Kansas. Their main objectives were identical: get the territory admitted as quickly as possible and make sure it was safely Democratic. Along with Oregon and Minnesota, also ready for statehood, Kansas might turn the scales in 1860. Douglas helped persuade Walker to accept the territorial governorship. A northern immigrant to Mississippi who became senator from the state, a land speculator on a large scale, an expansionist, and secretary of treasury under Polk, Walker on the record was much abler than his predecessors in the territory. His appointment indicated the high priority that Buchanan placed on Kansas. Whatever the President's private views on how early in the territorial stage popular sovereignty began to operate, he had committed and for some time would continue to commit himself positively on the right of residents to ratify their constitution. "Who contest the principle," he had asked in a campaign speech, "that the will of the majority shall govern?"

As ambitious as the Little Giant (Walker hoped to become Senator from the new state and had definite presidential aspirations), he saw eye to eye with him on popular sovereignty and Kansas. Determined to have a fair election and submission of the constitution to residents for ratification, he affirmed in his inaugural speech — to the infuriation of southern ultras — that climate would make the territory a free state. On his way west in May he stopped in Chicago for a long talk with his senator friend, particularly about his economic program which he hoped would unite the rival factions.

When the Little Giant asked him if he had in writing the President's concurrence on submission of the constitution, the Governor showed him his inaugural address with annotations in Buchanan's own hand. Walker had accepted his appointment with specific assurance, widely published in the press and included in his instructions that "you [Buchanan] and all your cabinet cordially concur in the opinion expressed by me, that the actual bona fide residents of the territory of Kansas, by a fair and regular vote, unaffected by fraud or violence, must be permitted, in adopting their state constitution, to decide for themselves what shall be their state institutions." The inaugural speech stated specifically that the Governor was authorized by the President and cabinet to say that Congress would reject the constitution were it not submitted to the people. At that stage no one thought of spelling out the details of submission, but events would prove that the crafty Senator had smelled the right rat. In July, four months later, the President was still writing Walker that "the

point on which your and our success depends is the submission
of the constitution to the people of Kansas. . . . On the question
I am willing to stand or fall."

Walker had not been on the job long before Calhoun took the
ball away from him and began to call the plays, with the results
described above. But other national developments of deeper impact during this crucial year influenced the policy of the administration. Congressional elections after the inauguration, mostly
in the South, gave the Democrats a safe majority in both houses,
but the outbreak of a serious depression caused elections later in
the year to go against them. Cries from southerners against
Walker, loud from the first, became a din when he threw out the
fraudulent votes in the October election. Open threats of secession were made in the South, whose ultras had never wanted
Buchanan in the first place. In near panic the frightened President, as weak in his own way as Pierce but more obstinate, let
himself become captive to a southern "directory" consisting of
cabinet members Jacob Thompson of Mississippi and Howell
Cobb of Georgia, and his recent campaign manager Slidell, an
unofficial power behind the throne.

Before the convention drew up the Lecompton Constitution
the Governor actually asked for a leave of absence to attend to his
business affairs in the East, with which the depression had played
havoc, but delayed his departure at the President's request that
he wait until the convention had finished its work. In Washington he learned from Buchanan that the President would accept
the Lecompton subterfuge on ratification over his protests. In his
own opinion, this gave the lie to the fine talk about submission,
and two weeks later he resigned. Walker had been defeated by
the territorials, like his predecessors in office, and he had every
reason to feel betrayed by the President.

The Little Giant had seen the breakers ahead as early as February, 1857, when the Lecompton legislature failed to require a
referendum on the constitution to be drawn up by a convention
later in the year. He concurred with Senator Charles E. Stuart

of Michigan (one of the few northern Democrats in the upper house to join him later in the bolt against the administration), who wrote him at once urging repudiation of the legislative action and a new enabling act, as provided earlier in the defeated Toombs Bill. "Utter destruction awaits the Democratic Party in the North and Northwest," predicted Stuart, "unless this course is taken early and rigidly adhered to." Repudiation was right on its own merits, he went on, and *it is the only mode in which what there is left of the party in the Northwest can be saved.* When the free-staters won the election for the legislature the next fall — just before the convention met — Douglas issued an unmistakable warning. An editorial in the Chicago *Times* demanded that prohibition of slavery be put into the constitution and that the constitution be submitted to the voters. The Douglas organ asserted that Kansas would accept "nothing less than a constitution which shall exclude and prohibit slavery."

The stubbornness of a Jackson at this point might have prevented civil war. But Buchanan feared that stubbornness might bring the war on sooner. In his own mind the President thought he was straddling a dangerous issue; in difficult moments straddling is often the essence of statesmanship. But he did not straddle; he surrendered completely to one side. He yielded to the greater pressure by giving the South what it wanted: protection of slavery in Kansas and seeming assurance of its admission as a slave state. Already in the summer he had written a public letter stating that, according to the Supreme Court, slavery "existed in Kansas under the Constitution of the United States."

To summarize the whole matter, Buchanan was reluctantly pledged to submit the constitution to the people and Douglas voluntarily believed in doing so. Since the President could not openly violate his pledge, it was decided to make pretense of "submission" by "submitting" a nonessential question rather than the essential one. Therefore the people were given no option to accept or reject the constitution, and no option to allow or ban slavery, but were presented with a *fait accompli* — a constitution allowing slavery. They were given only the option of voting on the further introduction of slaves.

This trick made a mockery of popular sovereignty — residents could not vote on the rest of the constitution, and, even if they voted against "slavery," property in slaves then in the territory was protected until the document should be amended. The President naïvely counted on party discipline in the North to carry the bill through Congress. Even more than Douglas in 1854, he failed to foresee the violence of northern reaction. Had not Douglas and his group bolted on the issue, the Democratic Party would have been destroyed above the Mason and Dixon Line. For, unpopular as the repeal of the Missouri Compromise had been, here was a Democratic administration clearly stacking the cards to make a slave state out of a territory against the expressed will of its inhabitants. Who now could deny a plot of the slavocracy, or that slavocracy was aggressive?

Calhoun engineered the subterfuge through the convention. At all times he was in contact with his allies in the cabinet, who in fact sent out an agent, Mississippian Henry L. Martin, as land clerk to assist him. The directory insisted upon some gesture which could pass for submission — the President had committed himself too positively — but the origin of the method cannot be traced. An editorial in the Chicago *Times,* quoted above, in October, 1857, suggested that both a free state and a slave state constitution be presented to the voters. In the spring Frederick A. Stanton, Walker's secretary, who preceded him to Kansas, had suggested a similar idea, and it was much in the air. Whatever the origin of the scheme, it suited the purpose of the cabinet directory who wanted a sure thing. Alcoholic Calhoun may have even thought it would save his face with his ex-patron Douglas, but he never dared write the Senator any explanation.

When news of the Lecompton steal reached the East all but one of the fifty-six newspapers in Illinois condemned it. The Senator at once announced that he would fight it, that he favored a new enabling act. Walker stopped by on his way east to give him the sordid details, and rumors abounded that the President would urge acceptance. Meanwhile, to strengthen his position, Douglas held conferences with Republican leaders in the state, since they would be forced to support his stand against Lecompton. To his friends he pronounced the whole business a scheme of his cabinet enemies to ruin him. At the end of November he returned to Washington for the opening of Congress, probably conferring on the way again with Walker in New York, with George Bancroft, another member of Polk's cabinet, and with John W. Forney, Buchanan's close Pennsylvania friend. Apparently he wisely decided to try first to persuade the timid executive to change his mind again, for he knew the hazards of a party split. In 1854 he had taken care to commit Pierce in advance to the Nebraska Act.

On December 3 the Senator called at the White House and urged the President "as a friend" not to recommend acceptance in his annual message. Buchanan said he must do so, and asked him to remain silent on the question until the results of the impending Kansas referendum were known. The Little Giant replied that he would "denounce it the moment the message was read." As the conversation became more heated the President pulled his rank: "Mr. Douglas, I desire you to remember that no Democrat ever yet differed with an administration of his own choice without being crushed. Beware of the fate of Tallmadge and Rives [two senators read out of the party by Jackson for disobedience]."

This was too much. Buchanan had already ignored him as the titular congressional authority on territories by telegraphing his approval of the Lecompton Constitution to Kansas without consulting him. The Little Giant was not a man to be pushed around by anyone, certainly not by a weakling in the presidency. "Mr. President," he replied defiantly, "I wish you to remember that General Jackson is dead."

V I I I

Lecompton and the Debates with Lincoln

THE fight over Kansas, both in the territory and in Congress, was the prelude to the American Civil War. The congressional debates over the admission of Kansas further inflamed the North and the South, increasingly engaged in "cold war." The two sections came to hold concepts of vital interests in Kansas, both symbolic and strategic. The Lecompton battle split the Democrats and brought the Republicans to power two years later. This was the immediate event which set off secession.

Minorities in both sections already favored drastic action, either to abolish or to protect slavery; the Lecompton struggle greatly strengthened their positions. At once Lincoln and Davis moved closer to the radicals of their respective sections and, in fact, became fellow travelers of the minorities. When Congress finally settled the Kansas matter by the English Bill in the spring of 1858, the majority of citizens in each section felt that they had been denied justice and injured in their vital interests.

The South had argued that the Lecompton convention, a duly constituted body, had full power to determine the method of adoption of the constitution it had drawn up. Free-staters had rejected the opportunity to vote for delegates, and submission of the constitution to the people was not legally necessary. Northern congressmen blocked admission simply because the Lecompton

Constitution protected existing slave property. Southerners concluded that the North would, in the future, on some flimsy pretext block the admission of any additional slave state. The North,
on the other hand, had contended that the Lecompton convention was the product of fraud and chicanery, its submission device
a palpable trick. Territorial residents had rejected the constitution by a two-to-one majority.* The same constitution had been
condemned without exception by territorial governors Walker,
Stanton, and Denver, all of whom were southern-born or prosouthern in sentiment. Yet the Buchanan administration, having
unfairly intervened like its predecessor against free-staters, now
sought to force a slavery constitution upon an unwilling territory
in order to bring another slave state into the Union. The southern intent, concluded most northerners, was clear: free territories
would be admitted only if they accepted slavery. Worse, the South
would not even abide by the fair compromise of popular sovereignty, to which it had given lip service; it would not even permit
territorial residents to vote on their own constitutions. In short,
each section believed that the other was determined to block the
admission of any new state which would decrease its voting
strength.

The hectic Lecompton debate in Congress lasted almost five
months after the President's message of December 8, 1857, set it
off. In its main outlines it resembled the battle over the Nebraska
Bill three years before; but this time the administration, defeated
in the end by a coalition of northern Democrats and Republicans,
was forced to substitute a face-saving compromise which passed
only by a narrow margin. In both instances the Little Giant of
Illinois led the victorious forces.

The first phase of the struggle lasted from December 8 until
February 2, when Buchanan formally recommended admission
under the Lecompton Constitution on the grounds that it had
been approved by a December plebescite in Kansas. The argument then revolved about the question of whether the mode of

* See Chapter VII, p. 156.

submission of the constitution was proper, and did not touch the slavery clauses. This was high ground deliberately chosen by Douglas. But in this period the basic positions were taken and ultimate strategy planned, since it was almost certain that the first Kansas plebescite would approve the constitution "with slavery" and that the administration would then attempt to force an admission bill through Congress. With a Democratic majority of fourteen in the Senate and twenty-five in the House, the White House seemed to have enough votes to do so.

In his annual message Buchanan shrewdly made no recommendations to Congress. He expressed "deep mortification" that the convention had not submitted the full constitution to the territorial residents. Nevertheless, he said, the action of the convention was legal since the original Kansas-Nebraska Act required only submission of the slavery question. By this lame technicality he prepared the way for his subsequent recommendation of admission once the constitution had been ratified, privately justifying his action on the grounds that the dangerous issue would thus be quickly removed from Congress and that citizens of the new state could at once amend their constitution as they wished.

The Senator from Illinois replied on the day the message was read in a clever, courteous, but firm address of three hours which even the unfriendly Washington *Star* pronounced the ablest forensic effort of his career. He approved the executive message, which left the decision to Congress where it belonged. Only on one point had the President fallen into error — a fundamental one — and that was in his assertion that the Lecompton submission of slavery alone was properly derived from the Nebraska Act itself. The Senator reminded his colleagues of his 1854 speech in which he had argued that territorial residents should have power over all their domestic affairs and not just slavery alone. The clear intent of the Act, by the repeal of the Missouri Compromise, had been to remove the single congressional restriction placed upon them: the right to decide about slavery. A territorial constitution, he agreed, had no legal status until Congress approved;

it should be regarded rather as a petition, but Congress should not approve unless it was positive that the document represented the will of the majority of residents. Lecompton did not!

He then reviewed its history, driving his points home with force and sarcasm. He cited the President's pledges and Walker's assurances on submission, which had been taken at face value until the convention met in October. The device it adopted offered the territorials only the choice which Napoleon gave his soldiers: to vote *yes* and live or *no* and die. This was no choice at all, for residents were not allowed to vote on the rest of the constitution, which would go into effect whether they voted "with" or "without" slavery. Delegates had openly admitted that they rejected a vote on the whole constitution because they knew it would be defeated. "Will you force it on them [territorial residents] against their will," he asked the Senate, "simply because they would have voted it down if you had consulted them? . . . Is that the mode in which I am called upon to carry out the principle of self-government and popular sovereignty in the Territories?"

The proper procedure was to ignore both the Lecompton and Topeka Constitutions and to start with a new convention fairly elected. Add to the defeated Toombs Bill a clause requiring submission or apply the recent Minnesota enabling act to Kansas, he urged. "But if this constitution is to be forced down our throats in violation of the fundamental principles of free government, under a mode of submission that is a mockery and an insult, I will resist it to the last. I have no fear of any party associations being severed. I should regret any social or political estrangement, even temporarily; but if it must be, if I cannot act with you and preserve my faith and honor, I will stand upon the great principle of popular sovereignty."

The Little Giant introduced a new bill for Kansas. Thereupon the administration opened all its guns upon him. The Republicans lent him strong support, but only two of his Democratic colleagues followed his lead. He now was attacked by two groups of his former friends, northern Democratic senators and southern extremists like Toombs. He took them all on at once; the gloves were off. His new enemies repeated all the charges previously made by the Republicans: he was inconsistent, selfishly ambitious, a traitor, and a scoundrel. They resorted to all sorts of insinuations and reflections upon his integrity, even falsely charging that he had earlier opposed submission.

Behind them, of course, stood the irate President, who insisted upon making Lecompton a party test and who proceeded to use the vast patronage and pressure at his command against those who would not conform. But the Senator could take care of himself. "What if I do differ from the President?" he asked Graham Fitch of Indiana. "I have not become the servile tool of any President to receive and obey his instructions against my own judgment and sense of right." He also replied in kind to his southern opponents and their press who read him out of the party with the same epithets they used for Seward and Sumner: "There are men here personal enemies of mine — men who would be willing to sink an Administration if they could kill off northern men, and get them out of the way in the future; such men are getting their tools to denounce me as having abandoned the party. Why? Because I do not desert my principles as freely as the masters of these editors do theirs."

Of necessity he formed an alliance with the Republicans. In a long conference at his home in the middle of December with Anson Burlingame and Schuyler Colfax, he outlined the strategy of the coalition, the same strategy in fact which the Republicans had tried unsuccessfully against the Nebraska Bill. The administration would seek to rush the Lecompton Act through. Since it could carry the Senate, the coalition must "fight a delaying game" in that body until sufficient public sentiment could be aroused to block the measure in the House. Insist first upon the admission of Minnesota, he suggested, then of Oregon; if the South resisted, block appropriation bills. Meanwhile he would push a Kansas act requiring popular submission, in whatever form the Republicans were willing to accept. To them, as to the President earlier, he gave his solemn promise that he "had taken a through ticket and checked all my baggage."

Douglas had complex motives in his break with the party; his ends were plural. Although he made his own realistic assumptions as to the outcome, he could not be certain what it would be. As a man of intelligence who loved his country and who knew that its very existence hung in the balance, he constantly chose what seemed to him the lesser evils.

President Buchanan asserted that had not Douglas bolted, the Lecompton Act would have passed and all would have been well. Citizens of the new state would in constitutional convention have outlawed slavery in Kansas. Senator Albert G. Brown, the Little Giant's admirer from Mississippi, made the same point. But passage of the act would surely have killed the Democratic Party in the North, and Douglas would have been defeated for re-election in his own state. More than a score of northern congressmen bolted on the issue, recalling the fate of their fellows who voted for the Nebraska Act. Most of them would have done so regardless of Douglas's action, but without his leadership the bolt almost certainly would have failed. The strength of his move lay in the fact that most northern congressmen would stand for re-election in 1858 — their southern fellows had just done so the year before — and they faced the hard choice of losing administration support or campaigning against their Republican rivals with Lecompton on their backs.

The wisdom of the Senator's action was sustained by its political consequences: he was re-elected in a close race in Illinois and nominated by his party for the presidency two years later, though southerners left the convention and nominated a candidate of their own. So many Democrats who supported the administration met defeat in 1858 that the party lost its newly gained majority in the House, and the successful anti-Lecompton minority held the balance of power.

Never in his mind was there any doubt from the first that opposition to Lecompton was mandatory. He was not a man to repeat his errors; with the best of intent he had been burned by the Nebraska Act, as Buchanan was now asking to be burned by Lecompton. In 1854 Douglas had yielded to southern opposition by making the concessions they demanded. The result had been a political earthquake; the party had split, a dangerous new party had arisen, he had been excoriated throughout the North, and had lost the next two elections in his own state. Now Buchanan, by an identical rationalization, was asking for the same fate. Douglas would not carry a dead hunchback on his shoulders.

Nor was his bolt due to mere political expediency, to the desire for re-election to the Senate and nomination for the presidency. A safer road to the nomination, were that his main objective, might have been support of the administration. As it was he arrayed the followers of Buchanan and the whole South against him. Although he carefully left the road to compromise open, he must have sensed that he was at his Rubicon. Probably he was reconciled, at the worst, to coming back to the Senate with the Northwest solidly behind him and to using its balance of power to force compromise and peace upon the two older, intransigent sections. If this was his last hope, it was thwarted. But in view of the odds, rarely has any bolter in American political life made the amazing recovery he did in 1860.

Douglas was beset by personal tribulations throughout this critical year. He was bedridden with his old throat infection, his wife had a miscarriage, and the depression forced him to mortgage his Chicago properties heavily. He had a near duel with Senator Fitch of Indiana, formal charges were made that he had abused his position as chairman of the Committee on Territories, and untrue but damaging insinuations upon his political integrity were publicized by his own colleagues. The Little Giant was tough, however; he usually anticipated and could take personal abuse, having given enough of it without rancor in his long congressional career.

To an extrovert in his forties, holding the deep loyalties which the Senator did — and the chief of these, next to the nation, was the Democratic Party — apostasy without great compulsion was impossible. When Pierce had banished him from the inner counsels, he had stuck by the party; when Buchanan had been chosen over him, he gave his energy and his money without stint for the party success. When the new President similarly ignored him and even gave Bright control of patronage in the Northwest, he still gave the administration his support, though privately he made his dissatisfaction known. His recurrent affirmations of devotion to the party must be taken at face value. His brave speeches concealed an undercurrent of sorrow. The sensitive new Republican Senator, James Dixon of Connecticut, was "more and more impressed with admiration for the man. I see more and more what a struggle it cost him to sever all personal and political ties, and take his stand on the foundation of eternal truth and justice. All sorts of blandishments and fascinations were applied in vain — and when promises proved unavailing, resort was had to threats. He could have had the assurance of fifteen States at the next Presidential election, with a good prospect of Illinois, Pennsylvania, and perhaps others. But he was decided and resolute. . . . The South never made a greater mistake than in provoking his opposition. He will prove a terrible foe."

To the younger Douglas, addicted intellectually as a frontier politico to the specious argument and to compromise as the end product, the Lecompton dodge might have appealed. But the mature statesman would not buy it with its hard skeleton protruding so openly. The matter had become one of intellectual consistency. Popular sovereignty had become a vital principle which he regarded as the only hope of Union and of peace. Personally he was a man of honor, yet his pledged word had been questioned throughout the nation. Shifty on his feet as he was, he belonged to the old nineteenth century school that had rather be right than President. The slurs on his integrity rankled. He had defended popular sovereignty, whatever the defects in his constitutional justification, when it proved unpopular in the North. He was not about to abandon it when it was challenged by the South.

In his dire emergency the Little Giant formed a working alliance with the Republicans. They used him and he used them, with all the patter that goes with a crucial trade. Some of the less astute believed that he would follow Frank P. Blair, Jr. into their party; others took him up the mountain and showed him the Promised Land, giving rise to embarrassing accusations that he had sold out for the promise of that party's nomination. Eastern Republicans like Greeley and Seward, seeing the import of a fatal split in Democrat ranks, tried to call their Illinois partners off his tail. Hungry for office and embittered by many clashes with the Little Giant, the Trumbull-Lincoln crowd refused to surrender their chances of local victory for the sake of national party advantage.

Douglas privately led the Republicans to think he might join them; some such statement led to Blair's unconfirmed but much-publicized charge that the Illinoisan informed him that he planned to go over to the new party in 1860. These tactics increased the pressure upon Buchanan and the party. Wiser heads in both parties expected the Senator to make peace once Lecompton was out of the way, and such was surely his intention all along. He had said as much forthrightly to Colfax and Burlingame in the December conference when he told them, "If this issue is settled right, new issues will come up hereafter and we will divide again. If this is not settled rightly . . . we can let the future determine our duties and positions." Leading Democrats continued their efforts to heal the breach and the Senator himself several times made moves to end it, but the petulant President refused to meet him halfway.

Both men were caught in a dilemma from which no easy escape existed. Had he acted otherwise the Senator would have lost his state and his section. Yet had Buchanan backed Walker to the end and insisted upon full submission, he would certainly have faced a southern bolt which would also have split the party. By his abject surrender Buchanan encouraged southern leaders to believe that they could continue to employ threats with impunity and with success. Thereafter his cabinet impudently overruled him at will. But having made his play for southern support to check a secession move, he made Douglas a whipping-boy for party ills, ousting the Senator's friends wholesale from Federal offices and even entering an administration candidate against him in the Illinois race. The Little Giant won the nomination despite Buchanan's opposition, but the party lost the next election.

Douglas knew that in fighting Lecompton he gave mortal offense to some southern leaders, but they were already his enemies and he had no choice. With them he pulled no punches in the heat of debate, so infuriating Jefferson Davis that the temperamental Mississippian allegedly on one occasion rushed at him on the floor of the Senate. Yet he continued to offer the South all that he had always offered it — an even chance in the territories — and he persisted in his calm tolerance of slavery. He would press just as hard for the admission of slave territory, if residents clearly desired slavery, he declared, as he would for free; he did not care whether slavery was voted up or down in Kansas. He warned southerners, however, that by backing Federal interference with popular sovereignty they endangered state rights. Discounting from long experience hot words spoken in Congress as part of the political game, he still hoped that the moderation of his position would in time impress the southern public and its more rational leaders. When passions cooled he expected to work out an acceptable compromise.

The broad issue upon which the Little Giant now took his stand was not the issue of slavery. It was rather the right of local self-government and the related concept of strict construction of the Constitution: specifically the denial of the power of Congress over local institutions. The strong national appeal of his position was indicated by the fact that Greeley and eastern Republicans at once rallied to his support, even though their motives were largely partisan. In the North, and particularly in the Northwest, local self-government was one of the fundamental tenets of the American democratic faith. This principle was equally dear to the South, with its insistence upon state rights, and for that reason Douglas hoped to maintain much of his southern popularity though he fought the admission of Kansas as a slave state. He merely extended the right of self-government to the territories as well as the states. Congressional noninterference was the fundamental premise of popular sovereignty as he defined it.

As a matter of fact, all along the Senator had sought to avoid a showdown on the question of slavery, and for good reasons. He had not pressed the question of how early a territory could act on the matter, not even when the Cincinnati platform had endorsed the southern interpretation. Any stand that he could have taken on slavery would have brought on a fatal fight with the South, but whatever his stand it would also have divided the North, where the subject was equally ticklish. Actually he regarded the question of when territories could act an abstract one. If slavery had reached its geographical limits as he firmly believed, it would make no practical difference whether a territory had to wait until its admission to decide the question. The reaction to the repeal of the Missouri Compromise, it is true, made him realize that it was not a matter of what he thought, but of what his constituents thought, and he continued in his speeches to insist that territories could act before statehood. This was the limit of concession which his own Northwest would accept. But he could say so for home consumption and still avoid a fight in the party or in Congress over what he was convinced remained an abstraction. What he wanted was speedy organization and statehood for the territories. How would the disputed question arise? It was not involved in Kansas, whose legislature had acted on slavery with the approval of the southerners. There were no signs that it would arise in New Mexico and Utah, and certainly not in Nebraska.

Like the President Douglas considered the possibility of an attempt at secession, but he would meet it boldly rather than retreat in panic. "Jeff Davis and other southern ultras are ready for disunion," he asserted in his December conference with the Republicans. "If they go on, we must form a grand Constitutional Union Party to stop them. . . . Our true policy is to put the disunionists in their real light before the country. We must put them in such a position that when the break comes, as come it must, they will be in the position of insurgents; instead of letting them create a situation, as they wish to do, in which *we* must revolt. We will let them be the rebels. Then the army and power of the nation will be against them."

On February 2, 1858, Buchanan formally recommended admission of Kansas under the Lecompton Constitution "with slavery," in the face of recent word that a second referendum in the territory had rejected the document by a two-to-one vote. The measure was referred to the Committee on Territories, in which Douglas was now in a minority. The administration also controlled the same committee of the lower house. Nevertheless, the strategy of the coalition ultimately succeeded. On March 25 the Senate, having refused an amendment of John J. Crittenden of Kentucky calling for a third territorial referendum, passed the Lecompton Bill with a single proviso guaranteeing the new state's right to change its constitution immediately. On April 1 the House voted 120 to 112 to send the measure back with an amendment identical to that proposed in the Senate by Crittenden. On this ballot the anti-administration bloc included 92 Republicans, 6 Know-Nothings, and 22 anti-Lecompton Democrats. Despite southern opposition to resubmission in any form, the administration was forced to compromise. With such an objective in view, towards the end of the month a conference committee reported the English Bill, which was signed by the President early in May.

This bill actually resubmitted the entire constitution to territorial residents, but in language which obscured that fact sufficiently to obtain the necessary southern support. Submission was now coupled with early admission. Should residents reject the constitution, admission would be delayed until the population reached the number required for a congressional seat. At this point most anti-Lecompton Democrats surrendered, including ex-Governor Walker, who in a long conference temporarily persuaded Douglas to accept the measure. The Senator was under such heavy pressure as he weighed his decision that drops of sweat poured from his forehead, pleas still came from home "to yield not one inch," and he changed his mind the next day when he faced the open contempt of his stanchest allies in the long fight. "Sir, I cannot understand you," exclaimed the stalwart Californian Broderick, livid with anger when informed of the decision, "you will be crushed between the Democracy and the Republicans. I shall denounce you, sir. You had better, sir, go into the street and blow your damn brains out."

This incident illustrated the difficulty of the Little Giant's position, arising largely from his realization that he could not with certainty estimate from Washington his own state's and section's reaction to his course. This indecision continued until he returned to Illinois after Congress adjourned. At this point, for reasons political in part, he returned to a strict consistency; the English Bill retained interference. In it, he told the Senate, for all his "anxious desire" to find an acceptable compromise which would restore party harmony, he could but see "intervention with a bounty on one side and a penalty on the other." A few months later the territory rejected the proffered terms six-to-one.

With Lecompton out of the way, he could concentrate on the coming Illinois election. Already he had suffered no little damage. For some time the President had been removing the Senator's friends in Federal office and denying official printing contracts to newspapers supporting Douglas. Leaders of the Buchanan state machine were the notorious "Ike" Cook, new Chicago postmaster, formerly a Douglas man but now his bitter enemy, and Dr. Charles Leib, an equally unsavory character. Getting nowhere at the Democratic state convention in the spring, which enthusiastically renominated the Senator and endorsed his anti-Lecompton stand, the Cook crowd held a rump convention early in June and put up its own candidates. Later in the month a convention of Republicans, who had formed a working agreement with the Cook forces, nominated Lincoln for the Senate.

In a Senate speech Douglas heatedly pronounced the alliance of the Republicans and the "Danite" Democrats as dirty politics. But the development so disturbed him that at the close of the session he made a conciliatory speech indicating that he was ready for peace with Buchanan were reasonable terms offered. To an administration agent who caught the Senator in the Washington railroad station as he was departing for home after adjournment, he demanded full support of the administration in the senatorial race. Soon his father-in-law Cutts and George Sanders, now as much Buchanan's man as he had formerly been Douglas's, wired him in Chicago that the President had accepted, though apparently the latter insisted in return on an open endorsement by Douglas of the English Bill.

The Little Giant had been busy selecting his staff and arranging for proper press support. On his leisurely trip home, accompanied by his lovely wife, he first borrowed one hundred thousand dollars with the help of New York friends. In his campaigns the Senator spent his own money freely, and he well knew that he faced the most desperate election fight of his career. But as he traveled through the northern states he became aware that the unpopularity of Buchanan and Lecompton was greater than he had realized. He concluded, therefore, that acceptance of the English Bill would drive votes over to the Republicans, both in Illinois and in the Northwest. Consequently, at a moving homecoming when he reached Chicago — his first triumph there since 1850 — he defended popular sovereignty all the way, and in the process replied to Lincoln's recent "House Divided" speech.

For Buchanan and the Directory this was the end; they would have the head of the traitor. The Washington *Union,* official organ of the administration which took its orders more from the Directory than the President, resumed its scathing attacks. When Congress reconvened, the Democratic caucus over the protest of a minority ousted Douglas from chairmanship of the territorial committee which he had held for more than a decade. The remainder of his friends were removed from office, and Slidell came to Illinois to manage the Danite campaign and thus to elect Lincoln. Washington heard the next winter that the Louisiana senator had been chosen in secret caucus to pick a quarrel with the Little Giant in a Senate bar and shoot him down. Such was soon the fate of his friend Broderick, who was killed by an ardent southern judge in a duel following a heated contest in California between the two Democratic factions. During the same period Douglas had his near-duel with Senator Fitch over his remarks about the appointment of the Indianian's son to an Illinois post.

Purging Douglas, from here on, was a top priority project of the administration and it went all out to defeat him, first in Illinois and then at the Charleston convention in 1860.

Lincoln had opened the Illinois campaign by an aggressive speech in the middle of June, accepting his party's nomination. To it Douglas replied on July 9 in Chicago. Far more than the later "debates" between them during August and September, these speeches express succinctly their divergent views on the problem of slavery. The Democrat's Nebraska Act, said the Republican candidate, had not stopped but rather had augmented agitation. This agitation, in his opinion, would "not cease until a crisis shall have been reached and passed. 'A house divided against itself cannot stand.' I believe this government cannot endure half *slave* and half *free*. I do not expect the Union to be dissolved — I do not expect the house to fall — but I do expect it will cease to be divided. It will become all the one thing or all the other. Either the opponents of slavery will arrest the further spread of it, and place it where the public mind shall rest in the belief that it is in the course of ultimate extinction; or its advocates will push it forward until it shall become alike lawful; in all the States, *old* as well as *new*, *North* as well as *South*."

Lincoln's previous speeches and his affiliation with the Republicans left no doubt about his strong desire for an immediate end to slavery expansion. Both North and South interpreted this new statement to mean that he desired also its extinction, but northerners got the warning that the institution might instead become completely national. He went on to hurl, for the first time, the radical charge already advanced by Seward and Chase of the existence of a plot to make the nation all slave. Using the homely metaphor of the construction of a building by different workmen, he concluded that "we find it impossible not to *believe* that Stephen [Douglas] and Franklin [Pierce] and Roger [Taney] and James [Buchanan] all understood one another from the beginning, and all worked upon a common *plan* or *draft* drawn up before the first lick was struck." The next step, if voters returned Democrats like Douglas to office, would be for the courts to declare that no state could prohibit slavery.

During the weeks in which Lincoln had been preparing his address his friends, except his abolitionist partner Herndon, urged him not to make such a preposterous charge. This prediction of civil war as the only alternative to the triumph or end of slavery placed Lincoln for some time on the defensive. It was only a prediction, he admitted in his Chicago speech three weeks later, "a foolish one, perhaps." He denied that he earlier expressed the desire that slavery "be put in the course of ultimate extinction. I do say so now, however." On the other hand he later denied that the North had any right to interfere with slavery in states where it existed; the process of emancipation, on which he offered no specific program other than exclusion of slavery from the territories, might require a century.

But when Seward within a few months repeated the prediction of "an irrepressible conflict between opposing and enduring forces," the new Republican strategy was evident. By his own admission the New Yorker made his statement purely for partisan political effect, and Lincoln at least subconsciously had a similar motive. The Republicans had lost Kansas as an issue when the territory was saved for freedom that summer by its residents' rejection of the English Bill. A new issue came conveniently to hand in the alleged Democratic plot to force slavery on the whole nation, a plot of which the Nebraska Act and Buchanan's efforts to make Kansas a slave state were used as evidence.

The Chicago homecoming, where thirty thousand people turned out, was a real tribute to the Little Giant. Exhausted from lack of sleep for several days, he nevertheless spoke effectively and without notes. He reminded the crowd that in the recent Lecompton battle, which had won their admiration, he was contending for the same popular sovereignty which had brought him their condemnation when he last spoke before them. He called Lincoln, who was in the audience, an "intelligent gentleman, a good citizen, and an honorable opponent. And whatever issue I may have with him will be of principle." Then he attacked the main contentions of the Springfield speech. By denying that the nation could endure half slave and half free, Lincoln called for a "war of extermination" between the sections, ignoring the "fundamental principle" of the Founding Fathers, in accordance with which they endowed each state with sovereignty over its domestic affairs. "Uniformity is the parent of despotism the world over," the Senator continued. Lincoln would destroy "the greatest safeguard which our institutions have thrown about the rights of citizens." The Republicans would convert the nation into a consolidated empire with a Maine liquor law everywhere.

Douglas declared the voice of the Court to be final; Lincoln would appeal constitutional interpretation to petty caucuses throughout the country. Republican objections to the Dred Scott decision were equally bad; whether the Republicans would admit it or not, they proposed Negro equality. The American government had been "made by white men, for white men, to be administered by white men." The inferior race had its rights, but only those "consistent with the safety of society," the extent of which each state must decide for itself. In a concluding peroration which brought thundering applause the Senator denied "that the States must be all free or must all be slave. I do not acknowledge that the Negro must have civil and political rights everywhere or nowhere." His issue with Lincoln was "unequivocal and irreconcilable. He goes for uniformity in our domestic institutions, for a war of sections, until one or the other shall be subdued. I go for the great principle of the Kansas-Nebraska bill, the right of the people to decide for themselves."

Both candidates had expressed their views publicly in the state for several years, notably in their recent remarks on the Dred Scott decision. In all but the first of their numerous campaign speeches before and after the joint debates, and particularly in the debates themselves, they were simply sparring for the advantage and changing their emphasis to suit the prejudice of the particular community in which they were speaking. For this reason the debates, with all their drama and political significance, added nothing to their basic arguments. The Little Giant stumped the state as vigorously as he had years before in his congressional race against Colonel Stuart, traveling over five thousand miles and making over a hundred speeches, all but two of which were in the open air and seven of which were in the rain. Little wonder that his throat began to bother him again, that Adele's best care proved of no avail, and that two years later he became a victim of inflammatory rheumatism. Never before had so formidable an array of opponents faced him. Besides Lincoln and Trumbull, Republicans like Chase and the abolitionist Lovejoy harried him at upstate points; the Danites, aided by funds from Slidell, set their stalwarts like ex-Senator Breese upon him throughout Egypt. "The Hell-hounds are on my track," wired Douglas to a friend who volunteered his support. "For God's sake, Linder, come and help me fight them." But speeches were only a small part of the public contacts demanded of a veteran politico seeking re-election.

The rival candidates were actually battling for the election of their party's nominees to the legislature, since that body would choose the state's next senator. With the northern third stanchly Republican and the southern third equally Democratic, central Illinois would determine the outcome. There the decisive factor would be the vote of the ex-Whigs and Know-Nothings, both of whom followed Senator Crittenden as Clay's successor. The Little Giant had vehemently attacked the Know-Nothings in 1854, but Lincoln had not come to their defense. In the course of the senatorial contest Crittenden came out strongly by letter for Douglas: "The people of Illinois little know how much they really owe to Senator Douglas," it read in part. "I say . . . there is a heroism about him that deserves the endorsement of all your people of every party." Many important Democrats from outside the state also gave him warm support, in defiance of the administration, including Alexander Stephens, Governor Wise of Virginia, and Senator James S. Green of Missouri, who had recently fought him over Lecompton. Even Vice-President Breckinridge gave him a lukewarm approval. The majority of party leaders in all parts of the nation agreed with an Illinois correspondent of Crittenden's who argued that "the very necessities of the Democratic party here and generally over the South and West must impel them to unite together on the Douglas platform. . . . Douglas is the only man who can do anything for them here; killing him, they die also."

Illinois Republicans had their troubles too. Eastern members of the party, Greeley in particular, insisted that the Little Giant should not be opposed because they hoped either that he could be induced or that he would be forced into their party. In any event they saw correctly that the permanence of the Democratic split would gain them national advantage far greater than the addition of one senator. At first they gave Lincoln's canvass little support. Illinois leaders refused to admit the slightest possibility that Douglas was sincere, and were unwilling to walk the plank to strengthen their party nationally. One of Trumbull's correspondents noted during the Lecompton fight: "The Republican papers in Chicago and elsewhere [are] denouncing Douglas and all his friends . . . for fear they may be left without a party. . . . To talk of such men being anxious to defeat the measure above all things is a mockery. They would sacrifice it [Kansas] a thousand times rather than forget a party advantage."

In the face of heavy odds and beset on both flanks, the Little Giant won re-election to the Senate, emerged as a greater hero than ever of the northern Democracy, and went on to the party's nomination, for which he had been twice defeated. True, the Republican legislative ticket polled a plurality of 4000 (roughly 125,000 to 121,000 for the Douglas Democrats and 5000 for the Danites), but failed to win since apportionment had not been changed to give the northern section representation for its population increase in the past decade. The new legislature, in control of the Democrats, by joint ballot the next winter voted for Douglas over Lincoln fifty-four to forty-six. In the previous races in Illinois, equally close, the Democrats had lost: Shields for the

Senate in 1855 and Richardson for governor in 1856. Yet when the master ran in his own right he won. The Democrats also won five of the nine congressional seats, but lost two state offices.

To Douglas it was just another battle, a crucial one, in a career full of hard fights. The whole nation knew from his Senate speeches where he stood. The enunciation of his "doctrine" at Freeport was old stuff; as it turned out, by his opposition to Lecompton he had probably already offended the South. But Lincoln, by his clash with Douglas, attracted national attention that he could not otherwise have attained. He rose immediately from a local Illinois politician to at least the second rank of national Republican leaders. Despite his loss, he had proved a match for the Democrats' top debater.

None of the famous personal rivalries of the young American Republic, neither the feud between Jefferson and Hamilton nor that between Jackson and Calhoun, are more dramatic than that of Lincoln and Douglas. Despite the physical contrast between them, the one extremely tall and gangling, the other short and heavy, they were actually much alike. Both were migrants to the state, both were self-made men, and both had completely acquired western attitudes and manners. Each was a "born" politician. The Little Giant's political success, of which his rival was so envious, may have been due only to the fact that he happened to choose the right party and that Lincoln did not. Certainly the latter possessed equal ability, intelligence, and sense of showmanship. On issues of the day, other than slavery, there was little disagreement between them.

In political fights they hit each other with all they had, but they actually held a genuine regard and respect for one another. "I shall have my hands full," the Senator told Forney when he heard that Lincoln had been nominated. "He is the strong man of his party — full of wit, facts, dates — and the best stump speaker, with his droll ways and dry jokes, in the West. He is as honest as he is shrewd, and if I beat him, my victory will be hardly won." Lincoln reciprocated this feeling. The rumor arose at one point that Douglas wanted to fight him over the Dred Scott conspiracy charges. The Republican candidate told an audience that the Senator was just excited; "he and I are about the best friends in the world, and when we get together he would no more think of fighting me than of fighting his wife." Right after the debates the victor wrote a personal letter to President Walker of Harvard, which Lincoln's son Robert had just entered, recommending the lad as the son of his friend Abraham Lincoln, "with whom I have lately been canvassing the State of Illinois." At the nervous President's inauguration in 1861 the Senator held Lincoln's hat when he seemed at a loss to know what to do with it. And the new executive wept openly when he learned shortly of his friend's death.

For a quarter of a century the two had lived with and fought each other on the stump. In their senatorial contest the chips were down; Lincoln was out to take the Little Giant's seat from him. (Lincoln's ambition, according to his partner Herndon, "was a little engine that knew no rest.") Both conducted themselves according to western standards of sportsmanship, by which anything went. Both used to the fullest their particular brand of the art of showmanship. Since Douglas dressed well and traveled in his private Illinois Central coach (for which he paid), his rival dressed shabbily and cried poor-mouth to gain the sympathy of the crowd.

In the early part of the campaign Lincoln followed the Little Giant around to take advantage of the larger crowds which the Senator attracted. Things were going so badly for the Republicans that they kept urging Trumbull to hurry home from Washington to join the attack. Then in late July they hit upon the clever ruse of a challenge to joint debate, a common western practice. The Senator reluctantly agreed, after some formal quibbling; as he told his own aides he had everything to lose, his rival everything to gain. Probably he had no choice, as a refusal would have hurt him in Illinois, but certainly his pride and sheer love of battle inclined him to accept. According to the terms one speaker would open for an hour, the other would reply for an hour and a half, and the first would conclude for thirty minutes. The debates would be held in each of the seven congressional districts in which they had not already spoken. As the challenged party, Douglas named the places and took four of the seven openings. Between August 21 and October 18 encounters took place at Ottawa, Freeport, Jonesboro, Charleston, Galesburg, Quincy, and Alton.

To offset the Senator's national reputation, Lincoln had many advantages. His party was not split, and as the underdog it was easier for him to appeal to the public's sympathy. He could concentrate fully on the Senate election, while the Little Giant was consciously campaigning also for the presidential nomination and election. The latter had spoken his piece so many times that it was a bit old to himself and his audiences; his rival was fresh, eager, and not yet affected by the law of diminishing returns. Douglas was in the position of the veteran boxing champion who, each time he defends the title, risks the off night or one lucky blow from the challenger. He lacked his opponent's pungent humor, he was long-winded and often inclined, as Mrs. Stowe pointed out, to go all around the periphery of the point before he came to the center. Both debaters had their assets, however. The Senator could upon occasion strike home forcibly, but in Lincoln he met a genius in the art of phrasing and the use of parables and Biblical quotations. The Republican was even trickier and shiftier, adept in concocting logic by which a horse chestnut became a chestnut horse.

Like two cautious wrestlers grappling for an opening, both men generally took the defensive in hopes that the other would commit a fatal error. While they spent much of their time defending positions previously taken and reiterating rebuttals, each was seeking to convict the other of inconsistency. They met charge with countercharge; each sought to trap the other by posing a series of questions and to anger his opponent, by occasional *ad hominems,* into dropping his guard for a moment. Representative of their milder banter was Douglas's statement that the young Lincoln could "ruin more liquor than all the boys of the town together," and that he had been a "flourishing grocery-keeper" at

Salem, which in western parlance meant bartender. The Republican denied both charges, though he admitted that he "did work the latter part of one winter in a little still-house up at the head of a hollow."

At one point Lincoln accused his opponent of complicity in forgery (in regard to an article in the *Illinois State Register*) and later of lying. He had taken offense at Douglas's statement that his friends had to carry him off the platform at Ottawa because he was so weak from fright. "I don't want to quarrel with him," Lincoln said — "to call him a liar; but when I come square up to him I don't know what else to call him, if I must tell the truth out." The Republican echoed Trumbull's charge that the Senator had plotted to deny Kansas residents the right of voting on their constitution, and again and again he accused him of conspiring with the Presidents and the Supreme Court to deny states the right to exclude slavery. It is highly unlikely that Lincoln himself believed either allegation.

In the first debate at Ottawa the Little Giant replied to Lincoln's earlier conspiracy charge by accusing Lincoln and Trumbull of plotting to split the Whigs and Democrats, and to unite the dissenters into a new northern abolitionist party. In 1855 he said, Trumbull had cheated Lincoln out of the nomination. Then the Senator read resolutions, quoted in the *Illinois State Register* (which his friend Lanphier had supposedly carefully checked) of the Republican State Convention at Springfield in 1854. These called for repeal of the Fugitive Slave Act, the abolition of slavery in the District of Columbia and its exclusion from all territories, and resistance to the admission of any new slave state, Kansas in particular. Then he asked his opponent a number of pointed questions. For the time being Lincoln simply denied being present at the convention and said that he had not authorized the use of his name as a member of the state committee.

Before the second debate, the Chicago *Press and Tribune* proved that the resolutions were not those adopted by the state convention, but rather by a local group in a northern county. The *State Register* had been in error. Caught in a serious blunder Douglas admitted the mistake, but showed by a dozen other local Republican resolutions that the radical platform truly expressed the sentiment of the new party at that time. When Lincoln answered the question at Freeport he asserted that he did not favor repeal of the Fugitive Slave Act, but he did positively favor formal congressional exclusion of slavery from all territories, and he "would be exceedingly sorry" to have to vote on the admission of any territory, previously free, whose constitution permitted slavery. If such an unlikely contingency should arise, he would reluctantly vote for admission.

Throughout the debates, with the vote of the conservative ex-Whigs in view, the Little Giant tried to make his opponent appear an abolitionist. Lincoln parried the thrust by hedging. In the antislavery northern section he emphasized the immorality of slavery and the Senator's lack of concern for the moral issue. "In the right to eat the bread," he said of the Negro at Ottawa, "without the leave of anyone else, which his own hand earns, he is my equal and the equal of Judge Douglas." Earlier at Chicago he had urged an "end to all this quibbling . . . about this race and that race and the other race being inferior . . . [Let us] once more stand up declaring that all men are created equal." But in the Negrophobe central section he denied the charge that he favored equality of the races. Thus at Charleston he came out strongly for white supremacy: "There is a physical difference between the black and white races which will forever forbid the two races from living together on terms of social and political equality. And inasmuch as they cannot so live, while they do remain together there must be the position of superior and inferior, and I, as much as any other man, am in favor of having the superior position assigned to the white race." His rival promptly accused him of being "jet black" in the north, a "decent mulatto" in the center, and "almost white" in Egypt.

At Freeport Lincoln retaliated with a set of questions of his own, the most famous of which asked how popular sovereignty could be reconciled with the Dred Scott decision. He had been saving the query for just such an occasion, although the Little Giant had given an explicit answer a year before. "I answer emphatically," the latter replied, "as Mr. Lincoln had heard me answer a hundred times at every stump in Illinois, that in my opinion the people of a Territory can, by lawful means, exclude slavery from their limits prior to the formation of a State Constitution. . . . It matters not what way the Supreme Court may hereafter decide as to the abstract question . . . slavery cannot exist a day or an hour anywhere, unless it is supported by local police regulations." In answer to a related question later in the debates, he stated he would fight to the last against a congressional slave code for the territories. Lincoln hammered away incessantly at Douglas's unconcern about the moral wrong of slavery and his acceptance of the institution as permanent. "I hold that the people of the slave-holding States are civilized men as well as ourselves," the Senator replied at Quincy, "that they bear consciences as well as we, and that they are accountable to God and their posterity and not to us. It is for them to decide, therefore, the moral and religious right of the slavery question for themselves within their own limits."

The Republican candidate continually repeated his contention that, since slavery was morally wrong, Congress should prohibit it in all territories as a proper and peaceful step towards its ultimate extinction. Again and again he assured his hearers that such action involved no risk of civil war. The Little Giant challenged this prediction and history soon bore him out. "I care more for the great principle of self-government," he concluded in his summary at Alton, "the right of the people to rule, than I do for all the Negroes in Christendom. I would not endanger the perpetuity of this Union, I would not blot out the great inalienable rights of the white man, for all the Negroes that ever existed."

The debates were less important for Douglas than for Lincoln. The Freeport Doctrine further alienated the South. Douglas's pointed repetition of his position widened the breach with southern leaders which began during the Lecompton battle. The debates were more critical, however, for Lincoln's career. What the Republican candidate said for northern consumption won him the party's nomination two years later, but it also convinced southerners that he was as dangerous as Seward. The result was the secession of the Lower South immediately upon his election.

Lincoln uncovered and hammered away at what was to prove a fatal weakness in the Senator's position. The morality of slavery involved a duality in that the Negro was both a person and a piece of property; the North regarded him in the former light, the South in the latter. Many northerners, including Lincoln, admitted that the contract of the Constitution among the states protected slave property in states which chose to legalize it; though only a very few agreed with Benjamin R. Curtis of Massachusetts, who challenged the antislavery forces "to show that the moral duty which we owe to fugitive slaves, when in conflict with the moral duty we owe to our country and its laws, is so plainly superior thereto, that we ought to engage in revolution on account of it." Even those northerners who recognized southern rights regarded slavery as an immoral institution. On the other hand, southerners regarded aid to fugitive slaves as deliberate theft of their property. Moral views, whatever their validity, are a potent historical force.

Lincoln proposed to deal with the moral evil of slavery in a positive way: limit it to the area in which it existed as the first step towards its ultimate extinction. Douglas, however, opposed any attempt to restrict it because he feared that civil war would be the consequence. He proposed only a negative solution: leave it alone and it would disappear in accordance with basic economic laws. But he was unable to convince the northern public that such would be the outcome.

I X
Candidate at Last

THE victory over Lincoln was the high point of the career of Stephen Douglas. For some time after the close of the senatorial race he remained optimistic — justifiably so in view of his distinct victory over both the Republicans and Buchanan, and of the many indications all over the North that his popularity had reached a new peak. In this interval, he hoped to unite moderates of all sections in support of his principles and his candidacy. His anticipation of success had much to warrant it. Just such a combination had won in 1852 and again in 1856, a year of bitter sectional crisis when two new parties confronted the Democracy. He continued to receive open and even enthusiastic support from parts of the South during the Lecompton fight and his campaign against Lincoln. By compromise he might win over the plain people of the southern region, as he had those of the Northwest, from leaders who called for a continuation of unyielding sectional conflict.

Yet 1860 found the Little Giant opposed by three parties: a sectional one in the North, a sectional one in the South, and a third group, composed of moderates from the border region whose program was identical in its essentials with his own. Thus he failed. But this failure did not stem basically from the man's personality. The tragedy of the Civil War, says Avery Craven, "must, in large part, be charged to a generation of well-meaning Americans who, busy with the task of getting ahead, permitted their short-sighted politicians, their over-zealous editors, and their pious reformers to emotionalize real and potential differences and to conjure up distorted impressions of those who dwelt in other parts of the nation." In time "good men had no choice but to kill and be killed." In the new white heat produced by John Brown's raid on Harper's Ferry and the immediate events which preceded it, no farsighted statesman had the slightest chance of forming a sufficiently strong national phalanx of moderates. None could have prevailed — and few would have even dared the attempt — against the array of enemies Douglas had aroused: northern ultras, southern ultras, and the President and cabinet of his own party. In such a tense situation the concessions necessary to hold any one group must inevitably have alienated the others.

As a consequence of the Kansas fight Douglas was forced into an open break with southern congressional leaders, a break as bitter as that with northern politicos after the Nebraska Act. Behind this break lay the growing divergence in interests and attitudes between the northwestern and southern sections, largely the product of an increased sectional consciousness and basic economic changes in the upper valley. For the sake of unity the Senator yielded as much — perhaps too much, judging by the outcome — as his constituents in the Northwest would permit.

Douglas long enjoyed a popularity in the South which persisted in the lower Mississippi Valley until the very eve of secession. (Memphis gave him its vote in 1860 and in New Orleans he ran second to Bell, ahead of Breckinridge.) Slidell, Davis, and other southern congressmen early opposed him, but he stood high with the mass of southern people. As late as September, 1859, the extremist Richmond *Enquirer* pronounced him honest but mistaken on Lecompton and his break with Buchanan. In the past, it reminded its readers, he had "borne the brunt of many battles and struggled manfully in the cause of party and in defense of the rights of the South."

But after the Dred Scott decision, with a southern clique dictating administration policy, slavery might gain in all the territories while popular sovereignty in practice did little for it. When the South demanded congressional action to force a slave code upon all the territories, in answer to unfriendly local legislation, the Little Giant had no alternative but to resist. Neither sentiment in his own section nor his devotion to consistency permitted any other course. He had risked southern disapproval in fighting for popular sovereignty in Kansas, and now he again did what he told Lincoln at Alton he would do: "I will never violate or abandon that doctrine, if I have to stand alone . . . fighting for it when assailed by Northern mobs, or threatened by Southern hostility. I have defended it against the North and the South, and I will defend it against whoever assails it, and I will follow it wherever its logical conclusions lead me."

Immediately after his re-election in the fall of 1858 he took steps to make his "doctrine" palatable to the South. First, he had his friend Sheehan in the Chicago *Times* correct an eleven-point summary of his position on slavery which the Richmond *South* had just published. In the Dred Scott decision, he contended, the court had guaranteed slave property an equality with other forms of property in the territories; but should it require "further affirmative legislation" from an unwilling territorial legislature, such a result would be "a misfortune attending that description of property for which the Democratic Party have no remedy and are not responsible." Then, on his way to Cuba with his wife for a much-needed rest and sea voyage ordered by his doctors, he reiterated his views in speeches at Memphis and New Orleans. Territories, like states, should decide the question of slavery for themselves, but their decision would actually be determined by the accident of soil and climate, for the Almighty had drawn a dividing line across the continent. Under the Constitution the older sections had no "rights in the territories," and slave property was as much subject to local law as drygoods. Southern hotheads were making the same appeal to prejudice as the abolitionists: "I have never thought proper to disguise the fact that, if the people desire slavery, they are entitled to it, and I am content with the result.

But I would not be instrumental in attempting to force a Constitution upon an unwilling people." Here he was stating for his southern friends the maximum concessions the Northwest would offer, in words almost identical with those used a decade before by Clay and Webster.

But the Senator characteristically sought to tone down their impact. He was not seeking the party's nomination, he announced, for it was the South's turn, and he took care to praise Breckinridge and Wise. In New Orleans he demanded the acquisition of Cuba, for the purchase of which the administration was then launching another formal effort, though he decried the method of filibuster. For the time being he was exercising caution. "Do not come here," his brother-in-law Julius Granger had written from Washington, "and pitch into all those *that deserve it*. You are great in a row, but your rows are so devilishly magnificent that you can't get over them the same day." But when he returned to the capital, after triumphant receptions in New York, Philadelphia, and Baltimore, he found that his senatorial enemies had ousted him from the chairmanship of the territorial committee.

Then southern senators proceeded to block a number of measures demanded by the North — a Pacific railroad bill, a homestead act, and increase in the tariff — and Buchanan vetoed a bill granting land to the states for agricultural and mechanical colleges. With the two houses deadlocked and northern tempers raw at the highhanded southern rejection of concession on any issue, Douglas's friend Brown of Mississippi called for the enactment of a slave code for the territories. Were this right denied, Brown openly admitted that he would "retire from the concern." When the Little Giant met him toe-to-toe on the issue, respectfully but nonetheless positively, Davis and other southern leaders joined the fight. The open break had come.

A month before Senator Alfred Iverson of Georgia, in a speech on the Pacific railroad bill, had pronounced the Illinoisan's popular sovereignty a ruinous and deliberately deceptive doctrine for the South, worse than the Wilmot Proviso, which had been "open, manly, and decisive." In the forensic melee over the slave code proposal southern Democratic congressmen in effect told Douglas that they would accept neither his platform nor his candidacy; moderates and ultras alike seized upon this as an expedient issue over which to fight him for control of the party. At least twenty of them were aspirants for the nomination. Naturally Douglas fought back with all his energy, and the publicity given his replies further alienated southern public opinion. In the fall of 1859 *Harper's Weekly* published a twenty-page article, drawn up after much careful research, in which he attempted a constitutional justification for territorial sovereignty.

The Little Giant repeatedly tangled with Jefferson Davis in the congressional sessions of 1858-1859 and 1859-1860, in which the two factions jockeyed for position in the approaching party convention at Charleston. "Allow me to inform him," replied the Senator from Illinois in one instance when the Mississippian had read him out of the party, "that I stand on the platform, and these that jump off must go out of the party." By a letter in June, 1859, to an Iowa editor friend, J. B. Dorr, he formally announced his candidacy for the Democratic nomination, but on the condition that the Cincinnati platform of 1856 be reaffirmed. Should his enemies succeed in their effort "to interpolate into the creed of the party such new issues as the revival of the African Slave Trade, or a Congressional Slave Code for the territories . . . I could not accept the nomination if tendered to me." In the heated session which followed John Brown's raid later in the year he pronounced that crime the inevitable result of Republican doctrines, and introduced legislation to protect states from domestic invasion. So far had the southern ultras lost their perspective that they accused him of indirect responsibility for the Harper's Ferry raid by denying the South equal constitutional rights! Early in 1860 a Democratic caucus in the Senate, with the President's aid, passed Davis's extreme state rights resolutions, including a demand for a slave code. Thus they presented the Little Giant and the Northwest with an ultimatum.

Congressman James G. Blaine later said that the argument about slavery in the territories was over "an imaginary Negro in an impossible place." A few sensible southerners recognized the absurdity of the territorial issue. Senator James Hammond of South Carolina opposed Lecompton as "an affair . . . rotten from beginning to end" and admitted that no territory then in the Union was suitable for slavery. Other real southern rights, he believed, were endangered, but "the South is and will be henceforth nearly united and we can always divide the North and govern it essentially . . . we can whip them *in the Union* and the attempt to do it will only the better prepare us to kick them out of it, if we fail." At the same time a minority group of disunionists, led by William L. Yancey and Robert B. Rhett, differed with Hammond about southern strength in the Union. Apparently they laid rough plans for a bolt of at least a few southern states at the next Democratic convention, in order to elect a Republican President in 1860 and thus produce secession of the whole section. But a far larger group of southern ultras believed that by pressing their demands, using secession as a threat, they could continue to dominate the Democratic Party. Either Douglas and the Northwest would yield on most points or they would take the party away from him.

In retrospect, these southern leaders appear irrational and inconsistent. Douglas's nonintervention had been first advanced by Calhoun himself, as the New Orleans *Delta* pointed out, when he argued against the constitutionality of congressional action on slavery in the territories. Territorial nonaction would be locally fatal to the institution, admitted the prominent congressman James L. Orr of South Carolina and Alexander Stephens of Georgia. Even Jefferson Davis agreed with this contention in a speech at Bangor, Maine, in the fall of 1858, though he soon reversed himself upon his return to Mississippi.

The Little Giant offered the South far more than any other northern leader who had a chance of winning the votes of his section. He insisted upon strict enforcement of the Fugitive Slave Act. He repeatedly stated that states had exclusive control over their own domestic institutions. He would admit new slave states without hesitation and he refused publicly to express any criticism of the peculiar institution. He even reiterated his unconcern about the spread of slavery and left the question of its morality to the southerners themselves. He incessantly condemned the Republicans for their injustice to the South. True, by popular sovereignty he knew that he was letting the South down easy, as Clay and Webster had, but if climatic factors blocked the spread of slavery into the West — as he and they believed — no other outcome was possible. To offset this inevitable loss, more than any national leader he pressed for the immediate acquisition of Cuba and other land to the southward, from which slave states might be admitted to maintain a balance in the Senate. Though he opposed reopening the foreign slave trade, so did a majority of southerners. No northern statesman could have granted more without destroying his leadership.

Many southern leaders still regarded him as a man of unquestioned honor. Stephens urged the South to support Douglas; Toombs in 1860 said of the Little Giant that "there has been but one greater [man] and he is the Apostle Paul." Brown, who started the slave code fight, congratulated him on his *Harper's* article for making "the best use of a bad cause." Pierre Soule in Louisiana, editor John Forsyth who fought for him in Alabama to the end, and Senator Archibald Dixon of Kentucky held him in equally high regard. Tennessee editor-politico James C. Jones called him "the truest and bravest of men, as pure a patriot as any living or dead." Much more to the point, these admirers saw clearly, as numerous editors in the lower Mississippi Valley kept insisting, that the ultras would commit suicide by killing Douglas, for like Sampson he would "pull down his enemies with him."

So large a group of men become irrational, as these southern ultras did in 1859, only under the compulsion of great stress or fear. Three events in particular deeply disturbed them: the publication of Hinton R. Helper's *The Impending Crisis* in 1857 calling on southern yeomen to rise in revolt against the planter class and the decadent institution of slavery; Seward's "Irrepressible

Conflict" speech the next year; and the attempt by John Brown in 1859 to incite a slave insurrection in the South. Though their section had completely dominated the national government since 1850, these men knew that it was increasingly falling behind in wealth and population. They knew that the loss of parity in the Senate had undermined their last line of defense against the evil day when a united northern majority should take over. This underlying fear for the future made them unduly suspicious of the Northwest, both because of its growing *rapprochement* with the Northeast and because of its new power and independence as an equal of the two older sections, with interests which increasingly conflicted with those of the South.

Should the southern section become politically isolated, its only security would be a scrupulous observance of its rights under the Constitution. Seward and Lincoln denied these rights openly, at least as interpreted by the court; Douglas, though protesting otherwise, would covertly deny what southerners regarded as their titular right of equality in the territories. Could he then be trusted to observe their other constitutional rights which he professed to acknowledge? If he would, could he induce the Northwest to follow him? The Little Giant was a traitor — thundered the radical Charleston *Mercury* — the real leader of the Black Republican cause in Kansas and much more dangerous than Lincoln. After all, in blocking the admission of Kansas as a slave state, he had given the South its only significant defeat since 1850. The irony of this charge was that, while southern ultras accused him of closing the territories to slavery, the Republicans asserted as loudly that he was opening them all to the obnoxious institution.

When southern leaders began their fight with the Little Giant early in 1859, months before Brown's raid, the Yancey radicals had by no means taken over. Unionism and conservatism were still strong in the South, particularly among the mass of the people. Should politicians discover that they had gotten ahead of the public, as many of them had in the Nashville Convention *coup* of 1850, either they would back down or they would suffer repudiation. By raising the slave code issue they hoped to unite their section behind a bold demand and to increase the pressure on Douglas for further concessions. Like Calhoun in 1850, they resorted to desperate tactics — again making use of the tacit threat of secession — to get the best terms possible when the Democratic convention met. Even the bolters at Charleston seemed to have been playing this game, for they were dismayed when the Douglas clan made no effort to induce them to return to the convention. Probably southern leaders intended to replace Douglas with some other nominee, but they definitely intended to control, not disrupt, the party. Shocked by Harper's Ferry, however, the southern public moved abruptly to a support of the most extreme demands of their leaders. Brown's invasion hardened the latter against terms of compromise which they might previously have accepted, and led many of them to consider seriously the merits of secession, which before they had used only as a bargaining lever.

In a deeper sense, most southerners were unalterably opposed to two governmental principles, implied by Douglas for some time in his speeches, which he now worked into a formal political philosophy: majority rule and territorial sovereignty. Both were principles in which the Northwest believed; they were basic premises to which the Senator was forced in order to justify positions — chiefly that of the Freeport Doctrine — he had already taken. Majority rule was particularly an anathema to the South as a conscious minority. Calhoun had long before attacked it with his strict construction and concurrent majority doctrine. He and most southerners cited the fact that the Founding Fathers had intentionally excluded majority rule from three of the four branches of the national government. They contended that the United States was a federal republic of sovereign states which had delegated certain powers to a common agent. Douglas's novel assertion of the sovereignty of territories, giving territories power equal with that of states to act upon slavery and upon other domestic matters, infuriated them even more.

The Senator reached this principle by his customary empirical reasoning, then cut the Constitution to fit. The Little Giant simply claimed for a territory, as a distinct political community, the same power that it could exercise once Congress had formally admitted it into the Union. At what exact moment, he might have asked, does an unsovereign group of people suddenly become sovereign? Were territorial residents any different the day before from what they were the day after admission? Could sovereignty be accomplished by a mere act of Congress? To illustrate his thinking the parallel of a common-law marriage might be cited. The partners in such a marriage produce offspring, maintain a domicile, own property, and participate in most social affairs like a lawfully wedded couple. True, the law places restrictions upon their rights to property, but Douglas denied that the Constitution placed any more restrictions upon territories than upon states. If it be argued that sovereignty of the territories was an assumption, so was sovereignty of the states, which had been long denied by John Marshall and many other Americans.

In the preparation of his article the Senator studied numerous sources, including Calhoun's works and Elliot's *Debates,* and solicited the help of his historian friend Bancroft. Undoubtedly he was trying mainly to refute Lincoln before the northern public, since *Harper's* had only a small southern circulation. He still supported the Supreme Court in the Dred Scott decision, which he maintained had only thrown out the power of *Congress* to prohibit slavery in the territories. Since he knew that Taney's arguments might be used against territorial prohibition of slavery, he cleverly defended his principle of local action on the grounds of territorial sovereignty. Were this premise granted, his conclusion was logical and he escaped the inconsistency which Lincoln's question at Freeport had alleged.

His argument, much compressed, stated that neither the colonies nor the states had ever surrendered jurisdiction over local institutions to a central government. The word "territory" in the Constitution was used in a geographical sense only. Congress derived its power over the territories purely from its function of admitting new states, and had jurisdiction over slavery only from the clause providing assistance to citizens of slave states seeking to recapture runaways to free states or territories. A master had no more right to take his slave into a free territory than into a free state. While Congress could set up territorial government by an enabling act, the territorial legislature could exercise powers forbidden to Congress, since the power to admit new states was delegated, whereas the power of Federal interference with domestic institutions was not.

It must be conceded that Douglas made an advocate's case of some cogency and of definite originality. The court had never passed on the question of the exact relation of the national government to the territories, even though legislation in 1850 and in 1854 included a provision for such a decision, nor had Congress clearly defined the relation by statute. In 1857 the court did not consider the power of territorial legislatures over slavery, nor did it ever pass upon the question. Lincoln attempted to refute the Senator's article in his Cooper Union speech in February, 1860, as did Attorney General Black the previous fall, but the famous Whig lawyer Reverdy Johnson formally sided with Douglas. Years later Black used the identical arguments of his former opponent in defense of the state of Utah against the United States.

The strategy of the southern ultras in their attack upon Douglas destroyed the very basis of their domination, the support of a northern minority. In spite of its potential danger, the South had never enjoyed such control over national policy as it did in the 1850's, nor had any other section ever done so. It had lowered the tariff, repealed the Missouri Compromise, and had gained full recognition of its rights in the territories from the Supreme Court — at least so far as congressional interference was concerned. Administrations of captive northern Presidents made repeated efforts to obtain Cuba from Spain and to admit Kansas as a slave state. Southern votes or presidential vetoes blocked all measures which the South disliked — a central or northern transcontinental railroad, homestead acts, rivers-and-harbor bills, and upward revision of the tariff. Southern unity alone would never have achieved this control without northern votes. But by highhanded intransigence and by rejecting Douglas, the South literally drove away its remaining northern allies at the very height of its power.

Perhaps chance, at least in the timing of events, determined the outcome as much as anything. But for Harper's Ferry the Little Giant might have won his greatest victory and averted war. He acted on the basis of experience, as an intelligent man must. Time and again he had won compromise at the last moment in the face of long odds, and won it with southern support. Surely the clouds had seemed just as dark in 1850 when, after a bold stand, the South retreated and stuck to the Union. Who could predict in 1859 that its temperamental politicos had not overshot themselves? In view of the stakes and historical probability, his game was well worth the try.

The Senator's consistency should not be overlooked. Even here he was not taking a stand against slavery but clinging to strict construction of the Constitution. The Dred Scott decision had denied Congress power over slavery in the territories. In calling for a mandatory slave code, the southerners were demanding that Congress exercise power over the territories to force slavery upon them. As the constitutional authority Reverdy Johnson observed, if Congress had no power over slavery in the territories, it lacked the power to establish as well as to prohibit the institution. The southern ultras had shifted their position, not the Little Giant.

Even a well man could not have withstood the strain to which the Senator from Illinois was now exposed. His rheumatic attacks became more frequent, his throat bothered him continually, and there were indications that he was no longer the happy, confident warrior. He indulged in heavier drinking, at times to such an extent that friends kept him out of the Senate when he was under the influence of alcohol. Particularly after the party conventions of 1860, he seemed morose and expressed the justifiable fear that his enemies were out for his political life. But publicly he continued to present a bold front; harassed and sick as he was, he carried out manfully his earlier promise to young McConnel to "stick to the old ship while there's a plank of her afloat."

In the midst of his struggle with the southerners the Little Giant still hammered away at the Republicans, who now returned to their former attacks upon him. Obviously the successful candidate in 1860 must either carry sufficient states in the North in addition to the South, or win practically all the northern states. The Republicans continued to gain in the elections in 1859, during which both Lincoln and the Senator spoke in the state of Ohio. On numerous occasions he battled them in Congress, particularly in his answer to Seward's speech softening the "irrepressible conflict" into an economic one between the "capital" (southern) and the "labor" (northern) states. In his speech on the admission of Kansas he effectively reviewed their inconsistency. At the same time the administration increased the intensity of its war upon him. Yet by throwing the support of Illinois congressmen to the party's candidate for the House speakership in the long contest in the winter, he kept the way open for the support of party regulars at the coming convention. Since no possibility existed of Buchanan's renomination, the President's influence would soon be ended.

Shortly after Douglas announced his candidacy in the summer of 1859, he took the unprecedented step of opening an unofficial headquarters in New York. Circumstances forced him to do so. Henry Flint, a young Chicago attorney, prepared a collection of his speeches and his friend Sheehan wrote a campaign biography for *Harper's,* which did not come off the press until the Charleston convention assembled. In the next six months, the Senator made such progress that he went to Charleston with Northwestern Democrats solidly behind him and his platform for the first time in his career. Elsewhere in the North he gained almost as strong support despite Buchanan's opposition, even in New England, and most important of all, in New York, though that state and his own Illinois sent hostile minority delegations which the convention rejected. His own personal canvassing in Washington during the winter led Greeley's *Tribune* to observe that "probably no other candidate for a presidential nomination ever played his hand so openly and boldly."

The New York editor admitted privately that he continued to praise Douglas, in a backhanded fashion, deliberately to arouse distrust of him in the South. Most southern states had instructed for local sons, but the Little Giant's henchmen there assured him that he would be their second choice. Forsyth informed him from Mobile that he was a thousand times stronger with the southern people than the attacks of the section's politicians would indicate. Professional gamblers in New Orleans found no takers for five thousand dollar bets at even money that he would win the nomination. Thus he was undoubtedly expressing his true belief when he wrote in February, "There will be no serious difficulty in the South." Never was a candidate more mistaken.

The Democratic convention which met in Charleston in the latter part of April, 1860, proved by far the most fateful in that party's long history; never before or since has such a body wrangled in so much confusion. Douglas's staff, with the veteran Richardson in command and Stuart of Michigan as floor leader, planned to yield somewhat on the territorial question by affirming the platform adopted four years before at Cincinnati, and to gain enough southern votes by giving the vice-presidency to that section. Stephens was Douglas's personal preference. Hoping to obtain a majority for the Senator in an early ballot, they expected then to get the necessary two thirds by the withdrawals usual in such circumstances of the remaining opposition. Douglas had magnanimously done so at Cincinnati when he failed to break Buchanan's bare majority. But the same senatorial trio of Slidell, Bright, and Bayard — which at the last convention had put Buchanan in — were again on hand, representing the President and the Directory and intent on blocking the Little Giant in favor of a compromise candidate. They had no intentions of defeating the party, but the Yancey delegation from Alabama did. Alabamans were determined both to stop Douglas and to force the adoption of a slave code plank; should they fail to do so, their instructions called for their withdrawal. Before the meeting convened six other delegations (Georgia, Florida, Mississippi, Louisiana, Arkansas, and Texas) agreed to follow them. But these anti-Douglas groups, who together disrupted the party, could not agree on a candidate.

The anti-Douglas forces scored first in the selection of the pro-southern Cushing as chairman, and in the control of the committee or organization when presidential patronage added Oregon and California to the fifteen slave states, thus constituting a majority of seventeen out of the thirty-three members (one from each state). Then the Douglas managers obtained a resolution requiring a unit vote only if state conventions had so ordered. Since most northern conventions had done so and most southern had not, this resolution increased the Senator's votes in both sections. At this point the Douglas crowd made the fatal error of agreeing to write the platform before selecting the nominee. After a week's battle, during which resolutions were drawn, redrawn, and modified, they rejected the majority report of the platform committee endorsing a territorial slave code by a vote of 165 to 138, and substituted one of their own leaving the question of the power of territories over slaves to the Supreme Court. Thus the Northwest and its candidate surrendered popular sovereignty for the sake of party harmony. This concession was not enough for the radical wing of southern ultras, who demanded all or nothing. When the convention reassembled on the morning of Monday, April 30, they withdrew.

Douglas men were incensed by the rejection of their olive branch. They were particularly infuriated by a speech of Yancey's on the previous Saturday in which he argued that they would have defended the morality of slavery from the first. "Gentlemen of the South," replied Senator F. Pugh of Ohio, "You mistake us — you mistake us — we will not do it." Murat Halstead, the able young *Tribune* journalist who reported the convention, wrote from Charleston that he had "never heard Abolitionists talk more rancorously of the people of the South than the Douglas men here." Then just before the bolt on Monday, Stuart delivered a bitter attack on the South, probably without obtaining the Senator's consent. Immediately after this speech the southerners withdrew. The convention was the prisoner of the fiery

Charleston audience. The bolters were greatly chagrined when the rump convention did not offer a bargain for their return, and everyone's plans went awry.

Responsibility for the debacle was shared equally between ideologues like Yancey and Rhett and a larger group of southern politicians who feared that the Douglas wing would cut them out of the patronage in favor of its own southern friends. The Little Giant's lieutenants may have hoped for a minor bolt to facilitate a majority and to increase their hero's appeal in the North, but probably Buchanan's senatorial trio, although dismayed at developments, were willing to disrupt the party if Douglas could not be stopped another way. At any rate the deed was done, and the analysis made at once by Alexander Stephens proved correct: "The party is split forever. The only hope was at Charleston. . . . The seceders intended from the beginning to 'rule or ruin,' and when they find they cannot rule they will then ruin . . . In less than twelve months we shall be in a war, and the bloodiest in history."

Fifty of the original 303 delegates had left, but many of the ultras remained to stop Douglas. With New York's help they ruled that the nominee must obtain a two-thirds majority of the original number, which actually amounted to five sixths of the rump convention. For fifty-seven ballots the Little Giant maintained a majority, reaching 152 at one point, and none of his rivals mustered strength. At this impasse his forces recessed the convention for six weeks, to reassemble in June at Baltimore. The bolters meanwhile scheduled a meeting at Richmond a week earlier. The New Yorkers were simply seeking sufficient time to work out a compromise or a compromise candidate in order to strengthen the party.

During the recess the Little Giant's enemies ganged him in the Senate, hoping to trick him into some indiscretion, but he would reply only to their leader Davis. Though he had opposed the southern bolt, the Mississippian was as adamant as ever for extreme southern rights and succeeded in getting the Senate to pass his earlier caucus resolutions. Never had he so goaded his Illinois opponent, whom he now told to his face that he would rather "have an honest man on any sort of a rickety platform" than a man he did not trust on a perfect one. Douglas answered that the break at Charleston had come over the platform; "Why did you not tell us in the beginning of the debate that the whole fight was against the man?"

The Senator did not withdraw at this point, as he soon offered to do at Baltimore, for several good reasons. He was the only candidate who had a chance of beating the Republicans in the North, and unquestionably he was the choice of a majority of Democrats in the nation. He was motivated also by his sense of obligation to his loyal followers in the Northwest, and he really felt that his personal honor was involved in the face of the attacks upon him by the administration. During the six-week recess all the southern states except South Carolina decided to send their delegates back to Baltimore, in effect postponing the Richmond gathering, but Soule and Forsyth succeeded in getting pro-Douglas delegations chosen in Louisiana and Alabama. At Baltimore the Douglas forces insisted that these be seated but agreed, after several days of wrangling, to let most of the other seceders return. When New York voted on the sixth day for this arrangement, after unsuccessful efforts to find some acceptable northern candidate, a hundred southern delegates withdrew, led this time by Virginia.

Then the convention proceeded to select a candidate. On the second ballot the Senator was declared the nominee when he received 182½ votes of the remaining 192½. Benjamin Fitzpatrick of Alabama was chosen as his running-mate, but when Fitzpatrick later declined Herschel V. Johnson of Georgia was selected in his place. The platform retained the previous Douglas concession, leaving the status of slavery in the territories to the Supreme Court. The seceders quickly nominated Breckinridge as their candidate and included in their platform a mandatory slave code.

The Senator yielded much in this crisis. At Charleston he surrendered his cherished popular sovereignty for the very Supreme Court power of decision which the southerners were recently supporting; in response they only raised their demands another notch. Fearing a repetition of the earlier bolt at Baltimore, on June 20 he sent his manager Richardson authorization to withdraw his name in favor of a compromise candidate, and two days later he sent a similar communication to Dean Richmond, the head of the New York delegation that was again making frantic efforts at compromise. "If my enemies are determined to divide and destroy the Democratic party, and perhaps the country, rather than see me elected," the message read, "and if the unity of the party can be preserved, and its ascendancy perpetuated by dropping my name and uniting upon a reliable non-intervention and Union-loving Democrat, I beseech you, in consultation with my friends, to pursue that course which will save the country, without regard to my individual interests. I mean all this letter implies." Neither Richardson nor Richmond used his authorizations because they could not comply with these terms. The New Yorker first pressed Horatio Seymour of his own state as a possible compromise candidate, but when he realized that the Northwest would oppose any nominee other than their hero he concluded that the best chance for victory over Lincoln was to stick to Douglas, even though the South bolted.

In the interval between the two Democratic conventions the Republicans met confidently in Chicago at the end of May. When they quickly picked Lincoln over the favored Seward, skeptics charged that the politicians had sacrificed idealism to expediency. The fact was that the Northwest forced its own candidate upon the two major parties. The Republican platform called for restriction of slavery and endorsed a homestead act, an increase in the tariff, internal improvements, and a Pacific railroad. This effective intersectional bargain with its multi-group appeal was enhanced by the choice of the Illinois "railsplitter" as the party's standard-bearer.

Lincoln's conduct before his nomination was that of an able politician. During 1859 he made more than a score of speeches through the North, by which for the first time he became well-known in the East. His Cooper Union address was designed for eastern conservative support, and he admitted it was not popular in his own section. But he deliberately made his chief appeal to western farmers and pointedly to eastern labor. In New Haven, where a shoe-workers' strike was on, he stated publicly his approval of labor's right to strike or to quit their jobs when they wished: "One of the reasons why I am opposed to slavery is just here." Both candidate and platform, therefore, gave the new party a universal appeal north of the Ohio and the Potomac. "Gentlemen," the Little Giant remarked to some Republican friends in Washington, "you have nominated a very able and very honest man."

Earlier in May ex-Whigs and Know-Nothings, mostly from the border states, had formed the Constitutional Union Party and passed over the aging Crittenden at his own insistence to nominate John Bell of Tennessee. With a strong attraction for the moderates of all sections, it was actually the first party in 1860 to nominate a candidate. Essentially it was a conservative response to the threat of secession made imminent by the bolt at Charleston, a southern opposition to the Yanceyites. Its platform called simply for the maintenance of the Constitution and the Union. The action indicated a lack of confidence in the Democratic Party, a fear of the southern ultras more than a distrust of the Senator from Illinois. These Whigs disliked their old foes the Democrats, and the new Republicans even more, but they split the conservative vote and put Douglas in a most difficult position as a national candidate. As a result he found himself opposed by Lincoln and Bell in the North, and Bell and Breckinridge in both the border region and the Lower South.

Only during the first two months of the campaign did the Little Giant hold any hopes of success; September state elections convinced him that Lincoln would win the North and the presidency. Nevertheless, he continued the speaking tour of all sections he had already begun, both to dissuade the South from

secession and to unite the Union against it should the event oc-
cur. His decision to "take the stump" was unprecedented in the
history of the presidency (Lincoln did not make a single speech
after his nomination), but it was by no means motivated by ambition alone. In contrast to the Republicans who fiddled while
Rome was about to burn with their repeated public assurances
that southern threats were empty, and to Buchanan who washed
his hands of the danger, Douglas battled singlehandedly against
the grinding of the fates which, as it turned out, he foresaw correctly.

PRESIDENTIAL ELECTION OF 1860

	Popular Vote	Electoral Vote	States
Lincoln	1,866,452	180	17½ (all northern)
Douglas	1,376,957	12	1½ (Missouri and ½ New Jersey)
Breckinridge	849,781	72	11 (Lower South plus Maryland and Delaware)
Bell	588,879	39	3 (Tennessee, Virginia, and Kentucky)

Analysis of the election returns shows that had not the South
bolted and had not Bell entered the race, Douglas as the candidate of a strong and united Democracy might have beaten Lincoln in a few northern states. Only two of the larger northern
states plus the fifteen slave states would have given the Democrats
the victory. When Buchanan had earned only five northern states
in 1856, astute Republicans had concluded that they could win
in 1860 by gaining only Pennsylvania and either Illinois or Indiana.

In view of the acute danger of a Republican victory, fusion was
considered by the other parties but accomplished only in a few
states. Since neither Breckinridge nor Bell had a chance in the
North, only Douglas could have stopped Lincoln. The Little
Giant himself attacked the Breckinridge party for being as sectional as the Republicans and would have no truck with them.

He correctly charged that though all of the Kentuckian's followers were not disunionists, most disunionists were in his party. This radical group, of course, would have blocked fusion in order to insure a Republican victory as a lever to secession. Less radical southern Democrats and some of the Bell men seemed to have hoped that the lack of a majority for any candidate would throw the election into the House.

Some southerners believed that, if the House were unable to choose a President from the top three, prosouthern Joseph Lane of Oregon, Breckinridge's running mate, might be chosen vice-president by the administration-controlled Senate and thus become the executive. Hopes of Bell and Breckinridge men for a House election would have inclined them against fusion had Douglas made the attempt. Jefferson Davis later wrote that he formally proposed fusion under a new candidate to all three of Lincoln's opponents, and that the Little Giant alone refused to withdraw. Douglas argued that the scheme would simply throw more votes to Lincoln, since Seymour — whom Davis had in mind and whom the New Yorkers had dropped at Baltimore as too weak a candidate — could not carry the northern Democracy. The plan was impracticable in that probably none of the three could have induced a sufficient number of their followers to vote for some other candidate. Bell and Douglas men did cooperate throughout the nation and in some states effected a joint ticket, each naming a portion of the electoral slate. As for an election by the House, the Senator from Illinois asserted that he would throw it to Lincoln first.

The Republican nominee defeated him decisively in the North by a popular majority of more than 600,000 out of the three million votes cast in that section. Four years before Frémont had carried eleven of the sixteen free states, winning in them by a popular majority over Buchanan of 100,000. But Douglas, who won a larger popular vote in 1860 than Frémont had in 1856, carried the electoral vote of only one state. The combined Douglas-Bell vote in the South exceeded Breckinridge's by 110,000, Douglas getting 160,000 votes in that region. Yet this significant increase in Republican strength was by no means due just to the different positions of Lincoln and Douglas on the question of slavery.

The North voted against the Democratic Party in 1860 for good reasons. They voted against the Buchanan administration, whose prosouthern bias had been conspicuous and whose corruption had been so recently exposed in the Covode Report. They voted against the party they held responsible for the recent depression. They voted against southern domination of the government and southern obstruction to legislation which they favored. They voted against the presence of Negroes in the territories.

Douglas, though he had openly attacked Buchanan and the southern ultras, had to carry them on his back. As their party was his, so were their sins. Many northerners who wanted specific legislation — a Pacific railroad, a homestead act, internal improvements, and tariff increases (the first three of which Douglas had actively supported) — did not vote for the Senator because his party in the past had rejected these measures. Without the South he could not get congressional action, and should southerners return to their former alliance with him they could block his program. The Republicans promised positive action on these very issues, action which as a new party they were more likely to carry out. Thus a new sectional alignment emerged in 1860, as it had at intervals before, and Douglas was its unlucky victim.

So far as peace and Union were concerned, the central question was slavery. On it Lincoln, during the four years he had expressed himself publicly, had talked out of both corners and the middle of his mouth. He had charged the existence of a slave state plot, with the connivance of northern Democrats, to force the institution upon the free states. But to avoid alienation of northern conservatives he carefully refrained from condemning the South; he admitted the insolubility of the problem, and he formally offered a constitutional amendment requiring the consent of a state to emancipation within its limits. At the same time he attacked the institution in such a way that he attracted both Negrophobes and Negrophiles in the North. Those who did not regard slavery as a moral, social, and political wrong, he asserted in the debate at Quincy, should leave the Republican Party. Prohibition of slavery in the territories tied all threads together; it would prevent the admission of more slave states; it would save migrating northern farmers and laborers from social intercourse with the despised black man when they moved west; it would save free northern labor from having its wages lowered by competition with slave labor; and it would be a practical step towards the ultimate extinction of slavery throughout the entire nation. He contended, in short, that the slavery threat was real, that slavery itself was an evil which could and should be stopped, and that the proposed method of nonextension to the territories would prove perfectly peaceful. In danger of being outvoted, the South was once again crying wolf.

Douglas scornfully pronounced the slave plot charge preposterous. As a domestic institution, he insisted, slavery was under exclusive state and territorial control. "If each state will only agree to mind its own business and let its neighbors alone," he answered Lincoln, ". . . this republic can exist forever divided into free and slave states, as our fathers made it, and the people of each state have decided." Since nature had excluded slavery from the existing territories, popular sovereignty would restrict it as effectively as the Wilmot Proviso. But congressional exclusion — and this was his significant difference with his Republican opponent — would *not* be peaceful; not merely was it unnecessary, it would lead to secession and civil war. In the eyes of those who accepted Lincoln's slave plot thesis, the Little Giant stood for appeasement of the South.

The candidate of the northern Democrats began his campaign in New England in midsummer, concentrating on the first state election in Maine, but before he left that section he admitted to Republican Henry Wilson his belief that Lincoln would be victorious. He continued his tour partly for party reasons; morale must be maintained to strengthen the Democrats in Congress in their efforts at compromise and for future elections. But he told Wilson and Charles Francis Adams he was convinced that disunionists, confident of winning Virginia and Maryland, intended to seize Washington by a *coup d'état* immediately after the election. For that reason he hurried South to save those states from Breckinridge, and to warn their citizens against an attempt at secession.

He did so dramatically in answer to two questions handed him at Norfolk in August. To the first, which asked if the South would be justified in seceding should Lincoln be elected, he replied "emphatically" no. "The election of a man to the Presidency by the American people in conformity with the Constitution of the United States *would not justify any attempt at dissolving this glorious confederacy.*" To the second, which asked would he advise coercion in such an event, he replied as boldly in the affirmative. The President must enforce the laws, "and I, as in duty bound by my oath of fidelity to the Constitution, *would do all in my power to aid the Government of the United States in maintaining the supremacy of the laws against all resistance to them, come from whatever quarter it might.*" A week later at Raleigh he expressed himself even more strongly: "Yes friends, I would hang every man higher than Haman who would attempt to resist by force the execution of any provision of the Constitution." Returning to the middle Atlantic region he continued his attack on both the Republicans and the Breckinridge Party. "I wish to God," he thundered to a New York audience, "we had an Old Hickory now alive in order that he might hang Northern and Southern traitors on the same gallows."

Douglas had already warned the South that "no Illinoisan would ever consent to pay duty on corn shipped down the Mississippi." At this point he decided to alert his own Northwest, which the Republicans were beguiling into false confidence with their scoffs at the prospects of a southern withdrawal. Early in October he spoke to a tremendous gathering in his own Chicago. "I'm no alarmist," he stated calmly, "I believe that this country is in more danger now than at any other moment since I have known anything of public life. It is not personal ambition that has induced me to take the stump this year." He was speaking in Cedar Rapids, Iowa, when a telegram from Forney informed him that the Republicans had carried the state election in Pennsylvania. "Mr. Lincoln is the next President," he told his secretary. "We must try to save the Union. I will go South."

The strain of speaking several times a day was telling on the veteran, despite the moral support of his ever-faithful wife who traveled with him. His throat became hoarser than ever. The national committee had been unable to raise more money and he spent heavily from his own depleted funds, but he never hesitated in the heroic task to which he had set himself. After speaking in St. Louis and then in Tennessee he invaded the lower cotton states, though open threats were made against him and several incidents indicated that attempts were made to wreck trains on which he rode. In a speech of introduction in Georgia, Stephens attributed to him greater moral courage than any other living statesman; he called the Senator the most powerful friend the South ever had. The Little Giant was sitting in his friend Forsyth's office in Mobile when he received official word of Lincoln's victory; vainly he sought to dissuade the editor from urging a call for a state convention. Towards midnight he slowly made his way back to his hotel, "more hopeless," recorded his secretary, "than I had ever before seen him."

X

The Good Fight

THE Civil War began in mid-April, 1861, when the Confederates fired on Fort Sumter in Charleston Harbor. Lincoln called upon the northern states for militia to put down the insurrection, and four of the eight slave states which had remained in the Union thereupon seceded. Within five weeks after his inauguration on March 4, the new President finally made up his mind to attempt relief of the Federal garrison. Prior to the inauguration several attempts at compromise had failed, the most important (Crittenden's) through Lincoln's expressed disapproval. Compromise efforts began as soon as the seven states of the Lower South, led by South Carolina, seceded during the two months after the Republican victory in the presidential election and united in the Confederacy.

These events marked the calendar of the last year of Douglas's life. He died in June, 1861, before the first major battle of the war had taken place; to a greater or lesser degree, he was involved in all these main events. For all his warnings to the South, the Little Giant worked steadily and with outward confidence for conciliation and compromise after the election. In the Senate action, as might be expected, he and Crittenden took the lead. "I trust we may lay aside all party grievances, party feuds, partisan jealousies," he told his fellow senators as the southerners began to leave, "and look to our country, and not to our party, in the consequences of our action. Sir, I am as good a party man as anyone living. . . . But . . . I do not desire to hear the word party, or listen to any party appeal, while we are considering and discussing the questions upon which the fate of the country now hangs." He asked the southerners for a bill of particulars as to their grievances.

Buchanan crossed himself out by holding that a state could not secede but that the national government could not coerce a state. Belatedly in January, after a reconstitution of the cabinet which brought in unionists, he did send the *Star of the West* to relieve Sumter. It was repelled by state batteries, but the northern public was not yet ready for the alternative of war. Several compromise efforts were already under way. Both houses of Congress appointed committees, and upon their failure the state of Virginia called a peace conference in Washington. Specific proposals from these three sources eventually failed because of opposition from the Republicans on one hand and from the secessionists on the other. In fact, these two extremist groups effectively passed the ball of obstruction back and forth to each other. Pressing constantly for compromise, on the contrary, were the Douglas Democrats in the North and the Bell men in the border states. Leaders in the effort were Senators Douglas and Crittenden, representing the two moderate parties in the recent election. They received aid from Seward, spokesman for the conciliatory Republicans, who was aghast at the threat of war he had done so much to produce.

The Senate committee of thirteen, appointed on December 20 (the day South Carolina seceded) consisted of five Republicans, three northern Democrats, three senators from the border states, and Toombs and Davis from the Lower South. Of the seven plans considered by it, Crittenden's — which extended the Missouri Compromise line — had the best chance. But the committee had adopted Davis's suggestion that no formula be reported unless it had the support of a majority of both Republican and Democratic members, and the former opposed it when Seward learned through his emissary Thurlow Weed that Lincoln did not approve. Toombs and Davis would probably have accepted this compromise had the Republicans done so. Thus the Senate committee made no report. When the Washington Peace Conference later included the 36°30′ extension in its plan, Crittenden and Douglas made strenuous efforts for its adoption in the Senate. But the Republicans remained adamant, and the only congressional action — towards the close of the session on the day of inauguration — was the passage of the proposed thirteenth amendment declaring that slavery could not be abolished in any state without its consent. This measure, in fact, came from the House's Compromise Committee of thirty-three.

The Senator from Illinois presented a plan of his own to the committee, but it never received serious consideration. He would freeze the existing territories as they were (Dakota, Colorado, and Nevada were formally organized in this session without exclusion of slavery) and would permit them to enter the Union with or without slavery when their population reached 50,000. Any new expansion would require a two-thirds vote of both houses of Congress. Included in his plan were certain other provisions identical with Crittenden's, but he added a prohibition of voting or office-holding by Negroes and the suggestion that the Federal Government buy land for their colonization.

Douglas had several strings to his bow. At first he was hopeful of compromise, since a majority of slave states had rejected secession and a sizable minority had opposed it in the seven that seceded. The northern vote for Lincoln in November could not be regarded as a mandate for coercing the seceding states, for that question had been carefully dodged by the Republicans. The new party did not control Congress, and northern Democrats could wield considerable power should Douglas and Buchanan men unite. The Senator maintained close contact with both Crittenden and Seward, hoping to induce or to force the victorious party to accept compromise. Believing that a majority of the public favored compromise regardless of the action of Congress, together with Crittenden he pressed hard for a national constitutional convention. In fact, he probably induced Lincoln to insert formal approval of such a convention in the inaugural address. But Douglas's major effort was directed at keeping the border states in the Union, and his introduction of a more effective fugitive slave bill on January 28 was designed to influence an approaching plebiscite in Virginia on secession.

The Little Giant did not deliberately delude his supporters in the border states. While he had consciously in mind the reduction of the strength of the Confederacy should hostilities commence, his main objective was to keep the door open for an ultimate reconstruction of the Union. This was also Seward's chief hope. Could a martial incident be avoided, the formation of the Confederacy need not eventuate in peaceable separation; the seceding states, either because of their weakness or in view of satisfactory concessions, might rejoin the Union. With reconstruction in mind — and as an alternative to war — Douglas at one point drew up a plan for a commercial union with the Confederacy which may actually have been presented in Montgomery by his old crony George Sanders. (He had already drafted an article proposing such a union, like the German Zollverein which he had seen firsthand, between the United States, Canada, Mexico, and the Central American nations.) This plan called for uniform trade and tariff regulations between the two republics under a supercouncil consisting of one member from each of their states. Surplus revenues would be divided by the two on the basis of population, and neither could add territory without the other's consent. He never published his plan, but after his death it was found among his papers.

The prospect of war "upon an abstraction," as the Little Giant put it, was abhorrent and unthinkable to him as to other intelligent patriots. But as a realist he admitted its increasing probability, though publicly he maintained his confidence in peace. Not until Sumter did he return to the support of coercion which he had boldly advocated during the presidential campaign. In the interval he may have wavered from week to week as to his ultimate position, torn between hope and fear while awaiting for the contingencies to evolve. His consideration of commercial union suggests that for a while he may have preferred peaceful separation to war. Chiefly he tried persuasion upon the Republicans and the southerners, though upon occasion he lost his patience at the latter's sneers and recalcitrance. He tried to shock the Republicans into an awareness of their terrible responsibility. War would be long and bloody, he warned. "South Carolina had no right to secede," he stated, adding that secession was unlawful and criminal, *"but she has done it.* The rights of the Federal government remain, but possession is lost. . . . *Are we prepared for war? . . .* prepared *in our hearts* for war with our own brethren and kindred? I confess I am not." But the victor in so many close congressional battles, fighting the good fight in this tragic hour, lost the one he preferred most to win.

After the failure of compromise in Congress and after the inauguration, Douglas logically concentrated his energy upon Lincoln, seeking to induce the new President to follow a passive course of action and thus avoid an incident which might set off hostilities. Of the Senator's sincere desire for peace and of his intimacy with his old rival during the period immediately before and after the inauguration there can be no doubt. Seward, it is well known, had a low opinion of the new executive and openly proposed to take the helm from him. Like the Little Giant, the New Yorker tried desperately to avoid any action which might provoke civil war. He even suggested to Lincoln that the United States instead initiate hostilities with European powers, and he exerted himself for the evacuation of the Federal garrison at Sumter.

But Douglas knew Lincoln too well to expect to dominate him. Certainly, in the interest of peace, he thought that he might influence the President towards caution and win him over to the constitutional convention plan, which at the moment offered the best hope for compromise. At first the Little Giant believed that he had succeeded, for the President told him in the middle of March that he intended to evacuate Sumter. In any event, Lincoln would have been forced to consult him as the leader of the northern Democrats who had polled well over a million votes in the recent election. Each may have sought closer contact to effect a bipartisan arrangement in case war should start. Douglas must have considered the possibility that, in the event of a Republican split, he might himself attain control by uniting his followers with the moderate wing. Unlike Seward, he well knew Lincoln's personality and potentiality.

To an acquaintance who commented on the weakness of the President-elect he replied, "No, he is not that, Sir. But he is eminently a man of the atmosphere which surrounds him. He has not yet got out of Springfield. . . . He does not know that he is President-elect of the United States. He does not see that the shadow he casts is any bigger now than it was last year. It will not take him long when he has got established in the White House. But he has not found it out yet."

On his way to Washington during February Lincoln made ineffectual speeches which revealed that he was still under the delusion that the South would not fight. True, he was sobered by the fact that seven states had seceded, but he underestimated the crisis and in particular he overestimated the strength of southern unionism, on which he and Seward counted until the last moment. Up to this point his most important action had been his rejection of the Crittenden Compromise in December, although false rumors persisted that he was reconsidering it. As leader of a new party come to power his criteria, like his problems, were chiefly political. On fugitive slaves and similar issues he would make real concessions, but not on the platform which bound his party together: exclusion of slavery from the territories. With compromise on that point, he wrote Trumbull, "all our labor is lost, and ere long, must be done again. . . . The tug has to come, and better now than at any time hereafter." Yet two years before, at the conclusion of the debates with Douglas, he announced he would willingly retire from the race should the Missouri Line be restored; and two years later, in a famous answer to Greeley, he stated that he would free half the slaves — or none of them — if by so doing he could save the Union. In all three instances he was much the man of the atmosphere surrounding him, as Douglas said, but his was the chief responsibility for the failure of the most promising terms of compromise. Characteristically, he maintained party harmony by including in his cabinet Chase, leader of the radicals, and Seward, leader of the moderates. In the running fight between these two factions Douglas saw his opportunity.

He called on Lincoln shortly after his arrival in the capital to assure him of their mutual desire for peace. The two discussed the crisis, in particular the peace conference then in session. At the end of the conversation the Senator referred to their long-standing political opposition, but added that "in our devotion and attachment to the Constitution we have never differed — in this we are one — this must and shall not be destroyed." Deeply moved, Lincoln replied "God bless you Douglas, I can't forget it." During the following month they held other conferences, the exact nature of which have never been revealed. The Senator read the inaugural speech in advance and became its chief defender in the short session of the Senate which followed. It was probably he, not Seward, who persuaded the President to insert the paragraph approving a national constitutional convention — a proposal which Lincoln had pointedly rejected in the original draft. During the inauguration ceremonies Douglas held the embarrassed President's hat and openly expressed approval of portions of the address. That night at the inaugural ball he was particularly attentive to Mary Lincoln.

Much of this intimacy was spontaneous and the motives of both men were high, but each was seeking at the same time to use the other for his own purposes. The Senator sought to bolster the President against the radicals in his own party, to dissuade him from a policy which in any way would appear aggressive in southern eyes, and to commit him to compromise. But the Little Giant was too wise about men to rely upon personal influence alone. In the Senate session following the inaugural he sought to produce a split in the Republican Party, in order to make certain that Sumter would be evacuated whatever the President might decide.

When Jackson had decided to coerce South Carolina, his advisers had persuaded him to ask for express congressional authority in the form of the Force Act. Lincoln's inaugural speech was as ambiguous as his earlier remarks about slavery. He pronounced secession unconstitutional, he announced his intention to use his power "to hold, occupy, and possess the property and places belonging to the government," but he assured southerners that he would not "assail" them.

Actually, Lincoln did have a plan of masterful inaction which he thought precluded any chance of an incident. Douglas defended the message as one of peace, cleverly putting words into the executive's mouth, and declared that all Union-loving men should thank the President for having "sunk the partisan in the patriot." He demanded that the Republicans admit and discuss their intentions. Even if the administration should decide upon relief for Sumter, he asserted, it lacked the power to effect it. Both he and Seward announced confidently that the fort would be evacuated; and at the moment all but one member of the cabinet and probably Lincoln himself favored such action. But the Republicans would not rise to his bait.

Though the Little Giant wooed the President, he took care to maintain his own dignity and independence. In his praise of the inaugural message he warned the Senate against any inference that he had "any political sympathy with his administration, or that I expect any contingency can happen in which I may be identified with it. I expect to oppose his administration with all my energy on those great principles which have separated parties in former times; but on this one question — that of preserving the Union by a peaceful solution of our present difficulties . . . if I understand his true intent and meaning, I am with him." At this point Douglas's hope for peace had undoubtedly revived. Steps were being taken in Kentucky, whose legislature was about to assemble, for the calling of a border state convention. Unionists still controlled the Virginia state convention which remained in session. In their recent territorial bill, as Douglas pointed out in debate with Breckinridge, who was trying to share the limelight with him, the Republicans had dropped the Wilmot Proviso by omitting the exclusion of slavery. This, he argued, was surrender to southern demands. The President himself was advocating a national convention.

In February Lincoln offered to evacuate Sumter if the Virginia convention, then considering secession, would adjourn *sine die;* as late as the middle of March he was of the same mind. When he assumed office he intended to hold both Sumter and Pickens in Pensacola as symbols of national authority. Evidently he thought he could do so without a clash, since it was believed at this time that the forts could sustain attack. But on March 5 word came from Major Anderson in Charleston that he would soon be forced to surrender because the Confederates had cut off his food supplies. This development placed the President in a dilemma which induced a modification of his formula for peace, since he feared that abject surrender of both forts — which his general-in-chief Winfield Scott recommended — would ruin his party in the North. Yet all but one of his cabinet favored evacuation of Sumter, so Lincoln first turned to a substitute plan of yielding it and seizing Pickens instead.

Meanwhile Seward, aware of Douglas's game and disturbed by the intimacy between him and Lincoln, embarked on a series of negotiations on his own to prevent hostilities. Unofficially, he three times gave positive assurance to southern commissioners in Washington that Sumter would be evacuated, to which he added a pledge that notice would be given of any decision for a relief expedition. The Buchanan administration had arranged a similar truce at Pickens, which Federal troops on the U.S.S. *Brooklyn* stationed offshore could probably seize at will. Therefore the Secretary of State warmly seconded his chief's plan to substitute the Florida for the Carolina fort.

A number of events caused Lincoln to change his mind, however. His orders to occupy Pickens were not obeyed by the captain of the *Brooklyn* because they were sent through the War Department instead of the Navy. Through his own agents he learned that unionism in South Carolina was almost nonexistent, and the Virginia unionists delayed in seeking a conference with him. On March 29 he issued orders for the preparation of a relief expedition to Sumter. During the next week he decided to send it, and on April 6 he notified the Governor of South Carolina that he was doing so. No attempt would be made to reinforce Anderson, he stated, only to supply him with provisions; but resistance to the mission would be met with force. Lincoln was learning the length of his shadow. Before the end of March Douglas must have suspected this, for conferences between the two ceased and on the twenty-fifth he told a Virginia unionist that he had "no political affinity with the administration." On April 10 he warned Secretary of Navy Gideon Welles that a terrible civil war was inevitable.

War began when the Confederates attacked and took Sumter on April 12. The President thus obtained at the outset of the war the full support of a majority of citizens united by an act of aggression — like Polk before him and Franklin Roosevelt later. In some Americans the event produced a deep conflict of loyalties. As Robert E. Lee decided to stand by his native state, so Stephen Douglas decided to stand by his nation, each with a heavy heart from what they regarded as a tragic and unnecessary war.

When word of the attack reached the capital on April 14, the Little Giant yielded to the urging of his wife and a congressman friend and called on the President again to offer his firm support. He heartily "concurred" in the executive proclamation calling for 75,000 men, adding that he would "make it 200,000." Soon he was stating publicly to his friends, "We must fight for our country and forget all partisan differences. There can be but two parties — the party of patriots and the party of traitors." He was frequently in consultation with the Chief Executive about military plans, and perhaps he desired a commission as he had during the Mexican War. Certainly, had he lived, his poor health and his experience in matters of state would have prevented this; his friend Forney later stated "by authority" that Lincoln planned to call him into the cabinet. Within a few weeks the President sent him on a mission to insure the loyalty of the Northwest. Time would prove the danger of disaffection in a region which had much love for the Union but little for Negroes.

On this, his last tour, the Senator spoke movingly at Bellaire and Columbus, Ohio, and at Springfield and Chicago in his own state. Rumor had it that he was to raise a large army for the invasion of the lower Mississippi Valley, and according to family legend he dissuaded U. S. Grant from accepting a Confederate commission. Never was he sadder or more effective in his speeches. The war would be bloody, he predicted; Virginia would become a charnelhouse and Washington a city of hospitals. But patriots had no choice in a war of self-defense against conspirators: "Every man must be for or against the United States. There can be no neutrals. . . ." Yet, just as he had earlier anticipated Lincoln's policy in his campaign speeches in 1860, he now anticipated the President's subsequent attitude of charity towards the enemy.

"May we conduct it, if a collision must come," he said at Springfield, "that we will stand justified in the eyes of Him who knows our hearts, and who will justify our every act. We must not yield to resentments, nor to the spirit of vengeance, much less to a desire for conquest and ambition." And to this he added at Chicago, "We are a Christian people, and the war must be prosecuted in a manner recognized by Christian nations. We must not invade constitutional rights. The innocent must not suffer, nor women and children be the victims."

Soon after his Chicago speech on May 1 he suffered a severe attack of rheumatism, followed by constant high fever. Delirious most of the time, throughout the month he grew worse though Adele summoned physicians from Washington and Cleveland. Apparently he refused mass from her bishop, James Duggan. After Douglas died on June 3 Duggan did conduct the funeral service "in full canonicals," but the night before Masonic rites were performed. Surely his fatal illness resulted from his indefatigable efforts of the previous year, aggravated perhaps by his despair at failure. A fitting epitaph would have been his delirious cry, "Telegraph to the President and let the column move!"

The Little Giant's wise and dispassionate contemporary Alexander Stephens, Vice-President of the Confederacy, observed in retrospect that had Douglas prevailed the war would have been avoided. The Georgian pronounced him the "foremost patriot and statesman of his time." It was Douglas who directed the passage of compromise through Congress in 1850 after Clay and the Whigs had failed. The crisis of 1860, in contrast to that of a decade earlier, ended in failure not because of the lack of a moderate leader with a plan, but because the majority in both sections which previously had supported compromise now rejected it. What made Douglas fail was what brought on the war. No one man, however great a leader, could have prevailed against the passions of 1861.

Had Douglas lived it is quite conceivable that the course of both war and reconstruction might have been somewhat different. As an ardent war Democrat, he would probably have been chosen Lincoln's running-mate in 1864 and would thus have become President upon the assassination. Had he chosen instead to run as a Democrat against Lincoln he might well have won the election, though it is unlikely that he would have accepted peace at the price of southern independence. By his influence with northern Democrats and his cooperation with Lincoln he could perhaps have shortened the war. While probably neither he nor Lincoln could have prevented the Radicals from exacting vengeance in the age of hate which followed the war, surely he would have been more successful in resisting their harsher measures than the southerner Andrew Johnson.

The unquestioned political consequence of the Little Giant's death — "the most disastrous loss of leadership ever sustained by a major American party" — was the lack of a strong leader in the Democratic Party for the next quarter of a century. In 1872 the party even threw its support to the liberal Republican Greeley, and not until Grover Cleveland won the presidency in 1884 did it again have a man of ability and force at the helm. The weakness of the Democrats in these decades hurt the nation — a weakness which Douglas might have prevented had he lived longer.

"Not for a long generation," observes Wilfred E. Binkley, "until the rise of William Jennings Bryan in the 'nineties, were the Democrats again to have such a dynamic leader, and even Bryan lacked the broad tolerance that enabled Douglas to combine in a single following big business, farmers, and workers."

In a human sense the story of Stephen Douglas *is* a success story — despite his failure at the end of his short life to attain his personal and national objectives. Arriving in Illinois a penniless youngster, he later made a fortune in real estate which, though debts encumbered it in 1861, would certainly have more than regained its value under his personal management during the war boom. When death took him, his political career — so recently the envy of Lincoln — was by no means finished. Politics were both his vocation and his avocation, but he crammed a lot of living into his forty-eight years. He married two charming women and fathered two sons. He traveled extensively in the United States and in Europe. Magnanimous and generous to a fault, he spent his money as freely as he made it. In the conviviality of the male world he indulged heartily and at times recklessly, yet not to the injury of career or duty. Still, in the salon he was by no means a boor. He made thousands of friends and many enemies, which he knew in the nature of things were but the reverse side of the coin. He loved to fight and he reveled in the din and blood of political battle, but he rarely trampled on the fallen foe. He engaged in combat only men as big or bigger than himself. From his country he received sufficient recognition, formal and otherwise, to suit his moderate ambition. Even though he never became President, for almost a decade he was in essence the parliamentary chief of his party — a "happy warrior."

The life of the man, which reached its climax in America's moment of high tragedy, could as well be a theme for the poet as for the historian. In many ways the Little Giant had a rare combination of qualities. Of high intelligence, he was not insensitive to the philosophic and scientific concepts of his day, though preoccupation with affairs of state left him little time for their pursuit. Possessing an amazing ability to concentrate upon his objective once he had made up his mind, he usually won when the chips were down, except in the last instance. In many ways typically American, as the leader of the group tritely calling themselves "Young America" he articulated for the common man of his day a vision of the destiny of the United States. Never doctrinaire except in party discipline, unlike his abolitionist adversaries he had too much humility to try to play God. As much as any soldier on the battlefield he gave his life for his country. He died in the arena as he would have wished, and he did so with the personal satisfaction of knowing in his own heart that he had fought the good fight.

A Note on the Sources

DOUGLAS's papers and letters are abundant but scattered.
The University of Chicago has a collection of fifteen thousand items,
mostly routine correspondence addressed *to* the Senator — the bulk of
it for the period 1857-1860. The Illinois State Historical Library in
Springfield has about two hundred Douglas letters, some of them in the
papers of his associates like Lanphier and McClernand. The National
Archives has some material. Robert W. Johannsen is now editing a
much-needed volume of Douglas letters.

Douglas's congressional speeches may be found in the *Congressional
Globe*. His campaign and other speeches appeared in the Illinois press,
mainly the Chicago *Times* and the *Illinois State Register* in Springfield.
He was frequently quoted in the Washington and New York newspapers, and in those of any city like Memphis and New Orleans where
he spoke. The Arthur Clark Company of Cleveland in 1902 published
the best edition of his debates with Lincoln with an index.

His brief autobiography, written in his twenties, is printed in the
Journal of the Illinois State Historical Society, V (1912), 323-342. His
article, "The Dividing Line between Federal and Local Authority:
Popular Sovereignty in the Territories," appeared in *Harper's Maga-
zine*, XIV (September 1859), 519-537. J. Madison Cutts, his brother-in-
law, claimed to have included many of the Little Giant's views and
reminiscences in his *Brief Treatise upon Constitutional and Party Questions* (New York 1866), but it is of course secondhand. George M. Mc-
Connel did the same in his "Recollections of Stephen A. Douglas,"

Illinois States Historical Society Transactions, 1901. The anonymous *Diary of a Public Man* has much on the intimacy of Douglas and Lincoln in the secession crisis. Its authenticity is now questioned by scholars, but I see no reason to discount it on this particular subject.

James W. Sheehan and Henry M. Flint both did campaign biographies of the Senator in 1860, and Flint included some of his speeches. In 1908 Allen Johnson published the first scholarly biography, a judicious account which is still quite good. William G. Brown did another in 1911, and Frank Hodder was on the point of doing an excellent one at the time of his death. George Fort Milton, who discovered a lot of new Douglas sources, has written the closest to a definitive work in the *Eve of the Conflict,* published in 1932 as part of a trilogy on the period. It, however, is an admitted apologia. I wish to acknowledge my extensive use of it. The *Journal of the Illinois State Historical Society,* XVI (1924) has a private life by Frank L. Stevens which includes pertinent material not to be found elsewhere.

Most of the sources and secondary works dealing with political developments in the 1850's and the background of secession and war are pertinent to a study of Douglas. Roy F. Nichols summarized the historiography of the interpretation of Douglas in "The Kansas-Nebraska Act: a Century of Historiography," *Mississippi Valley Historical Review,* XLVII (1956), 187-212. I have used in particular the following secondary works:

Allan Nevins, *Ordeal of the Union,* 2 vol., New York, 1947.
  Emergence of Lincoln, 2 vol., New York, 1950.
Roy F. Nichols, *The Disruption of American Democracy,* New York, 1948.
Avery Craven, *The Coming of the Civil War,* New York, 1942.
Albert J. Beveridge, *Abraham Lincoln,* 2 vol., New York, 1928.
P. O. Ray, *The Repeal of the Missouri Compromise,* Cleveland, 1909.
James C. Malin, *The Nebraska Question,* Lawrence, 1953.
James G. Randall, *Civil War and Reconstruction,* New York 1937, and his later biography of Lincoln.
David M. Potter, *Lincoln and His Party in the Secession Crisis,* New Haven, 1942.
Richard Hofstadter, *The American Political Tradition,* New York, 1949.
Wilfred E. Binkley, *American Political Parties,* New York, 1945.
Gerald W. Johnson, *The Secession of the Southern States,* New York, 1933.

The following articles examine more fully the controversial issues involving Douglas:

George D. Harmon, "Douglas and the Compromise of 1850," *Journal of the Illinois State Historical Society,* XXI (1929), 453-499.

Holman Hamilton, "Democratic Senate Leadership and the Compromise of 1850," *Mississippi Valley Historical Review,* XLI (1954), 403-418.

Frank H. Hodder, "The Authorship of the Compromise of 1850," *Mississippi Valley Historical Review,* XXII (1936), 525-536.

Frank H. Hodder, "Genesis of the Kansas-Nebraska Act," *Proceedings of the State Historical Society of Wisconsin,* 1912, 69-86.

Frank H. Hodder, "The Railroad Background of the Kansas-Nebraska Act," *Mississippi Valley Historical Review,* XII (1925), 3-22.

No major American figure, not even Andrew Johnson, has been as unfairly treated by historians as Douglas, although recently Milton and Hodder have come to his defense. Oddly enough, two of Lincoln's biographers — Albert Beveridge and James Randall — are quite objective in their treatment of the Little Giant. Nevertheless a number of contemporary historians, Allan Nevins in particular, continue to show bias in their treatment of him.

Because Douglas would have appeased the South, the Republican historians in the post-Civil War decades treated him almost as a traitor. Von Holst began the stereotype, but the scholarly James Ford Rhodes, author of a multi-volume history of the United States beginning with the Compromise of 1850, was most prejudiced. His father was named by Douglas as executor of his estate; but the elder Rhodes mismanaged it so badly that the Senator's sons later brought suit against him. The younger Rhodes took revenge by depicting the Senator as a scheming politician who sold out his own section in order to gain southern votes for the presidency.

Any biographer of Douglas necessarily makes certain assumptions about the causes of the Civil War. The subject remains controversial, but the brevity and the nature of the present volume has prevented any detailed consideration of it. No statements of fact and no interpretation can be advanced which will not meet immediate challenge from some quarter. I belong to the group which rejects all monistic hypotheses, but which holds that the war resulted from two basic causes: the struggle between the several sections for control of the national government — a struggle as old as the Union itself — and the divergence among them in their attitude towards slavery. Probably neither by itself would have led to secession and war, and it is impossible to measure the relative potency of either. Even the Beards, who advance a thesis which borders on economic determinism, throw up their hands and admit *"felix qui potuit rerum cognoscere causas."*

Two main schools have arisen on slavery as a causal factor: one which emphasizes divergent moral attitudes towards slavery in the different sections as the basic cause of the war; and a second — consisting of latter-day abolitionists like Nevins — which insists that it *was* the immorality of slavery which brought on the war. Since Douglas the compromiser tried to preserve peace and Union by concessions to the South and since he refused to condemn slavery publicly, this group regards him as the villain of the epic. They make him the foil to Lincoln; they fail to discount sufficiently the libelous charges of the Senator's various enemies, and they pass moral judgment upon him on the basis of criteria which they fail to apply to his contemporaries. They emphasize his intemperance, his alleged moral obtuseness, and his trickiness and his use of invective in debate. They condemn him for attributes they ignore in Seward, Toombs, Sumner, and other public figures of the day, especially Lincoln.

Nevins, for example, in his four-volume opus at first pictures Douglas (in the period when the Senator was making concessions to the South) as an energetic, ambitious politician without scruple as to methods. He does not mention the fact that the Little Giant was almost the first statesman to attack the nativist movement of the decade, while Lincoln remained silent. Nevins even cites a letter to prove that Douglas betrayed his senatorial colleague Shields in 1855; the letter cited clearly proves the reverse — that the Little Giant rejected the pleas of his lieutenants that he drop Shields for another candidate. But when the Senator broke with the South over Kansas, Nevins changes his tone and presents him as a man of stature. Later in an article in the *Journal of the Illinois State Historical Society* in 1950, Nevins praises Douglas highly for his efforts to prevent a southern *coup* against Washington in the fall of 1860.

Since I have been so critical of bias in other biographers, perhaps I should state that when I began this study I was quite neutral towards the Little Giant and had no intention of coming to his defense. I have done so (in contrast to my biography of Calhoun which will appear shortly) because of my belief that the biographer must insist that his subject be judged — not on the basis of hindsight — but in the light of the standards and events of his own times as they unfolded; that is, in his own milieu. No biographer can be truly objective; as he delves into the sources he is bound to develop sympathy or antipathy; and he cannot be a good biographer unless he responds to his man. He can only be on the watch for his bias as it subtly arises, recognize it as such, try to evaluate it with some degree of objectivity, and then abide by it.

I wish to acknowledge my great obligation to two of my friends who read this manuscript critically: David Potter of Yale and Oscar Handlin of Harvard. For its typing I am indebted to members of the clerical staff at Tulane: to Zelia Dimitry of the Newcomb administrative office and to Ann Hayward and Mildred Stouse of the Graduate School office.

Index